Reach for Joy

How To Find the Right Therapist and Therapy for You.

by Lynne D. Finney, J.D., M.S.W.

The Crossing Press • Freedom, CA 95019

Many wonderful people contributed information and provided feedback for this book, and I would particularly like to thank Rosemary Murray; Robin Frederick; Professor Hugh Allred, D.Ed.; Joan Borysenko, Ph.D.; Laurie Brussow and her family; Ann Bogdanich; Jim Fadiman, Ph.D.; David Schell, D.Ed.; and Marcia Harrow for their enthusiasm, comments and support—and, most important, for their sustaining friendship.

I was also privileged to have a number of experts in child psychology advise me on the chapter entitled "How do I find a good therapist for my child?" I am very grateful to David Schell, D.Ed.; Doug Goldsmith, Clinical Director, Children's Center; Nancy Reiser, M.Ed; Sam Goldstein, Ph.D., Neurology Learning and Behavior Center; Trudy Bach-Whitehead, L.C.S.W.; Leslie McDonald White, L.C.S.W.; and Katy O'Banion, Ph.D., for helping to insure that this chapter included the most helpful and up-to-date information.

I appreciate the assistance I received from experts in brain wave biofeedback, including Steven Fabrion, Ph.D., Director of Research, Life Sciences Institute of Mind-Body Health Inc.; Topeka, Kansas; Dennis Campbell, EEG Spectrum, Inc., Los Angeles, California; Carol Manchester, Ph.D., Freshwater Clinic, Columbus, Ohio; Sebastian Striefel, Ph.D., Utah State University, Logan, Utah; and Martin R. Smith, M.Ed., Culver City, California.

I also want to thank Professor Gerald Corey for his superior textbooks which I used in graduate school and also as a reference for some of the therapies described in this book.

I am especially grateful to Randi Wagner for creating sensational art for the cover of this book.

And very special thanks to Elaine and John Gill, Dennis Hayes, Brigid, Amy, Karen, Dena, and all of the exceptional team at Crossing Press whose dedication and kindness showed me that working with a publisher could be fun. Elaine's editing skills made a significant contribution and I greatly appreciate her caring and effort.

Copyright ©1995 Lynne D. Finney
Cover art by Randi Wagner
Cover design by Amy Sibiga
Printed in the U.S.A.

Library of Congress Cataloging-in Publication Data

Finney, Lynne D., 1941-
    Reach for joy: how to find the right therapist and therapy for you. /
by Lynne D. Finney.
       p.   cm.
    Includes index.
    ISBN 0-89594-745-5 (paper)
       1. Psychotherapy—Popular works. 2. Psychotherapists—Evaluation.
3. Consumer education. I. Title.
RC480.515.F56 1995
616.89' 14—dc20   95-66
                                                                                                               CIP

*This book is dedicated with love to Jim who encouraged me to write it,
my mother and Dale who encouraged me to keep writing,
and Jackie and Bill who encouraged me to have fun.*

> *"The unexamined life is not worth living."*
> —Plato

Contents

IMPORTANT INFORMATION 1

I. CHOOSING A THERAPIST 5

How do I know if I need a therapist? 6
   ✔ Self-evaluation questions 9
What happens during therapy? 13
How long will therapy take? 22
How often do I need to see a therapist? 28
How much will therapy cost
   and how can I pay for it? 33
How do I find potential therapists? 39
   ✔ Checklist for obtaining referrals 42
What qualifications should my psychotherapist have? 44
   ✔ Basic qualifications checklist 53
How do I choose a therapist who is right for me? 55
   ✔ Interview questions 64
   ✔ Checklist for evaluating your candidates 66
Should I choose a male or female therapist? 69
Group Therapy 72
   • Special note for adolescents 74
   • Therapeutic groups—
      counseling and psychotherapy 75
   • Encounter groups 76
   • Marathon groups 76
   • T-groups 78
   • Self-help and support groups 79
   • Family groups and strategic therapy 79
   ✔ Interview questions and
      evaluation checklist for groups 80

II. SPECIAL CONCERNS 83

Will what I tell my therapist be kept confidential? 84
Can therapy make me worse? 90
What if I'm sexually attracted to my therapist
    or my therapist makes advances toward me? 96
Can therapy destroy my creativity? 100
How can I tell if I am making acceptable progress
    or if I should change therapists: resistance,
    codependency, transference, counter-transference 103
    ✔ Self-evaluation questions during therapy 111
    ✔ Checklist for assessing your progress in therapy ... 113
What can I do to make being in therapy easier? 115
How do I know when I no longer need therapy 120
What if I need to be hospitalized? 126
    ✔ Questions to ask before going to the hospital 133
    ✔ Hospital forms for your protection 135
How can I help a loved one who needs therapy? 140
How can I help a loved one who is in therapy? 144

III. SPECIFIC PROBLEMS 155

Depression—Therapy and the use of drugs 156
Alcohol and drug addiction treatment programs 161
    • Twelve-step programs 162
    • Rational Recovery 163
    • Other outpatient programs 163
    • Inpatient treatment programs 164
Sexual and physical abuse 167
Rape and domestic violence 183
Multiple personality disorder and ego states 187
Eating disorders: anorexia nervosa, bulimia and obesity .. 192
Anxiety disorders: panic attacks and phobias 198
Relationship problems—couples and marital therapy 203

IV. THERAPY FOR CHILDREN 209

How do I find a good therapist for my child? 210
    • How to find candidates to interview 210

- Qualifications 211
- Experience 212
- Finding the right therapist for your child 212
- Types of therapy for children 215
- Assessing whether the therapist is sensitive to your child's needs 217
- Preparing your child for the first appointment 217
- What if your child does not want to go to therapy? 218
- How long will your child's therapy take? 218
- Medication (attention deficit hyperactivity disorder and depression) 219
- Autism 221
- ✔ Interview questions for child therapists 223
- ✔ Evaluation checklist for your child's therapist 224

V. HOW DO I CHOOSE THE RIGHT TYPE OF THERAPY? 227

Psychoanalysis/Freudian analysis 229
The Neo-Freudian approach 232
Gestalt therapy 234
Transactional analysis 236
Behavior therapy 238
Rational-emotive therapy 241
Reality therapy 244
Hypnotherapy 246
Brainwave biofeedback 254
Breathing techniques for releasing emotions 260
Eye movement desensitization and reprocessing (EMDR) 266
Spiritual and transpersonal therapies 269
Prayer 275
Past-life regression 277
Neurolinguistic programming (NLP) 279
Art and music therapy 284
Body work and massage therapy 289
- Polarity massage 290
- Swedish massage 291

- Acupuncture and Shiatsu (acupressure) 291
- Chiropractic—spinal and cranial
  sacral adjustments 292
- Touch for Health 293
- Educational Kinesiology (Edu-K) 294
- Reflexology 294
- Mothers of Mercy 295
- Trager 295
- Reiki 296
- Feldenkrais Method® 296
- Rolfing 297

EPILOGUE 300

RESOURCES 301

ENDNOTES 309

INDEX 320

Important Information

Congratulations! If you are reading this book you have already taken a large step toward healing. You have recognized that your life is not working the way you would like and that you might benefit from help in making changes. Attaining this awareness is the first and often the hardest step to recovery.

Recognizing a problem enables you to do something about it. But you have gone even further: you have decided to take action to solve your problem and you are taking the sensible step of finding out how to get the best help possible. Your action means that you are motivated, which is essential to success in therapy; you have a healthy attitude and you are intelligent. So even though you may be in pain, frightened, depressed or confused, you have a lot going for you.

Since you are considering going to a therapist, you may be afraid you are "crazy," but the reality is that you are healthier than most people. The people who are in the worst shape are those who deny their problems, repress their feelings and reject help. They live in their own private hells where they hurt themselves and others. People who seek help tend to be the most creative, adaptive and highly functioning.

Seeing a therapist does not always mean you have a serious problem or that you are "abnormal." Studies show that the majority of us have low self-esteem and could benefit from therapy. Even if you do not have low self-esteem, you can use therapy to teach you new skills, to further your spiritual growth, increase your potential and reach greater heights of happiness. So if you decide to try therapy, you will be one of many people taking advantage of the advances in psychology and other sciences to make their lives more enjoyable.

The other good news is that you can be helped. I am sure some of you are thinking, "How can she possibly say that when she doesn't even know me?" I say that because as a therapist who has worked with clients who have been subjected to the most serious and prolonged types of physical, sexual, emotional and ritual abuse, I have seen healing take place even in the most severe cases. Perpetrators of sexual abuse, criminals, and people suffering from hallucinations, phobias, and so-called "personality disorders" can all heal.

You may have heard some therapists contend that certain criminals or pedophiles cannot be helped. These therapists are wrong; they are simply saying *they* do not have the skills to help. Other therapists do, as I found from talking to therapists all over the country when I do trainings on the treatment of childhood trauma.

I also know from my own personal experience that anyone can heal. I went to some of the most prestigious and expensive psychiatrists in the country for *fifteen years* because I was driven, depressed, suicidal and angry. My relationships were disastrous. I also had no memories of the first eleven years of my life, and I knew that was not "normal." Because I was a successful Washington, D. C., attorney and later a federal banking executive, these psychiatrists told me I was only "slightly neurotic" and that I should just get on with my life. But I knew something was very wrong because I was miserable all of the time, despite my professional achievements and awards.

It was not until I was over forty years old that a gynecologist recognized my symptoms as evidence of childhood sexual abuse and sent me to a therapist who used hypnosis. Under hypnosis, I quickly discovered that I had been physically and sexually abused by my father, which accounted for my years of amnesia. My story as well as other case histories and healing techniques are documented in *Reach for the Rainbow: Advanced Healing for Survivors of Sexual Abuse*.

When I first discovered my abuse, I fell apart. I found it difficult to believe my father could have done such things to me and I cried every day for six months, and on and off for many days afterwards. I trembled with fear and much of the time did not go out of the house. I thought that no one could ever recover from the kind of brutality I had endured from the time I was six months old until my eighth birthday.

I finally found a wonderful therapist, a psychiatric nurse, whose caring and creativity helped me deal with the pain. In a little more than a year, the shock of recovering years of repressed memories diminished and I began to be able to function again. I continued to work on the abuse issues with therapists for another year and then on my own, occasionally seeking help from colleagues when I felt I needed another perspective or a different technique. And I did heal. I feel so much better and more peaceful than I ever have in my life. If I can heal, so can you.

I have had many therapists, some good and some bad, just as I have found good and bad plumbers, doctors, lawyers and automobile mechanics. I have tried various theories of therapy, countless techniques, and innumerable self-help methods. I have seen what works for me as a person. I have also learned from my professional training as a therapist and from talking to hundreds of other therapists. I hope my experience will help you distinguish the good therapists from the bad ones, choose what will work best for you and keep you from making the same lengthy and expensive mistakes I made.

You have an advantage over me simply because so many revolutionary discoveries have been made since I was in therapy, advances in the understanding of our psychological and neurobiological makeup that have substantially improved the effectiveness of psychotherapy. During the last decade, scientists and clinicians have made significant breakthroughs in understanding how painful events, especially those in our early years, are imprinted in our minds and can affect us throughout our lives. This new understanding of our emotions, actions and behaviors, coupled with progress in therapeutic techniques, has made therapy much easier and results much more rapid. Therapy no longer needs to be as lengthy, expensive, or painful as it was in the past.

When selecting a therapist, one of the most important things to keep in mind is that *your therapist works for you*. Sometimes when you are looking for a therapist you may be so depressed and feel so bad about yourself that you no longer trust your own instincts. I lay on the couch of a highly recommended psychiatrist, the president of the psychoanalytic society, for three years, four days a week. I knew I wasn't improving, but it was not until my friends pointed out that I was getting worse and urged me to change therapists that I had the courage to leave him. Since my confidence in myself was so low, I thought the lack of progress had to be all my fault. Now I understand that the lack of progress lay in psychoanalytic theory itself and also in my psychiatrist who never uttered a word. I have since learned how to tell if I am getting what I need from therapy.

Research indicates that the most significant factor in successful therapy may be your relationship with your therapist. Studies show that a warm, caring therapist who does no therapy is more effective than a therapist who does therapy but is not warm. Your therapist should be a compassionate friend. The fundamental rule for choosing a therapist is to pick one you *like*.

I have found with my own clients that we all know what is best for us. Our minds know exactly what we need to heal. So in choosing a therapist, use your common sense as well as your instincts. If you are not comfortable with your therapist during the first two or three sessions, leave, no matter how highly recommended that person is. If you look hard enough, you will find someone who is right for you.

There is no one "right" therapist. There are many people and techniques that can help you in different ways. This book will help you understand various theories of psychology and some of the hundreds of healing techniques that are available today. Although deciding to seek help may seem like a scary experience, I found it can also be a fascinating adventure into the wonders of the human mind.

I have learned that no matter how dysfunctional or "crazy" our thoughts or actions seem, everything we do has a logical explanation, usually based on something that we experienced as children. Explosions of anger, destructive relationships and addictions can be explained by painful incidents from our pasts. Once we become aware of what we are doing and the causes, we can change our actions and our attitudes.

Going through therapy can be challenging, but it can also be a learning experience—and at times even fun. This book will assist you in finding a therapist and a therapy to meet your needs, a person and process to help you as painlessly and effectively as possible. It will also help you find a therapist who will be your friend to accompany you on your journey.

Lynne A. Finney

Choosing a Therapist

How do I know if I need a therapist?

Almost everyone could benefit from some type of therapy because there are now so many wonderful methods available to help us improve the quality of our lives. If you are reading this book, you probably could be helped by a therapist. We are usually drawn by our subconscious minds to what we need. The fact that you are thinking about seeing a therapist indicates it is likely that a problem is bothering you, which you have not been able to resolve on your own. Or you may be seeking meaning in your life or a new stage of growth.

Your first concern might be whether therapy really works. An early study indicated that while people with a wide range of psychological disorders improved after therapy, about the same proportion of people who received no treatment also improved.[1] More recent studies have contrary findings.[2] For example, researchers analyzed almost five hundred studies and found that the average person who received therapy had fewer problems and symptoms than eighty percent of people on waiting lists to obtain therapy.[3] Other studies show that the more therapy people receive, the greater their improvement. One study examined data from almost 2,500 people who had received psychotherapy for anxiety, depression and a variety of borderline psychotic states. As the number of sessions increased, the improvement increased.[4] It is reasonable to assume that the increased improvement is due to advances in treatment and that future studies will show even more dramatic improvement as therapy becomes more effective.

You might be asking why you can't simply talk to a spouse, partner or friend instead of paying a therapist. You can; I have received invaluable help from my friends, but often it is more helpful to talk to someone objective. Loved ones who are involved with us emotionally sometimes cannot see our problems clearly. And since our problems usually take time and sustained work to resolve, loved ones who have their own problems may become burned out listening over a prolonged period of time to our problems. Loved ones expect reciprocity, while professionals do not expect any emotional rewards or personal interaction; good therapists maintain a healthy objectivity and are totally present for you, concentrating on your needs.

Lastly, loved ones usually are not equipped to deal with displays of strong emotions, especially for long periods of time, even though experiencing your emotions, past and present, is generally what you need most in order to heal. Loved ones want you to be happy and so will encourage you not to cry or be angry and to "cheer up," which may not be what is best for your healing. While loved ones can be supportive and helpful in the healing process, a good therapist has the technical expertise to help you release any repressed trauma and speed the healing process.

Many of us, especially those whose trust in people was betrayed in childhood, try to tough it out and do everything on our own.

But the absurd image of "pulling ourselves up by our own bootstraps" shows us how foolish it is to ignore the help available all around us. Try pulling yourself up by straps on your shoes. You can't; but someone else can lift you up. The support of a therapist can make your healing much faster and easier.

So how do you determine if you really *need* therapy? You do not need a therapist if your life is generally working well. If you are content *most* of the time (no one is happy all the time), if most of your relationships are satisfactory, if you feel successful most of the time in your job or occupation, and if you like yourself, you probably do not require therapy. My rule is that if it's not broken, don't fix it. You may want to discuss a particular issue or learn additional skills for improving your life but it is unlikely that you need to delve into your past or engage in any prolonged therapy. You might have fun exploring some of the new self-help books or methods for expanding your mind and making your life even more enjoyable, but the only thing you really need to do is enjoy what you have.

One word of warning. Even though your life is satisfactory or even wonderful right now, if you review your life and find that you have frequently been in crisis and that your happiness does not last, you may want to consider therapy so that you can avoid sabotaging what you have this time around. You may want to break out of a self-defeating pattern caused by happiness anxiety.

"Happiness anxiety" affects approximately 90% of the population. Our culture has made most of us believe we do not deserve to be happy and that we cannot be happy all the time. Some western religions have brainwashed us to think that we are placed on earth to struggle and suffer—and most of us have adopted this belief, either consciously or unconsciously, and so we feel guilty, anxious or uncomfortable when we are happy.

Have you ever felt really close to someone, really happy, and picked a fight? Happiness anxiety is at work. If you see a pattern in your life of things falling apart whenever you are happy, you might want to explore overcoming this phenomenon with a therapist.

Sadly, most of us do not fall into the category of having lives that generally work well. There are many reasons for this but the most common reason is the poor self-esteem we developed usually from childhood experiences which invalidated us and artificially limited our natural potential.

Why do most of us have such low self-esteem? Mainly because we were not given the love, nurturing and validation we needed as children to develop a healthy view of ourselves. We are only now beginning to realize the devastating effects neglect, abuse and physical punishment have on children and we have hardly begun the mammoth task of training people to be effective parents.

Studies also show that most of us have suffered some type of trauma as children and are still suffering the destructive effects, mentally, physically and spiritually. The conservative studies indicate that one in every three or four adults has been sexually abused under the age of 18.[5] That means more than fifty million Americans were sexually abused as children. Many studies place the number even higher. Similar statistics are available from Canada, England, Australia, France and Belgium. In fact, one out of every five trials in the Cours d'Assises in France involves incest.[6]

Studies further indicate that more than half of the population has suffered some form of child abuse, if physical abuse and neglect are added to sexual abuse. Events which produce emotional harm to children are more difficult to quantify and record, but most children in our society are subjected to emotional trauma. Very few of us have escaped some sort of childhood trauma that may have damaged our self-esteem and produced behavior patterns which adversely affect our adult lives.

To make matters worse, in western culture we are also brainwashed with the terrifying spectres of hell, original sin and damnation. Even if the religion we follow does not espouse these psychologically damaging beliefs, we hear about them as children and they haunt us all of our lives. Since there are no easy-to-follow rules for getting into heaven, we live in a state of unconscious fear, which sometimes creeps into consciousness, believing we can never be good enough to avoid burning in hell. Such beliefs can hardly be expected to make us feel good about ourselves or allow us to enjoy life.

Healthy self-esteem is the single most important factor in living well and being happy. Virtually all dysfunctional behavior comes from low self-esteem usually resulting from some kind of childhood trauma. The primary purpose of therapy is to develop good self-esteem. People who love themselves do not hurt themselves or others.

The psychological importance of loving ourselves was recognized centuries ago. The *Bible* counsels us to "Love thy neighbor *as* thyself," acknowledging that unless we love ourselves *first*, we are unable to really love anyone else. But most of us don't really like ourselves and so we engage in behaviors which are destructive to ourselves and others. These behaviors range from violence and alcohol, substance and sexual addictions to marital problems, abusive relationships and sabotaged happiness.

There are no hard and fast rules to determine if you need therapy, but if you see yourself in one or more of the following categories, I believe some form of regular therapy would be beneficial.

✓ Self-evaluation questions

1. You don't like yourself, think you are not good enough, constantly criticize yourself, or feel you have to be perfect.
2. You think about hurting or killing yourself or someone else.
3. You are physically violent, or suspect you are abusing someone.
4. You are having flashbacks or hallucinations, seeing things or people that are not there, or hearing voices.
5. You have fears which keep you from living a satisfactory life, such as fears of going outside, riding in elevators, or of animals, people, or everyday objects.
6. You know or suspect that you were physically or sexually abused or neglected as a child, or that your parents abused drugs or alcohol.

7. You are addicted to or are abusing alcohol or drugs, including prescription tranquilizers and sleeping pills.
8. You are presently in a relationship where you are being emotionally, physically or sexually abused, or you have a pattern of relationships which end unhappily.
9. You do not trust people or you feel that people are constantly betraying you and taking advantage of you.
10. You become angry out of proportion to the circumstances.
11. You are frequently depressed, hopeless or listless, or your life seems empty, without meaning.

    (If you answered "yes" to this question, please use the depression checklist on page 156 to determine if you fit that profile.)
12. You are unable to express or feel emotions.

All of these conditions can be healed; you do not have to continue to suffer with them. And all of these conditions have a logical explanation, usually based on painful experiences in your past.

People are often afraid of spending years of misery in therapy. Most of us have already been unhappy for longer than we would like and just want to put our problems behind us. However, the harsh truth is that you can't ignore your problems because untreated, they usually don't get better, they only grow worse.

We are miraculous mechanisms, and our minds and bodies work constantly to bring us to a state of perfect health. If we ignore our problems, our minds and bodies remind us to face them by developing mental and physical symptoms and diseases. We humans also have an uncanny knack for creating situations for ourselves again and again which force us to deal with our painful issues. We can't get out of our pain by ignoring it.

An enlightened friend, Gary Acevedo, recently gave me the best reason I have heard for the existence of suffering. He said that just as missiles are kept on course by a complex guidance system, humans also have a built-in guidance system. Our guidance system is suffering. Pain, fear and anger are the signals which tell us when we are off course so we can adjust our thoughts and actions and get back on track. The farther we wander from our course, the more suffering we experience. Sometimes we need experts to help us understand these signals so that we can correct our course and return to our path of fulfillment and happiness.

You do not "catch" psychological problems like a cold. They arise from your reaction to something distressing, something you had difficulty coping with. We often ignore symptoms which indicate we need help because we feel we should tough it out or grin and bear it, when by finding the cause we could solve the problem.

Your life doesn't have to stop just because you are in therapy. Some people believe that you have to be miserable during therapy. While it is true that therapy may bring out some painful emotions, you can still enjoy life. Your therapist can show you ways to enjoy the present by improving your life and relationships even while you are working out past hurts. I tell my clients as a general rule, with exceptions, of course, that while they are in therapy they are allowed to be miserable a maximum of two hours per day. Then they have to do something they enjoy.

The purpose of therapy is to help you learn to be happy in the present and you can start doing that right away. You have already lived through the worst you will ever go through and now all you have to do is deal with the memories—past thoughts. The reality is that you have already survived and you can enjoy life now, even if you have some learning to do and changes to make.

The old stigma of therapy as being only for weak people or those who are "crazy" has thankfully almost disappeared. These fears are being replaced with the more rational, scientifically confirmed knowledge that appropriate therapy is effective and beneficial, and that most of us can benefit from it. We are finally becoming aware that we need to clear the past in order to enjoy the present—and to reach new levels of experience.

You do not need to have a problem to take advantage of the many forms of therapy available today. Many people are now using therapy as a mind-expanding experience and to increase their present happiness. People searching for meaning in life are finding it through transpersonal therapy and other techniques that increase spiritual awareness. The trend of spiritual growth, the search for enlightenment, is sweeping the world. The best-selling book on spiritual development, *The Celestine Prophecy*, emphasizes that "clearing the past" is an essential part of spiritual growth; we cannot reach our maximum potential without dealing with the psychological limitations imposed by our past experiences.

Going to a therapist means that you have a healthy desire to improve and grow. The real question is not whether you *need* a therapist, but whether you want to take advantage of ways to help you grow further and faster. Exploring yourself is a fascinating adventure, one which will change you forever.

What happens during therapy?

The primary purpose of therapy is to help you develop positive self-esteem and become consciously aware of your feelings, beliefs, thoughts and actions so that you can have freedom of choice. Most of us are puppets, blindly reacting to childhood misconceptions and ancient wounds. We may believe we act with a great deal of deliberation and thoughtful planning, but the truth is that without help, most of us rarely overcome the mental programming instilled in us by childhood trauma, because as children we were unable to analyze and assimilate our painful experiences.

We think we are free but we are not. Freedom comes with awareness. You have choices only when you know what you are doing and why.

Much of therapy is spent acquiring awareness of our dysfunctional patterns of behavior and the thoughts and beliefs about ourselves and the world that destroy our happiness. The main way therapists uncover these obstacles is by finding out about our lives, usually by asking us to describe our histories, families and significant events.

You may feel awkward and even embarrassed talking about your most private thoughts and feelings and the painful events in your life, but therapists need this information so that they can piece together the patterns in your life that are holding you back. I assure you that whatever you tell them will not be anything they have not heard before. The more honest and open you are, the faster you will heal.

The most dramatic advance in psychotherapy has been the discovery of the lasting effects of childhood trauma. Psychologists studying the effects of trauma on veterans of the Korean conflict and the Vietnam War observed that soldiers subjected to bloody combat or tortured as prisoners of war displayed a cluster of similar symptoms, including loss of memory, inappropriate anger, nightmares, insomnia, depression, flashbacks and alienation from others. The soldiers' repressed memories usually returned to consciousness within a few years of their return home, and recovery of the traumatic memories normally resulted in elimination of the other symptoms.

The same symptoms were found among people who were victims of natural disasters, accidents and violent crimes. The syndrome was named "post-traumatic stress disorder (PTSD)."

An accurate and moving example of post-traumatic stress disorder and its treatment was portrayed on television in the last episode of *M*A*S*H*, where surgeon Hawkeye (played by Alan Alda) is in a hospital being treated by Sidney, the psychiatrist. Hawkeye is angry, unable to function as a surgeon. He becomes very upset when Sidney tries to talk to him about an experience on a bus. Just mentioning a bus throws Hawkeye into a rage and state of panic, although he does not know why.

When he begins to recover the traumatic memory, he recalls being on a bus with refugees in enemy territory. Since an enemy patrol was in the area, everyone on the bus had to be very quiet to avoid detection. A refugee woman was holding a cackling chicken. Terrified that the chicken would attract the patrol, Hawkeye told her repeatedly to keep the chicken quiet. She finally kills the chicken.

As his session with Sidney continues, Hawkeye suddenly recovers the complete memory of the traumatic event, screaming when he remembers that the "chicken" was actually the woman's baby. He cries in anguish that she smothered her own baby to save the people on the bus.

Hawkeye goes through a catharsis, a release of the pain and grief over the death of the baby. The dialogue makes it clear that Hawkeye has subsequent sessions with the psychiatrist to alleviate his pain and feelings of guilt. When we see him later, he is calmer and rational, ready to return to his MASH unit.

This incident shows how PTSD works, how painful events become imprinted on our brains, how emotional reactions can be triggered by ordinary events (such as the mention of a bus for Hawkeye), how our minds erect defenses to conceal the trauma and our painful emotions, and how the destructive effects of repressing traumatic events can be successfully resolved in therapy.

An essential element of post-traumatic stress disorder is the fact that memories of traumatic events are repressed so that the person cannot remember them consciously. Neurobiologists have now isolated some of the brain functions responsible for imprinting a traumatic event in the subconscious while blocking that event from the conscious mind. Their studies, including ground-breaking research by psychiatrists at Harvard Medical School, indicate that intense emotions interfere with information processing, leading to amnesia.[1]

Traumatic events are not processed by our minds in the same way as ordinary events; they *bypass* the part of our brains that analyzes what we experience, going directly to another part where the experience is recorded *exactly as it occurred* with all of the information we receive from our five senses, including the intense emotions.

People may experience fear, anger or grief and confusion so intense that their minds cannot analyze the event and will block it from consciousness, but the event does not just disappear. The memory is indelibly recorded. Our minds store memories of traumatic events until our subconscious determines that we are ready to deal with them at a conscious level. The memories and associated feelings remain frozen in our brains just as they were when the event occurred.

In fact, researchers have found that memories created under intense stress and fear are far more accurate and detailed than ordinary memories of everyday events. When repressed memories are recovered, the person may experience them as though reliving the event with all of the violent emotions, although the physical pain is far less.[2]

Clinicians and researchers have found that children also experience post-traumatic stress disorder. When children experience traumatic events, such as a death in the family or abuse, they are subjected to intolerable stress and overwhelming emotions; they are unable to cope with what is happening to them and in most cases cannot understand it. The part of these children's minds that analyzes and processes ordinary events cannot cope with the flood of emotions and is bypassed. The memory is shunted to another part of the child's mind with the attendant emotions where they are imprinted, but blocked from consciousness.[3]

When these traumatic memories are recovered, people experience them at the age they were when the events occurred. A forty-year-old woman will experience the feelings and thoughts she had when she was beaten at the age of three and, under hypnosis, will even talk like a three-year old.

Many children die each year from abuse, an average of four a day in the United States, not just from the physical effects but from the mental trauma. Most abused children cope by suppressing their traumatic memories so that they can survive and grow up.

As adults, people may have totally forgotten the sexual, physical or emotional trauma they suffered as children, and start therapy because they are having nightmares, body memories or flashbacks of events they do not recall, or because they are depressed, angry or caught in patterns of victimization.

Children do not have to be abused to suffer trauma sufficient to result in post-traumatic stress disorder. Children can be traumatized by events that might not be overwhelming to an adult because children's minds, especially in the very young, lack the capability to process the experiences.

One of my clients, whom I will call Julie, recalled with a great deal of pain how she wanted desperately as a small child to be closer to her busy and rather distant mother. When she was five, Julie thought long and hard about what she could do to win her mother's approval and love. Her mother collected pictures of horses, so Julie spent weeks in kindergarten laboriously drawing a picture of a horse for her mother. When Julie finished the picture, she ran home to give it to her mother, but her mother was on the phone and pushed her away without looking at the drawing.

Julie was devastated by feelings of rejection, anger, disappointment, failure and grief which she repressed, feelings so overwhelming that she blocked them from her conscious memory. When she recovered those feelings under hypnosis as an adult, Julie found that she had concluded as a child based on this incident that her mother would never love her, that *no one* would ever love her, that she was inherently unlovable, and that it was not worth working hard or planning anything because whatever she did would not be appreciated—*and she acted on these beliefs for her entire life!*

This situation may not seem traumatic, but it was to five-year old Julie. The core beliefs created by her mother's general lack of attention combined with rejection of the picture controlled Julie's life, destroying her relationships and keeping her from completing her goals, like a college degree. Once she recovered the memories and released the pain she felt when her mother pushed her away, Julie was able to view her mother's actions from a more adult, realistic perspective. Julie was able to understand that her mother's actions did not mean she did not love her, but simply that her mother was raising eight children and was simply too exhausted to fulfill Julie's needs.

After changing her childhood decisions and substituting more positive beliefs, Julie blossomed almost immediately. She realized there was nothing wrong with her and was able to reconcile with her husband, finish college and take charge of her life.

When children are traumatized, they repress their memories longer than adults who suffer trauma, like Hawkeye, and many do not recover their memories until their thirties or forties. It appears that our subconscious minds somehow know when we are mature enough to process the memories consciously.

Memories can be repressed in various ways. Some people block out both the painful event and the emotions surrounding it. Others remember details of the event, but suppress the feelings they had. Those who block only the emotions are often harder to treat because they assume that since they have no feelings, the event did not affect them. Unfortunately, the opposite is true. Suppressed emotions can establish destructive unconscious behavioral patterns which wreak havoc on our adult lives even if we consciously remember what occurred.

Children who are repeatedly abused over a long period of time may block out whole years of their childhood from memory, as I did. And some children are so severely abused that they survive not only by blocking memories of the abuse from their conscious minds, but also by creating a number of new, distinct personalities to deal with their abusers. This coping mechanism is known as multiple personality disorder, and it affects many more people than therapists previously recognized.

Many of our traumas remain hidden from us until our minds or bodies give us hints that something is wrong. Scientists have found that we not only store traumatic memories in our minds but in our bodies as well. People often experience unexplained body sensations that are related to childhood trauma, such as pain with intercourse if the person was raped or pain in the anus if sodomized. Abuse victims are sometimes diagnosed with somatization disorder because they suffer from multiple recurrent physical complaints over a period of years for which no medical cause can be found.[4] The stress of trauma can create a multitude of physical ailments such as headaches, heart palpitations, impotence and gastrointestinal problems.[5]

But the most damaging result of repressing traumatic events is that children also suppress the erroneous conclusions they make about those events, conclusions which affect their view of themselves and their world for the rest of their lives. A common example is the conclusion reached by abused children that they are somehow responsible for their abuse. Young children are at a developmental stage when they are egocentric; they believe that they are the center of the universe and that they cause everything that happens to them. They also quickly learn that they are punished when they are "bad," and since abuse seems like a punishment, they draw the "obvious" conclusion that they must be really bad.

Most children go one step further: they hear that God protects "good little children" and so conclude that if they are being abused, they must be so bad that God does not love them and is punishing them. Such beliefs destroy their self-esteem and inculcate a frightening view of an unsafe, punitive universe which ruins their lives, until they absolve themselves of their "guilt."

Other common traumatic events also have fairly universal effects. For example, if your parent, sibling, abuser or other important person died when you were young, you may have concluded that you were somehow responsible for the death, because young children believe they cause everything that happens to them, even that angry thoughts can kill. In a recent interview Maya Angelou, renowned poet, educator, author, actress and civil rights activist, revealed how she had concluded as a child that she had killed her abuser: "When I was seven and one-half years of age, I was raped. I told my mother about it and the man responsible was put in jail. For some reason he was released soon afterward and a couple of days later he was found murdered. My child's mind informed me that my voice (as a witness at the trial) had caused his death, and as a result of that belief I didn't speak a word again until I was thirteen."

Obviously a belief that you killed someone will have a devastating effect on your self-esteem and cause guilt that will negatively affect your life. If you are fifty years old, you might think that the death of a brother when you were three is no longer important, but the past continues to haunt us until we deal with it.

When I started my therapy, I found it hard to accept the fact that events in my early childhood could continue to have such an enormous impact on me as an adult. I didn't want to believe that I was still repeating the painful patterns established in my childhood. I screamed at my therapist that I couldn't believe I wasn't even as smart as Pavlov's dog; at least he stopped going to the place where he received electric shocks while I was unconsciously drawn to repeat my destructive patterns and relationships over and over. It was only by recovering the memories of my abuse and bringing to consciousness the emotions and decisions responsible for my harmful patterns of behavior that I realized the extent to which my childhood trauma dominated my adult life.

Many people assume that a child will "grow out of" problems and that if they don't talk about unpleasant experiences, the effects will just go away. Unfortunately, research shows that the exact opposite is true. These repressed memories and emotions remain frozen, trapped inside us, festering and ruining our lives until we release them to consciousness where we can resolve them.

Although we may not remember the repressed incidents or how we felt about them, the emotions we suppressed will surface when triggered by later events and influence our lives and decisions. Have you ever erupted with anger out of proportion to the situation? Your reaction was probably exaggerated by old anger you repressed from an earlier experience.

Therapists work to help you uncover the true cause of your emotions. When you resolve your childhood problems, your old feelings no longer influence you and you become free to deal with present events on their own merits.

Many adults would rather not believe that their early childhood experiences still have such a profound effect on their behavior, insisting that you can't blame everything on your parents. While it is true that *blaming* your parents is unproductive, understanding your reaction to your parents' actions can help you become aware of patterns of behavior that you may want to change—and take responsibility for them. We may have been abused when we were young, but no one is abusing us now. We are responsible for our own actions and healing now.

In some cases, simply recognizing how you felt about a childhood episode can help you break out of a lifelong dysfunctional pattern of behavior. For example, Bill, a successful businessman in his fifties, wanted to find out why his relationships were unsatisfactory. His wife and children thought him cold and domineering because he never talked about his feelings or his problems. He would not let his family or his employees help him; he always had to do everything himself. Bill's inability to share his feelings or rely on others left him isolated, especially after his wife left him.

Under hypnosis, Bill recalled his terror and grief at being left alone during the Depression when he was four years old by his parents who worked in the family hardware store. A fifteen-year-old aunt looked in on him for a few minutes each afternoon. He remembered his aunt telling him that if he cried or complained he would be left all alone forever. She also told him he had to be good and take care of his infant brother if he wanted his parents to return.

Bill realized that his entire life had been organized around his childhood conclusions based on his aunt's admonitions: if you want to be loved and you don't want to be alone, you have to be stoic, never show your feelings, and help others without asking anything for yourself. His awareness of these childhood decisions changed his life almost immediately.

Bill worked on getting in touch with his feelings and sharing them with his family, including problems he was having in his business. His family and friends responded warmly when he started asking for their help. After less than three months of therapy, Bill said, "I feel wonderful about the changes in myself; it's amazing, I feel so good. I enjoy life."

Bill was an intelligent man who had tried using logic and will power to break out of his dysfunctional patterns of behavior before coming to therapy. But only after he recalled his childhood trauma, expressed his feelings about being left alone, and *reassessed the unconscious decisions he made as a child*, was he able to change his behavior.

It is not enough to simply recover the memory and emotions of traumatic events. We must also uncover the cluster of conclusions we made based on those events and substitute new positive decisions both in our adult mind and in the child part of our mind that contains the repressed memories.

You may be wondering if all psychological problems are based on responses to traumatic experiences. The answer is the vast majority, according to recent research and clinical experience. Psychotherapists have found that there is a reason for dysfunctional behavior; it does not happen at random. In the absence of a physical explanation such as a brain tumor or drugs, the reason is usually childhood trauma. In fact, recent studies indicate that certain genes carrying defects require extreme stress in order to be activated; many people with the genetic defect never exhibit the trait if not subjected to trauma. Other studies show that the majority of people who seek therapy have experienced some sort of childhood trauma.[6]

We were designed to function perfectly; our minds and bodies are miraculous mechanisms which are constantly working to bring us to a perfect state of mental and physical health. We were born to be happy and loving, as therapists have found who regress their clients under hypnosis to infancy.

If we hurt ourselves or others, there is a reason that can usually be traced to childhood trauma. We used to think alcoholism was a physical disease, but recent studies have shown a high correlation between alcohol or drug abuse and child sexual abuse. Sexual abuse is a learned behavior that is frequently passed from generation to generation. Although alcoholism also appears to run in families, the chain may be due to abuse rather than genetics, or the type of gene that requires trauma to activate it.

So the new emphasis in therapy is to find the reason for harmful behavior. The most effective therapy helps you to do the following:

1. Become aware of your traumatic experiences which are causing harmful behavior.
2. Release from your mind and body in an appropriate and safe way the suppressed emotions surrounding traumatic events.
3. Recall and reevaluate the erroneous decisions you made about yourself and the world.
4. Replace unhealthy decisions, thoughts, behaviors, and spiritual beliefs with positive ones.
5. Recognize your strengths, love yourself, develop a positive view of the world, and learn new behaviors and creative ways of interacting so that you can enjoy life.

These basic therapeutic goals can be achieved in many ways. Various theories and techniques are described in Part V.

Your therapist will do her best to use the techniques that you need at the moment, but she is only a guide. You are responsible for your own therapy and need to be open and honest about what you feel and what you want. Your instincts about what you need are usually reliable and a good therapist should help you follow them. One of my best therapists frequently asked me what I thought we should work on next and what would work best, and I have found these questions to be very effective with my own clients. It is amazing how our minds seem to know how to heal us.

Therapy is a safe place to explore your feelings and behaviors so that you can become aware of the choices you are making and why you are making them. Then you will be truly free to decide what you want and obtain it without being sabotaged by your past.

How long will therapy take?

It is impossible to estimate precisely how long your therapy will take, but because of the growth in our understanding of human psychology and new techniques that are available, the length of therapy is generally much shorter than it used to be. You no longer have to spend many years in therapy; in fact recent studies indicate that prolonged therapy may be less effective than shorter-term therapy and may even be counterproductive.

Interminable therapies, such as Freudian psychoanalysis where you spend an hour a day four or five times a week on your analyst's couch for five to eight years, have been discredited. Studies show that most of the gains in long-term treatment are achieved early in the treatment, often by the fifth or sixth session. Psychotherapists have developed methods that focus on the causes of problems and resolve them more directly and efficiently.

I believe that with the discovery or rediscovery of techniques such as hypnotherapy, breath work which releases repressed emotions, enlightened theories of marital intervention, and a more holistic view of psychology, most therapy should not take more than a year or two. Some conditions such as multiple personality disorder may take longer, but even these conditions and others resulting from severe trauma can be successfully treated in a couple of years using new methods. I specialize in the treatment of adults and adolescents who have been sexually abused as children and my own rule is that I will not treat a client for more than two years.

Seeing the same therapist for more than two years may create an unhealthy dependence. The purpose of therapy is to help you feel good about yourself and teach you the skills you need to handle problems on your own. If you think your progress is too slow, you can change therapists to obtain a new perspective and break through blocks. No one therapist has all the answers. There are many approaches and many techniques which can help you. If the one you are using is not working for you, try something or someone else.

One of the questions you should ask a therapist in your initial interview is how long therapy will take. You may also want to ask how long the therapist has been seeing some of his clients. If the therapist starts talking in terms of several years, you may want to cross him off your list.

How long your therapy takes will depend on many factors including the number and type of problems you want to resolve, the length and severity of abuse as a child, whether you consciously remember traumatic events in your life, and whether the use of drugs or alcohol impedes your progress in therapy. There are many variables that make it impossible to predict a termination date.

The most important factors are your own attitude and commitment to healing—you have control over those. *You* determine whether or not to make healing a priority in your life, whether you attend your sessions regularly, whether you are willing to face painful issues, and whether you will take the time to work on your own outside of the sessions to make your life better.

One word of warning: While you naturally want to heal as quickly as possible, it is important to maintain a balance and not push yourself too fast. Our minds can process only so much information at a time and, especially if you are dealing with painful events, you may need to rest periodically to absorb what you have uncovered. Trust your instincts and take care to ensure that you do not go faster than is safe for you.

Your expectations of how long you will take to heal can have a significant effect on the time you spend in therapy. In fact, new studies indicate that your expectations may be the most determinative factor in the speed of your recovery.

I was reading studies about the effect of expectations on progress in therapy when one of my clients dramatically brought this point home to me. Carol had been neglected by her parents and raped by a neighbor who was a boy scout leader, father and "upstanding" member of his church and community. The neighbor also abused Carol's siblings and, according to the police investigation, over a hundred other children. Carol had repressed many early memories and recovered some of these memories using hypnosis. Highly motivated and willing to face the painful memories and emotions, she made spectacular progress. In a little over six months, Carol dealt with her abuse and family issues (her family participated in the therapy), overcame her feelings of being evil and worthless, regained her self-esteem, resolved issues about her career and marriage, and took positive steps in other areas of her life. She glowed with happiness. We began to talk about terminating therapy and started to see each other less frequently.

Almost immediately I noticed Carol's happiness disintegrating as she requested more frequent appointments and started rehashing issues we had already resolved. I thought perhaps she was feeling anxious about having her life go so well and began exploring my concerns with her. It turned out that she was sabotaging herself with beliefs about how long therapy should take.

Shortly before we began to discuss termination, Carol had asked my advice about joining a sexual abuse support group at her university. I was enthusiastic about the idea because I thought meeting other survivors of abuse would reinforce the progress Carol had made and help her see that she was not alone. Carol shared the speed of her recovery with the group. Several members who had been in therapy for years told her that healing from sexual abuse so fast was impossible and that she must be avoiding painful issues. Carol believed her fellow group members and thought she must have missed something. She was looking for more problems.

After she realized that she needed to trust her own feelings about whether or not she had resolved her problems, Carol bounced back to her former state of happiness. Carol is now in Hawaii where she has started a new life with her husband and child, and she has sent me several letters describing how wonderful she feels. I am grateful to Carol for teaching me how important our expectations about healing can be; I now spend time discussing my clients' beliefs on these issues early in therapy so I can help them reevaluate any assumptions that may hinder their progress.

Although we may consciously think we do not know how long we need to be in therapy, our unconscious minds seem to know. My favorite therapist, a psychiatric nurse, asked me how long I thought my therapy would take. When I said I didn't know, she proposed a six-month deadline. I felt very uncomfortable with that estimate, but I did not know why. At the time, I had only uncovered memories of the sexual abuse by my father; I was unaware of the torture I discovered later. The severity of my abuse extended my therapy to two years, and I have gone to other therapists for short periods to discuss specific issues since then. My subconscious mind knew I had more to work on than my conscious mind was aware of. It knew that my healing would take longer than six months.

I have found that you can consciously program your mind to make your recovery quicker and easier. I often have my clients mentally repeat daily affirmations like, "Healing and learning are quick, easy, and fun." Clients with repressed memories may add, "I let go of my past quickly and easily." Even if you don't consciously believe these statements, repeating them often in your mind will begin to override your unconscious limiting beliefs and your subconscious will start to accept and act on what you tell it.

You can also accelerate your therapy by keeping yourself in good physical condition; therapy can be stressful and you can reduce the stress by getting plenty of rest and exercise, and eating well. Studies also show that exercise is *the* most effective antidote for depression. Other ways to facilitate therapy can be found on page 115.

Finally, you can expedite your therapy by doing work on your own. Bookstores and libraries are filled with self-help books, tapes and videos, and you can find information on any psychological issue. Learning more about your problem can reduce your fear and give you a clearer picture of issues you need to address in therapy.

The truth is that you have complete control over your therapy including how long it takes even though that control may not always be conscious. If you are not progressing as fast as you would like, you need to sit quietly and ask yourself what is stopping you. Do you believe you deserve to get well and be happy? Are you afraid of success? Are you sabotaging your success because you don't want your parents to be proud of you? Are you afraid of facing a problem because you think you will lose someone you love?

In most cases, people are responsible for their own progress in therapy or the lack of it. Therapists don't heal you; you heal yourself. Therapists merely guide you, giving you an objective perspective and suggestions. What you do with what you hear determines how easily you heal.

In some cases the therapist will be the chief obstacle to your progress. The best time to determine if your therapist is helpful is at the beginning of the therapy. Generally, you should begin to feel better after one or two sessions. After the first couple of sessions, you should at least have an increased understanding of your problem and behavior. When I finally found therapists who knew how to help me, I made noticeable progress immediately. I began to recover memories of my childhood abuse and became aware of how the abuse had negatively affected my view of myself and the world. Although at first I was more emotionally distressed because of these revelations, I also felt some relief because I found logical explanations for so many events in my life that no one had been able to explain during years of futile therapy.

After three or four sessions, if you do not feel better, or at least feel you have made substantial progress in discovering the reasons for your problem, you should consider finding another therapist.

Finally, your progress in therapy is strongly influenced by your relationship with your therapist. In fact, some studies indicate that a warm, trusting relationship with the therapist may be the most important factor in attaining a successful outcome. You should feel that your therapist truly cares for you and is a friend. After two or three sessions, you should feel comfortable with your therapist. In deciding whether you have found the right therapist, ask yourself whether he listens to you, whether he treats you with respect, whether he is kind. If the answer is no, find another therapist.

Sometimes we don't like someone or think they don't like us because we find it hard to trust or like anyone. If you believe your therapist does not like you or you are considering leaving, it is wise to talk about these feelings. You may have a misconception about the therapist that can be easily cleared up through open discussion.

Expressing your feelings is a healthy learning experience; most of us don't know how to talk about feelings and problems. Your therapist's response to your concerns, whether he takes them seriously and tries to work them out or belittles you and blames you for the problem, will give you more information about his competence and personality.

I want to stress that just because you are in therapy, you should not assume that the problem must be yours. There are bad therapists just as there are bad plumbers, lawyers and automobile mechanics. Therapists are human and have their own problems which sometimes interfere with their professional responsibilities. A therapist may be exceptionally competent and still not be the right one for you. Trust your own instincts; if you do not feel the therapist or the type of treatment is right for you, LEAVE.

Although finding the right therapist can seem like a life-or-death decision, it really is not. Nothing is irrevocable. If you make the wrong choice, you can change. If changing turns out to be a mistake, you can always return to the therapist you left. Therapists who have worked out their own insecurities know that the needs and perceptions of their clients may change and they understand that clients may change therapists for a variety of reasons. They are not hurt if clients leave and they will welcome them back if they return. I have referred my clients to other therapists who I thought could help in a different way. A couple of clients left because they thought I pushed them too hard. When they returned, they said they had not made progress with their new therapists and realized that they needed to be pushed. I was delighted. The fact that they had left for a while did not in any way affect our relationship.

If you are not satisfied with your progress, it's not the end of the world; you can always try another therapist. The time you spend looking for a therapist you like will not be wasted; it is part of your learning process. You will be discovering how to find what you want and how to give yourself what is best for you.

How often do I need to see a therapist?

If you choose traditional individual psychotherapy, you would normally attend a fifty-minute session once a week. Fifty minutes gives the therapist ten minutes between appointments to keep up with record keeping, go to the bathroom and take a short break between clients.

However, the fifty-minute session for adult individual therapy has come under increasing criticism because it simply does not allow sufficient time to complete the emotional release and processing found to be the most effective in addressing many problems. Adhering to a rigid forty-five or fifty minute session can be a way for therapists to avoid dealing with a client's intense emotions and painful issues. Scheduling appointments every hour also means that the therapist is frequently late because he is forced to run over into the next session in order to finish what his client is working on or, worse, cut the client off prematurely, leaving the client in an emotional or depressed state in order to adhere to his schedule.

One of my clients whom I will call Jeanne reported being an inpatient in one of the most prestigious psychiatric hospitals in the country where she underwent treatment for depression and trauma resulting from childhood sexual abuse. Her psychiatrist saw her for fifty minutes once a week and refused to exceed his fifty-minute limit no matter what emotional state he left Jeanne in. At times she left his office so distressed that the staff on her ward would call the psychiatrist and ask him to see her again. The psychiatrist refused and told the staff to give Jeanne drugs to "keep her quiet" until her appointment the following week. Needless to say, Jeanne's condition deteriorated.

Therapists often find that a ten-minute break is not long enough to make a transition between clients; many therapists burn out trying to juggle six to eight clients a day, one right after the other. Frankly, I find it very difficult to keep clients separated in my mind or even remember their names if I see so many so close together.

To avoid these problems, many therapists are adopting schedules of two-hour sessions every two weeks, with longer breaks between clients. The two-hour session ensures that the client has ample time to resolve an issue.

Hypnotherapy and breath work sessions almost always require more than an hour to be effective. It is simply not possible to have a client catch up on what has happened in the past week, go into a state of self-hypnosis or begin the breathing process, complete emotional release and recover memories, reframe damaging decisions, come to a positive state of mind and process the session in fifty minutes.

At the beginning of a session, clients generally want to discuss what has occurred since the last session and what is currently going on in their lives. This preliminary discussion can last a half-hour or more and often eats up most of a fifty-minute session so that no actual therapy is accomplished. Although a client may appear to skip around to a variety of topics, the narrative usually has a theme such as outbursts of anger, or a repetitive pattern like feelings of betrayal. This information is valuable in that it allows the therapist *and* the client to choose a particular issue to resolve during the remainder of the session. Clients also need this preliminary time to vent emotions about problems they are having, to lead into the issue they want to work on and to overcome any anxiety they may have.

A two-hour session also provides adequate time for the therapist to use various techniques to resolve all or a part of an issue, and allows the client time to release emotions and then return to a stable, positive frame of mind before leaving. I believe therapists should be flexible and finish working on an issue however long it takes. It is usually difficult to return to a state of mind or emotion at a later session.

Carol, a victim of sexual abuse by a neighbor, had extremely low self-esteem. When she was under hypnosis, the child part of Carol revealed her feelings that she was bad because she had not stopped her abuse which occurred for several years. She felt that if she had done so, her younger brothers and sisters might have been spared. I asked her what she could have done at the age of five. She remembered trying to tell her father about her neighbor's actions but her father did not understand and would not believe her. Usually retrieving such a memory would remove the child's guilt, but in this case Carol's opinion did not change. After more probing it became apparent that both the child and adult part of her believed that she was responsible not just for her siblings' abuse, but for the abuse of all the children molested by the neighbor over more than twenty years.

Even though the two-hour session had expired, I could not leave Carol with such a damaging belief after having uncovered it. I spent another hour helping Carol and the child part of her understand that there was nothing she could have done at this age to stop her neighbor and that she had done the best she could by trying to tell her father. When she realized she was not responsible for what her abuser had done to other children, the change in her was dramatic and well worth the extra time we spent. Her whole personality went from timidity to confidence and joy once she let go of the terrible burden of guilt she had been carrying. She was able to terminate therapy soon afterwards.

Perhaps I could have waited for the next session to work on the second part of Carol's problem, but I was not sure that her mind would go back to the same age and the same emotion. I felt it was important to work out the whole issue at once. I did not want to leave Carol with such a harmful negative belief simply in order to adhere to a schedule.

While therapists cannot always spend an extra hour with a client, the good ones are willing to bend a little to meet the needs of their clients, to be available in a crisis. You should ask your prospective therapists about their willingness to schedule longer sessions and their availability in emergencies.

New research indicates that we operate most effectively on a ninety-minute to two-hour cycle and that we automatically go into a natural hypnotic state or state of relaxation for about twenty minutes during that time. In his groundbreaking book, *The 20 Minute Break*, Dr. Ernest Rossi describes the biological or "ultradian" rhythms that regulate our waking hours; these are similar to the nocturnal rhythms discovered by scientists studying sleep disorders. Therapists are learning to use these natural daytime cycles to help clients recover memories and change decisions at a deeper level while they are in the twenty-minute period of mental rest. A two-hour session also corresponds to the optimal length of time for maximum work efficiency.

Another benefit of two-hour sessions for people who interrupt their work or travel long distances to come to the therapist is that they have to travel only once every two weeks.

Although two weeks may seem to be a long time between therapy sessions, many clients need that time to digest what they have learned and adjust to their new discoveries. The best therapists also give "homework assignments," usually self-help and self-esteem building techniques that clients can do on their own.

If you are sufficiently disciplined and knowledgeable about your own treatment, you may arrange to see your therapist less often, perhaps once a month or on an as needed basis. This arrangement usually works best after you have had regular sessions for a few months so you and your therapist have a clear idea of your issues and the goals for your therapy. You may be able to work out a treatment program with your therapist where you work by yourself at home in between sessions.

There are an infinite number of self-help techniques you can use at home. However, if you have repressed traumatic memories, are suicidal, are being abused, have multiple personality disorder or are actively engaging in a destructive behavior, such as substance abuse, you should see a therapist regularly on at least a weekly basis until you and your therapist agree that these problems are under control.

Shorter sessions of fifty minutes or less on a weekly basis are preferable for children and adolescents because their attention spans are more limited. Part of the sessions may be used for consultation with their parents.

Two-hour or longer sessions work well for marital and family counseling and other groups because all participants need time to be heard. It often takes longer than an hour for barriers to dissolve and for patterns of interaction to become clear to the therapist. The new family therapy called strategic therapy brings together as many family members as are willing to attend. It has achieved amazingly rapid results in many situations. (See page 79.) Such sessions are often two to four hours long, performing like a pressure cooker to bring up feelings and problems.

Finally, various group sessions can last anywhere from an hour to several days depending on the type of group. Regular group therapy sessions held with a therapist usually last $1^1/_2$ to 2 hours. Studies show that time-limited groups which have a set deadline for termination, such as twelve weeks, may be more effective than open-ended groups in some situations. On the other hand, groups that provide support for people in similar circumstances such as alcoholics, single parents, or victims of child abuse are usually more successful if they are open-ended.

It is up to you to decide what length of session works best for you and how frequent your sessions should be. During your initial interview you might explore whether the therapist is willing to try a two-hour session if you feel it would fit your needs. You have to determine what makes you most comfortable.

Be aware, however, that, unless you work consistently on your own, appointments more than two weeks apart may be less efficient because you may start to block out events or spend too much time during a session bringing your therapist current on what has happened in the interim. It is wise to keep some pressure on yourself so your therapy does not drag on interminably.

Keep in mind that everyone has different needs and works at his or her own pace. Please do not compare yourself to others. The best advice I can give is to trust your instincts about what you need and find a therapist who will schedule sessions in a way that allows you to obtain the maximum benefit.

How much will therapy cost and how can I pay for it?

Therapy is expensive. Most therapists charge for each session of fifty minutes. In 1995 the cost of an individual session was between $55 and $125 a session. In most cities it is difficult to find a therapist who charges less than $75 to $85 a session. Only psychiatrists charge $125 per hour (more in New York) because they have a medical degree. If you do not need medicine prescribed for you, that expertise is not necessary. Psychologists generally charge less than psychiatrists and clinical social workers sometimes charge even less.

So how do you pay for your therapy if you are not a rock star or an oil magnate?

First of all, it is important to get your priorities straight. Is it more important for you to have a new boat, car, house, or dress than to get rid of the problems that are keeping you from feeling better and finding satisfaction in life? What are you willing to give up to have a happier life? What do you want most?

I know how painful such questions can be because I have had to ask them myself many times over the years. I used to think if I had a husband, a lovely home, or an interesting job, I would be happy. But when I was living with a handsome husband on eleven acres of redwoods in the Santa Cruz mountains and had a job I loved as a law professor, I was miserable. A therapist told me that until I worked out my problems, I would be miserable wherever I went. I hated him, but he was right and I knew it.

I had to decide what my priorities were, and I made a vow to get well no matter what it took. I left my husband because we were not happy together, moved to Washington, D.C., and took a job as a Congressional investigator, not because I wanted to be there, but because I learned that the Government insurance would pay 80% of my therapy bills. (Unfortunately, the Government insurance has been substantially reduced for mental health services since then.)

It is not necessary to give up your spouse or your family in order to get help, however, you do have to be willing to make sacrifices and you have to place *your* well-being first. The *Bible* says, "Love thy neighbor as thyself," not more than thyself. You can't be much help to your family if you don't help yourself. Your unresolved issues, especially those of low self-esteem, mistrust, anger, hatred, fear of loving, and substance abuse will destroy your relationships until you resolve them. If you are willing to make recovery a priority in your life, if you will take some risks and make some compromises, there are ways to obtain therapy.

If you are in a low income bracket, you may qualify for a publicly funded mental health program available in all states. Some public agencies charge no fees at all or offer a sliding scale for fees. You may qualify for Medicare or a state program. Some therapists are willing to undertake the outrageously burdensome process of obtaining reimbursement for services from government agencies, but others are not. If you qualify, ask candidates if they accept payment by these agencies before your first interview.

Private nonprofit agencies, such as local mental health centers and family service association centers, also may have a sliding scale based on your ability to pay. The availability, cost, and expertise of services provided by public and nonprofit agencies vary greatly from state to state and community to community, but these agencies are certainly worth exploring if you are on a limited budget. The only drawback is that you may not be able to choose your therapist, but most agencies will try to place you with someone with whom you feel comfortable. You must thoroughly investigate the reputation of the agency you select by checking with other local agencies and hospitals and, if possible, with clients of the agency. If you know the nature of your problem, you should request a therapist experienced in that area.

Sometimes public and nonprofit mental health agencies have graduate student interns as therapists. These interns are supervised by a licensed therapist who reviews the intern's cases each week and who may listen to tape recordings of actual sessions or sit in on one. You have the added advantage of having many people looking at your problem. The intern, supervisor, and in some cases the entire staff may review your case.

If you are assigned to an intern, that fact should be disclosed to you and you should be given the option to reject him or her. However, do not automatically assume that an intern will not do a good job. I believe that good therapists are born, not made, and although education can help, competence does not depend on completing any graduate program. A compassionate, dedicated intern can be far better than a senior therapist who has lost enthusiasm and does not keep up on new developments or who has burned out and is simply going through the motions. Interview the intern and see if you like him or her. If you don't, do not hesitate to make your feelings known to the agency and ask for another therapist. Do not be afraid of hurting the intern's feelings. The intern will not be penalized—agencies recognize that clients have different needs and may change therapists for many reasons besides incompetence.

Another way of saving money is to join a therapy group led by a psychotherapist. Such groups cost considerably less than individual sessions, with average fees ranging from $15 to $45 per weekly session. The relative benefits of individual versus group therapy are discussed in the chapter on Group Therapy, page 72. You might join a therapy group for weekly sessions and also have an individual session with the same therapist once a month.

If you cannot pay at all for therapy and do not qualify for state services, you can still get help through support groups. Support groups differ from therapy groups in that support groups are not led by a therapist. The healing in support groups comes through similarity of experience and interaction with the other members. These support groups can be very powerful, although usually not as effective as groups led by a competent therapist. (See page 79, Group Therapy.)

Many organizations and businesses provide insurance which covers a portion of the cost of therapy for members and employees, although most policies have a substantial deductible and some have limitations on the number of visits and on the overall cost. Most policies pay only 50% of the amount they consider to be reasonable for each session for a maximum of thirty or fifty hours per calendar year.

Insurance companies are still in the dark ages when it comes to psychotherapy. They have not yet accepted the recognized connection between mental and physical health and so they continue to pay huge hospital and medical bills which might be unnecessary if their clients' underlying psychological problems had been resolved in therapy.

If you do not have mental health insurance where you work, find out what companies in your area have group health insurance plans which cover such therapy and consider changing jobs. State and local governments and school districts usually have the most comprehensive mental health policies. It may seem strange to choose a job based on insurance coverage, but that may be your best option for financing therapy, and you might be surprised at how many wonderful jobs there are which have mental health insurance coverage. People in clerical jobs have the largest number of choices and can easily find openings in government or large companies. If you need help in finding a job you like, I highly recommend Richard Bolles' classic guide to job hunting, *What Color is Your Parachute?*

Check the insurance plan so you know how soon your therapy will be covered. There may be a waiting period after you are hired before the policy begins to cover your expenses and in some cases preexisting conditions may be excluded. Some misguided insurance companies restrict coverage to therapists on their list, which often results in cronyism and inferior service.

If you are reluctant to ask a prospective employer about such coverage, simply obtain the name of the insurance company. You can telephone the company and ask for details. Your employer will never know.

WARNING: IT IS IMPORTANT TO OBTAIN INFORMATION ABOUT INSURANCE COVERAGE AND APPROVAL FOR YOUR THERAPIST IN WRITING. The easiest way to do this is to send a letter to the insurance company certified mail, return receipt requested, so you will have proof it was delivered. Simply write the following:

"This is to confirm our telephone conversation in which you told me that your policy would cover 50% of the fee of $___ per hour for individual therapy (or group, marriage counseling, etc.) for (name and address of therapist) (kind of degree or license, such as M.A.F.C., L.C.S.W., Ph.D., etc.) for fifty sessions per calendar year. I understand my deductible is $500. (State exactly what your total understanding is. If this is a new policy, add:) I understand my coverage will begin immediately (or in six months, a year, etc.)

If this is not correct, please let me know in writing immediately. If I do not hear from you within two weeks from the date of this letter, I will assume this is correct and I will begin therapy."

This letter puts the burden on the insurance company to let you know if your assumptions are incorrect and gives you written proof of your agreement if problems arise. You should send a similar letter to prospective insurance companies before buying a policy.

You may already belong to a group or organization that has insurance covering therapy. Almost all colleges and universities have in-house counseling programs or student health insurance plans. You may be able to save money by enrolling in a class or two or even in a part-time degree program in order to get the college insurance coverage. You might really enjoy the classes you take; you could even find when you finish your therapy that you have a degree and a whole new career!

Most professional groups have plans, such as associations of independent artists, writers, alumni associations, etc. I joined the local branch of the Farm Bureau because I live in a rural area to obtain my medical insurance and I have certainly never milked a cow! The possibilities are endless: you only have to be creative and find out what is available in your community. Your local mental health facility may have some suggestions and your public library and chamber of commerce could be fertile sources of information.

If you cannot find a group that provides adequate insurance, there are still other alternatives. Depending on your credit record, you may be able to obtain a loan for your therapy. It will be easier if you can use equity in your home or other assets for collateral. But if you have lived in your community for a while, have a good credit history and know your banker or credit union executive personally, you may be able to obtain an unsecured loan. Again, whether or not you want to go into debt for therapy depends on how committed you are to getting help.

What if you cannot find insurance or obtain a loan? Most therapists are fairly understanding about problems in paying for therapy, especially since many insurance companies have reduced mental health coverage over the last few years. Many therapists will try to work with you to find a mutually acceptable method of payment. Some therapists work on a sliding scale of fees based on the client's ability to pay.

Another possibility is arranging for deferred payment. This is often easier if you have been working with the therapist for some time and have a record of making regular payments. If you know that you will be graduating and getting a job, or getting a raise or receiving a large bonus, some therapists will let you defer payment. I have always been grateful to my therapist in Utah for waiting for a large portion of her fee until the sale of my house in Washington, D.C. It took more than a year and she never even mentioned it.

Some therapists reserve one or two hours a week for pro bono work. These therapists have usually chosen their profession because they wanted to help people. I know one wonderful therapist who was very poor as a child and was given help when he needed it badly. He has helped several clients who could not afford to pay, putting back in what he took out. Some of his former patients are paying him back years later, and he is using the money to help more people.

But not all therapists can afford to be that generous and certainly not with every client or they would starve. The only thing therapists have to sell is time. They have only a limited number of hours to see clients because the strain of helping people in emotional crisis is exhausting. A great deal of time is also consumed in paperwork, record keeping, and returning telephone calls for which there is usually no compensation. So you should not take it personally if a therapist says that he or she cannot see you for free or on the basis of deferred payment.

It would be better for the progress of your therapy and your peace of mind to select a therapist you like and find a way to pay him or her. I am convinced that a monetary commitment increases motivation. People who pay the full amount attend sessions more regularly and progress more rapidly than those who do not pay or who pay less than the usual fee.

There are many ways of paying a therapist if you are creative. Perhaps you have something that your therapist would be willing to barter for. You might find a way of working off your therapy fees.

And if you are game for a really radical solution, you could follow in the footsteps of a few courageous souls I know and move to a country that has national health insurance like England, Australia, or Sweden. If you meet the requirements, your therapy would be absolutely free for as long as you need it. But be sure to check the country's work requirements and mental health insurance requirements carefully before you hop on the plane.

Obtaining the help of a therapist is not a question of money, it is a matter of commitment. If you are sufficiently committed and want to get help, you will look hard enough and ask enough people for help and a way will open up for you.

How do I find potential therapists?

The best way to find potential therapists is to obtain as many recommendations as possible from as many people as you know and trust. Talk to your friends, your rabbi or minister, your lawyer, school counselors, your company personnel office, your doctor, and especially anyone you know who is currently in therapy. Ask them whom they would go to if they had your problem.

All of the therapists I interviewed for this book agreed that the worst way to find a therapist is through a directory like the Yellow Pages. It is unwise to consider a therapist or any other professional whom no one has personally recommended.

One productive way to find competent candidates is to visit public and nonprofit agencies in your area which deal with cases like yours and ask for the names of therapists who specialize in such cases. If you have an alcohol or drug problem, your local chapter of Alcoholics Anonymous could be a fertile source. Support groups generally are excellent referral sources. You can attend a session or two and ask other participants whom they have seen and would recommend or avoid.

If you or your child has been sexually abused, your community sex abuse treatment center and child protective service workers could be excellent sources of referrals. These centers are usually aware of some of the most competent therapists in your area, but they do not know all of them, or they may limit their recommendations to therapists associated with them. So do not rely solely on these referrals; simply add the names they supply to your list. Childhelp USA, a national organization, maintains a list of child abuse and cult abuse specialists in most states. Various national organizations to call for help are listed in the References section at the end of this book.

Your local mental health association may have some recommendations. Various professional organizations for therapists maintain lists of their members and make referrals from these lists. These organizations include NASW (social workers), AAMFT (marriage and family therapists), APA (psychologists), and AMA (psychiatrists). However, professional association referral services generally are not very useful because they typically do not rate the ability or expertise of their members and often do not even specify whether the member treats particular problems. You merely get the next name on the referral list which usually includes all members who ask to be on it. If you use these recommendations, be sure to obtain a confirmation of the person's ability from another source.

A very effective way of adding to your list of candidates is to ask the therapists you call and interview for the names of *other* therapists they would consider seeing if they had your problem. If you think a therapist would be offended by that question, let me assure you that generally the opposite is true. Most therapists are happy to recommend other therapists because we know that a good personality match is essential and that clients who interview a number of therapists are more likely to stay with the therapist they finally choose.

Make your list as exhaustive as you can and be sure to write down the names of people who made the referral and what they said. Also record how well your source knows the therapist. Obviously greater weight should be given to recommendations of people who have used the therapist personally or worked closely with her.

Then read over your list. If a couple of names keep popping up, you may want to put those at the top of your list to be interviewed. If you particularly like what one source said about a therapist or have great faith in the source, put that therapist on your interview list.

You will probably want to narrow the list down to a half dozen possibilities. No, you will not have to interview all of them; at least a couple of them may not be able to see you right away. And you may eliminate one or two because of the way they treat you when you try to set up an appointment.

If you need to make special financial arrangements, you may want to compile a longer list so you have a better chance of finding someone who is willing to treat you for a reduced fee or delayed payment.

Once you have assembled your list of a half dozen potential therapists, you can begin the process of evaluation by setting up appointments for interviews.

You can learn a lot about a candidate when you call to make an appointment. How long did it take you to reach the therapist? If the therapist had a secretary, answering machine, or answering service, how long did it take for the therapist to get back to you? This is an important question because it gives you an idea of what may happen if you try to reach the therapist in an emergency. Whether the secretary or answering service is polite or rude to you should also be considered. A therapist who permits employees to be rude to clients may not have much concern for clients' feelings.

Did the therapist take the time to talk to you personally on the phone or was the appointment made through a secretary? If you were able to talk to the therapist, analyze how you felt about the conversation. Phone conversations are sometimes awkward, but the therapist should not be abrupt or peremptory. How much time was he or she willing to spend talking to you? Did the therapist ask if you had any questions or concerns? Were all your questions answered?

The therapist should try to put *you* at ease and give you the feeling that your problem is important. If you do not like the therapist on the phone, don't make an appointment. First impressions are usually valid.

Before you spend your money on an interview, check with your state licensing authority to see if your candidate has a valid license and if any disciplinary actions have been taken against him or her. Unfortunately, most state licensing authorities will not disclose complaints on which no action has been taken, so you cannot place too much reliance on the fact that a candidate's record is clean. The appalling fact is that few states have the resources to monitor the various trades and professions they purport to regulate.

If you want to double-check any of your candidates, you can always call your referral sources and ask if they know your candidates and have an opinion about them. The more checking you do at the beginning, the more secure you will feel about your choice.

If you uncover any negative information about a candidate, you can always cancel the appointment. However, it is important to cancel appointments at least 24 hours and preferably 48 hours in advance so that the therapist has a chance to fill the slot. Some therapists will bill you for the lost time if you do not show up for your appointment without notifying them in advance.

One of the advantages of setting up several appointments for interviews is that it takes some pressure off you. You will feel more free to ask important questions during your interview if you know that other qualified candidates are available. Always keep in mind that there are many people who can help you and that you will find someone you like if you look hard enough.

Photocopy this form and make enough copies so you have one for each of your candidates. Compare responses for each to decide which you would like to interview.

✓ Checklist for obtaining referrals

1. Name of candidate, address and phone number.
2. Name of person recommending and phone number.
3. How does the person who makes the recommendation know the therapist, e.g. client, neighbor, friend—personally or professionally?
4. Comments of person recommending.
5. Qualifications.
6. Experience—number of cases like yours.
7. How long did it take for the therapist or secretary to respond to your call?
8. Were you treated courteously and sensitively?
9. How much time did the therapist spend talking to you and answering your questions?
10. Did you feel comfortable talking to the therapist?
11. Did you *like* her/him?
12. Did anything make you uncomfortable, nervous, or fearful? Be as specific as possible in describing how you felt.
13. Was the therapist willing to suggest the names of other professionals?
14. Was the therapist willing to answer your questions?
15. Did the therapist prepare you for the session or give you any helpful information?
16. Does this therapist have an opening at a time that is convenient?
17. What are the fees per hour or per group session?
18. Does this therapist accept payment through Medicaid, Medicare, insurance, etc.?

19. Is the therapist willing to discuss a reduced fee, delayed payment or barter?

    (Answer the following questions after calling your state licensing department.)

20. Does this candidate have a valid state license to practice psychotherapy?

21. Have any disciplinary actions been taken against this therapist?

What qualifications should my psychotherapist have?

Your first task in choosing the right psychotherapist is finding qualified candidates to interview. You want your therapist to have adequate training and experience to help you resolve your problems as quickly and effectively as possible. There are many different kinds of therapists and the alphabet soup of letters after a therapist's name which represent qualifications can be confusing. There are L.C.S.W.s, M.D.s, M.A.s, M.S.W.s, Ph.D.s, M.A.F.C.s and a host of others, depending on academic degrees, certificates and state licenses. So how do you sort out various kinds of therapists?

In most states, psychotherapists are licensed and regulated, which tends to ensure a minimally greater chance for competency than if therapists are unlicensed. You will want to find out if the person is licensed to practice psychotherapy in your state. You can verify whether a therapist is licensed by a phone call to your state licensing agency. However, in some states, anyone can call himself a "therapist," "psychotherapist" or "hypnotherapist" without having any training or license.

As a practical matter, licensing is of dubious value because most states do not have sufficient funds to follow up on complaints or to police their licensees, so incompetent and even flagrantly unethical therapists rarely lose their licenses. A license merely demonstrates that the person holding it has completed a course of study and had the ability to memorize facts and theories in order to pass a state licensing examination in his field.

Licensing examinations do not measure whether or not the person has any skills as a counselor, only that she has a certain amount of education. In fact many talented people are practicing psychotherapy without a license—holistic healers, massage therapists, chiropractors, motivational trainers, and others who conduct workshops and seminars. One of the best psychotherapists I found is a massage therapist without any formal training in psychology. He uses a combination of conscious connected breathing, massage, energy healing and psychological principles with his clients. Through his own study and self-healing, he has become so clear of his problems that he has an exceptional sensitivity to traumatic issues and the ability to help others release their violent emotions.

On the other hand, the worst therapist I went to was a psychiatrist in Washington, D.C., with all of the most impressive degrees and references; he had an M.D. degree and was president of the national organization of psychoanalysts. I lay on his couch, freely associated, and cried in every session, four times a week for three years. This doctor never had a clue as to what was wrong with me, nor did he say one thing that was helpful.

In the state where I practice now, there is a psychologist who teaches at a university and is recognized as an expert in hypnotherapy. Although this therapist's academic credentials are impeccable, my experience and the experiences of several of his former clients are that this person is arrogant and abusive.

The best therapists are born, not made. While knowledge of psychological principles and techniques is obviously a fundamental qualification for psychotherapists, the most important qualities are sensitivity, insight, compassion, and empathy, and *whether the therapist has worked through enough of his own problems to be able to help you with yours.* These qualities cannot be taught in any school nor are they evaluated by any licensing agency. Degrees and licenses may give you a false sense of security and that is why it is essential to thoroughly interview your candidates.

A rudimentary understanding of the type of training a therapist has *is* helpful in distinguishing among psychologists, social workers, psychiatrists, psychiatric nurses, and pastoral counselors.

Psychologists

Psychologists usually have a Ph.D. (Doctor of Philosophy) degree which means they have completed an academic graduate program and written a dissertation (a research paper). Although they use the title "Dr.," they do not have medical degrees. Their education includes therapeutic theories and techniques but tends to be heavily weighted toward research, testing and experimentation in the area of psychology rather than counseling. Psychologists are trained to administer a variety of psychological tests. Most states require psychologists as well as all other psychotherapists to have clinical experience under the supervision of a licensed psychotherapist. These states grant a preliminary license until the requisite number of hours are completed and the final license is awarded.

Some states permit people with an M.A. or M.S. (Master of Arts or Master of Science degree which usually takes two years of graduate study) in psychology to practice psychotherapy after they have passed an examination and trained under supervision. Some states also recognize an M.A. or M.S. in counseling and school counselors frequently have this degree.

Psychiatrists

Psychiatrists have an M.D. (Doctor of Medicine) degree and have completed medical school and a specialty in psychiatry. Their emphasis is on the physical causes of mental illness and the medications which can cure them. They are trained in some therapeutic techniques, but their training may lead them to perceive their therapeutic relationships in an authoritarian doctor-patient mode, where you are sick and they have the power to make you well. You should explore whether your candidates have this attitude before making your decision.

In most cases, only psychiatrists can prescribe drugs, but other therapists have access to psychiatrists so their clients can obtain medication if necessary. Psychiatrists charge significantly more than other psychotherapists.

Clinical social workers

Clinical social workers have an M.S.W. (a Master's degree in Social Work) and have completed a graduate program which in many universities is specifically designed to emphasize providing services for people. I chose this program because at my state university the M.S.W. program seemed to have the most comprehensive curriculum in counseling and new theories, techniques and practices of therapy.

The term "clinical" means that the therapist does therapy directly with clients as distinguished from someone who specializes in research, social service, or administration.

Some social workers also have a D.S.W. (Doctor of Social Work) which is equivalent to a Ph.D. This means they have taken more graduate courses and written a dissertation. In some states, clinical social workers are licensed as L.C.S.W.s (Licensed Clinical Social Worker) to practice on their own, or C.S.W.s (Certified Social Worker) which requires a state examination and enables them to practice under the supervision of another therapist until they have completed a certain number of hours of practice and have passed a second examination to become an L.C.S.W.

Social work has been referred to as the profession which serves as the nation's social conscience. The focus of clinical training is not on research or medicine, although social workers learn some of both subjects, but on helping people with a variety of mental, physical, spiritual, family and social problems. Social workers are taught to use an eclectic approach in practice, employing a variety of therapeutic models and techniques designed to address a client's individual needs. This discipline stresses short-term therapy and developing a relationship of equality and trust with clients. Social workers are trained to teach a broad array of skills to improve people's lives, and, as in other disciplines, to deal with serious mental problems and diseases, including childhood trauma and repressed memories and emotions. As a social worker, I have an obvious bias in favor of social workers if they have the appropriate experience. However, most academic programs, whether in social work, psychiatry, or psychology, emphasize theory rather than practical skills; I learned most of the methods I use in professional courses and workshops outside of graduate school.

Psychiatric nurses

Some states permit psychiatric nurses to practice psychotherapy in hospitals under certain conditions. Most psychiatric nurses have completed a graduate nursing program. My favorite and most effective psychotherapist, a woman skilled in hypnotherapy and in handling cases of sexual abuse, was a nurse practitioner who practiced under the supervision of a psychiatrist. She had more sensitivity and ability than any other therapist I have encountered and is certainly evidence that the person, not the license or type of training, is what counts.

Marriage and family counselors

Some states license Marriage and Family Counselors with the designation "M.A.F.C." These therapists are required to complete certain courses in family therapy and to be certified by their national organization. They may be social workers, psychologists or have Ph.D.s in education. Absence of the certificate does not mean that the therapist lacks training in marriage and family counseling; most therapists who specialize in counseling practice take courses in family therapy but may not apply for the certification.

Sex counselors

A growing number of therapists are advertising themselves as experts in treating sexual problems. Some may have extensive professional training in the field, but others may only have attended a weekend workshop. At this time, there is no state licensing requirement for sex counselors. It is crucial that a therapist who is working with such an emotionally charged area has extensive training and has worked out his or her own sexual hangups. It is important to inquire into a sexual counselor's training as well as his beliefs as to what constitutes a healthy sexual relationship.

Pastoral counselors

Priests, rabbis and ministers of all religious denominations are allowed by virtue of the First Amendment Freedom of Religion to counsel their followers without having any training or license; they are sometimes called "pastoral counselors." The advantage of pastoral counselors is that they usually provide their services without cost to members of their congregations. Pastoral counselors may be familiar with your family and may share a common bond with members of their congregation because of similar religious beliefs and values which can create the basis for a relationship of trust.

Some theology colleges provide training in counseling and some religions require that their pastors complete courses in counseling and even provide special training for their leaders in areas such as substance abuse, sexual abuse and suicide prevention. Those religious officials who have training often have the letters D. Min. (Doctor of Ministry) after their names but some officials call themselves "Doctor" without having any doctoral degree. You need to check the educational background and training of your spiritual leader.

Most ethical religious counselors limit their counseling to spiritual matters unless they have training in psychotherapy, and most will refer their clients to psychotherapists for mental and emotional help and to physicians for physical care, but many do not. Some church leaders are nonjudgmental, compassionate and knowledgeable about psychology, while others have little or no knowledge of psychology and are authoritarian and judgmental, heaping guilt rather than forgiveness on their unfortunate flock. Labeling someone as a sinner and creating illusions of hellfire and damnation are hardly conducive to therapeutic healing. It is important to keep in mind that ministers and priests are merely human beings with the same human flaws and frailties as the rest of us. Unfortunately, those who have not worked out their own problems often dump their bad feelings and guilt on others. The most essential elements of healing are love, caring, forgiveness, and acceptance—the same elements most religions espouse. If your pastor does not practice what he or she preaches, find one who does.

Hypnotherapists

Hypnotherapists are psychotherapists who use hypnosis in therapy. They can be members of any of the disciplines described above. Most states do not require people who use hypnosis to be licensed: some require a license if hypnosis is used in psychotherapy or for age regression (the process of having the client go back in his mind to recover the memory of a childhood event).

Some private organizations have sprung up which purport to certify hypnotherapists, but such certifications have little value. These certifications simply mean the therapist has paid for the organization's training program which may be only one course for one day. Other professional courses and books such as those of psychiatrist Milton Erickson, the "father" of hypnosis, provide equally or more effective methods of obtaining training in this area.

A word of warning: Do not confuse a hypnotherapist with a hypnotist. Hypnotists are not psychotherapists, do not have degrees in psychology or related fields, and are not trained to treat serious psychological and emotional problems. Some certifying organizations issue certificates which state that the recipient is a hypnotherapist even if the person has no training or degree in psychotherapy. If you want to use hypnosis to recover traumatic memories, you will want to choose someone who has a degree and a license in psychotherapy and who is trained in using hypnosis as a therapeutic tool.

In most states hypnotists and unlicensed hypnotherapists are permitted only to use hypnosis to help people achieve certain goals, such as relaxing, stopping smoking and losing weight. Even in these cases, however, new studies show that using hypnotic regression to uncover the reason for cigarette addiction and weight problems is more effective for permanently curing smoking and weight problems than the simple suggestions used by hypnotists to reprogram behavior.

Body work, breath work, and massage

Although body work, massage, and breath work are not considered to be part of traditional psychotherapy, their proven results in healing emotional and psychological problems, as well as physical illnesses of unexplained origin, mandate their inclusion in any up-to-date book on therapy. Some states require massage therapists to be licensed, but the majority of people who do massage, breath, and body work are not licensed. Most are trained in particular techniques or one theoretical school.

The best way to find competent people in these fields is by referrals, interviews, and a one-time trial of their methods. You should get results in the first session and, especially with massage and body work, feel noticeably better. Trust your instincts in deciding whether to return and do not sign up for any long-term expensive courses before you are sure that you want to continue. (For more information about body work, massage, and breath work, see pages 289-299, 260-265.)

In general, when reviewing the qualifications of therapists, I view training in much the same way as two of the most respected family therapists, psychologist Augustus Napier, Ph.D., and psychiatrist Carl Whitaker, M.D., authors of *The Family Crucible*: They state: ". . . the psychiatrist spends an inordinate amount of time learning medical skills that are of little use in any psychotherapy. He becomes biased to thinking in terms of illness and symptomatology, attitudes that must be unlearned as he tries to understand and work with social systems. We still speak of the family as our 'patient' largely out of habit, but it is a bad habit. The tendency to compare human psychological distress with physical illness is an often destructive use of metaphor.

"The psychologist who becomes a family therapist also finds that much of his training was peripheral or irrelevant. The hours spent studying statistics, research design, neurophysiology, and learning theory may have an occasional relevance to the family, but I have to strain to find it. . . . But the skills I need in order to be able to work effectively with families had to be acquired largely at my own initiative and after the 'necessary' training was over.

"It is possible that the social worker's training is the most appropriate education of all for family therapy since social systems are the direct focus of this field."

In spite of my personal preferences, it really does not make any difference whether you choose a psychiatric nurse, social worker, psychiatrist or psychologist, as long as you like the therapist and he or she helps you.

A WORD OF WARNING: Most mental health insurance policies cover only licensed psychotherapists: psychologists, psychiatrists, clinical social workers, and marriage and family counselors. The therapists in these categories who do hypnotherapy are usually covered. Some insurance covers visits only to certain psychotherapists.

Fees paid to massage, body and breath work therapists, hypnotists, and other unlicensed healers are usually not reimbursable by insurance, although sometimes massage may be covered if prescribed by a physician. Be sure to check with your insurance company to verify whether the therapist you choose qualifies for your insurance coverage.

Experience

After ascertaining your therapist's basic qualifications, you need to determine whether he or she has the necessary expertise and experience in handling cases such as yours. Has the therapist successfully treated cases involving obsessive-compulsive behavior, prescription drug abuse, eating disorders, ritual abuse or whatever your problem is? Does the candidate keep up on new developments in the field? The best therapists are the ones who are always learning, constantly looking for new ideas to help their clients. These therapists are creative, open to new healing techniques such as art or dance therapy, and, if they do not use a particular technique, will encourage you to find someone who does.

Although I believe anyone can learn anything, I would not want to be the first person a therapist has treated with a particular problem. Someone experienced in the field can quickly cut through defenses and deal with the seemingly tangled web of memories and emotions which might take many times longer for a novice to figure out.

Expertise and experience are important concerns and are areas where you should ask very specific questions and demand very specific answers in your initial interview. Sample questions are listed at the end of this chapter.

If you use the services of a public or nonprofit agency, you may be assigned to a trainee under the supervision of an experienced practitioner. This can be successful *if* the trainee is receiving ample and appropriate supervision by someone experienced in the type of problem you face. I encourage you to ask such questions if you are assigned to an intern. And if you are not satisfied, do not keep quiet in order to spare the trainee's feelings. You are entitled to competent, effective therapy.

Sadly, some therapists may be ignorant about certain problems, but will take the cases anyway. I sat in on a mental health provider meeting in my state where the various heads of divisions were discussing the fact that they were getting an increasing number of sexual abuse cases and were overwhelmed because the agency did not have enough therapists with the experience or training to treat them. One official suggested that the cases be transferred to divisions which had the expertise or to other mental health facilities in the area. But a more senior official responded that the agency should keep the cases because the agency needed the business and because "sexual abuse cases are just like any other problem and any therapist can handle them."

I was astonished that any professional would fail to recognize the special knowledge and skills needed to adequately deal with sexual abuse cases. Many states are studying legislation to require additional training and a special license for sexual abuse therapists because of the unique and complex nature of some of the issues and methods of treatment. Since I was still in graduate school and was only an observer at the meeting, there was little I could do to prevent the senior official from imposing his decision on the agency and making guinea pigs of its clients. I can only hope that therapists will speak out in the future and ensure that clients obtain better treatment.

You can avoid being the first by simply asking your prospective therapist how many cases of your type he or she has handled. Do not feel that you have to be the first because someone has to play that role; beginning therapists can obtain appropriate training by handling cases under the supervision of an experienced therapist. That way novices are able to learn and clients are protected. I strongly recommend that you select a therapist who has handled several cases in the field and who has seen at least a couple of those cases through to a successful termination.

It is also essential to find out what the therapist believes about your condition. If you have been sexually abused, you obviously do not want to go to someone who does not believe in ego states or multiple personality disorder. Even if you do not have multiple personality disorder, someone who rejects the concept, despite its general acceptance by the psychiatric profession, probably does not have the skills to help you. A psychiatrist recently appeared on a television talk show about sexual abuse and announced that there was no such thing as post-traumatic stress disorder. He apparently is unaware of the numerous studies of veterans of combat and other disasters with the disorder, the many psychological journal articles recognizing the same symptoms in victims of abuse, or the inclusion of this disorder in the American Psychiatric Association's Diagnostic and Statistical Manual of Mental Disorders, the basic diagnostic bible for psychotherapists.

Unfortunately, some therapists are ill-informed, and television shows tend to select guests who cling to outlandish minority views just so they can create controversy. If you find one of these kooks, or your instincts tell you that what the therapist believes is bizarre or harmful, leave.

If the candidate you are interviewing is defensive, antagonistic or in any way reluctant to answer these legitimate questions, this is a good indication that the candidate has his own problems and a poor attitude which will impede your progress in therapy. You can simply say that you are considering other candidates and leave, or you can be honest and tell the therapist that you are leaving because he is unwilling to answer your questions. If you have the courage to be honest, you may help the therapist alter his attitude, but, more important, you will be taking a large step toward speaking up and asserting yourself. Do not hire anyone who will not respond openly to the questions in this chapter and the next one.

✓ Basic qualifications checklist

1. Are you licensed by the state?
2. What license do you have?
3. What degree or education do you have?
4. What professional workshops or trainings have you recently attended? (This is a way to ascertain if your candidate keeps up on recent developments. You may want to follow up with:)
5. What do you do to keep up with new developments in the field?

6. How long have you been practicing?
7. Do you handle cases involving (insert your problem—alcoholism, child sexual abuse, depression, fear of cats, etc.)?
8. How many such cases have you handled?
9. How many cases have you completed successfully?
10. How long did those cases take?
11. Do you enjoy handling such cases? (The response to this question will give you an idea of how enthusiastic your candidate is.)

Be sure to record meticulously the candidate's answers either during your telephone interview or immediately afterward. You will also want to include your reactions—your feelings—about the answers. Put in as many details so you can remember the candidate later when you are making your comparisons. If you believe you did not get a complete answer or need more information, jot down those questions you need to repeat on your list of questions for your face-to-face interview.

The next chapter will provide the questions you need to ask in your first face-to-face interview and an evaluation checklist to help you determine which one of your qualified candidates is right for you.

How do I choose a therapist who is right for me?

Finding a therapist who is right for you is not an exact science. Even therapists have difficulty choosing other therapists to whom they can refer clients. One of my friends, a therapist in Alabama, told me that, despite her own training and experience, she has found referring people to other therapists and physicians to be hit-or-miss. She has learned to discuss the person she is referring with several possible candidates and to interview each one thoroughly. But most important, she relies heavily on her intuition, her gut feelings. In making your selection, you have to be a detective and ferret out as much information about your candidates as you can.

Once a candidate's basic experience has been established, the next areas of inquiry are almost totally subjective. The most important factor is *whether you like the therapist*. This depends on whether there is a good personality match. No one can make this decision for you. In deciding whether or not you like a therapist, you must trust your feelings rather than your intellect. For some of you this will be a new experience. I can provide some questions to ask and things to look for, but your feeling of comfort with your therapist is something only you can determine.

If everyone you know thinks a certain therapist is a saint, but you are uncomfortable and want to get out of the office, leave. Do not try to be rational, or do what you think you *should* do. Trust your instincts, those vague little feelings you've ignored for so much of your life. Those are the ones that warned you not to do something but you did it anyway because you thought you *should* do it—and later wished you hadn't. Choosing a therapist is a little like choosing your spouse; only *you* can decide whether you like the person or not.

It is often easier to make a decision if you can make a comparison. You need to shop around. You probably would not think of buying a new car without test-driving several models, so why would you hire a therapist without interviewing several to sample their styles and methods?

It is advisable to interview at least two or three therapists before making your final choice in order to compare different personalities and attitudes, as well as to obtain a greater understanding of your problems. You will find that diagnoses may vary widely and you need to question your candidates thoroughly until you understand the nature of their diagnosis, its basis and the proposed treatment. Each interview will provide valuable information and give you more experience about therapists so you will become more confident about your ability to make a wise choice. Even interviews where you decide you really don't like a candidate are useful, if only to be used as horrible examples!

If you have difficulty making a selection, you may want to have two interview sessions with your finalists before you decide. Yes, it may cost you a few hours, not counting travel time, and perhaps $200 to $400, but if it prevents you from making a mistake and enables you to find a therapist you really like, it will be well worth the effort and the price.

Having your partner or a friend accompany you to your interviews and your first sessions can provide support and another perspective. Therapists are beginning to be more sensitive to the needs of people seeking therapy and many encourage prospective clients to obtain the assistance of friends and loved ones. However, although input from others is useful, *you* are the one who will be in therapy and you must rely on your own feelings and preferences in making the final selection.

In some cases, you may have to interview more than two or three candidates, but I believe if you look hard enough, you will find a therapist you can work with comfortably. If you begin to feel that you have interviewed too many therapists and that perhaps the problem stems from you, it may be time to listen to your feelings and make a choice.

The most important question to keep in mind throughout your interviews is whether you like the therapist as a person. Often we are so self-conscious and concerned about whether someone likes us that we overlook our own needs. You are going to be spending a lot of time with this person. If you do not like him or her, you will be miserable and probably find excuses to miss appointments and arrive late, or you will quit. It is harder to start again with someone new and you will have lost the time and money. No matter how highly recommended and qualified someone is, or how desperate you feel, DO NOT HIRE A THERAPIST YOU DO NOT LIKE.

Most public and nonprofit agencies try to assign therapists who will be a good match, but most do not permit you to interview more than one therapist. Of course, if you do not like the therapist who is assigned to you, you can always request a change and most agencies will comply with your request. If you don't like the second therapist, you can request another transfer or you can try another agency if there is one in your area. Do not be afraid of offending anyone by your efforts to find a therapist. Remember, *you* hire your therapist, and you are entitled to someone who is competent and with whom you feel comfortable, regardless of your financial condition or the type of problem you have.

It may help to realize that therapists are also nervous during the initial interview and want to make a good impression. Some therapists warm up when they are not under the pressure of knowing that they are on trial. Keep in mind that your candidates are human, not superhuman.

The initial interview with a therapist is critical because you can obtain many clues about how he or she will treat you in future sessions and you will gain some idea about how the two of you will interact. I follow a general rule about selecting therapists, similar to my rule for choosing a spouse: if you become aware of a problem, prejudice or annoying personal habit, magnify that problem five hundred times, because it will never get better; it will only get worse. If you can live with the problem magnified, then stay with the relationship or keep that therapist. If not, cut your losses early.

On the other hand, you will never find a therapist who is perfect. Therapists are only human. If you are looking for a therapist who has it all together and has resolved all her or his problems, you will be looking for a long time. I heard a woman say of a therapist who lives in her neighborhood: "I'd never go to her; she can't even control her own kids." I, on the other hand, would never go to a therapist who did *not* have problems. How could such a paragon possibly understand my pain?

Sometimes therapists have problems which actually increase their effectiveness in treating similar problems. Most alcohol and drug abuse counselors are recovering alcoholics and addicts. Their personal experience combined with professional training often gives them an exceptionally astute understanding of the causes of addiction and the difficulties of facing and overcoming addiction. The same is true of sexual abuse. An increasing number of people who have been abused are becoming therapists and are bringing with them a sharper knowledge of the patterns of reactions to abuse, the ways the mind works to repress and later release memories, how ego states and multiple personalities function, and how to best unravel the tangle.

On the other hand, a therapist who is not an alcoholic or has not been sexually abused may be quite competent to help you. The specifics of the therapist's personal experience may not be as crucial as the therapist's self-awareness and understanding of human emotions. But only a therapist who has faced pain and loss and is comfortable with the depth of these feelings can be helpful.

Although we all would like a magic answer and a quick solution to our unhappiness, most emotional problems do not have a simple solution; most take time and effort to work out. Beware of a therapist who leads you to believe in a quick fix—such solutions are usually temporary or illusory.

During and after the interview, you should ask yourself: Does this therapist treat me with sensitivity and respect?

Whether the therapist is on time for sessions is always important but even more so at the first one because the client is nervous and in a strange environment. If the therapist does not have a secretary who can welcome new clients (many capable therapists don't), the therapist should arrange to be ready a little ahead of the scheduled appointment so that he can immediately bring you into the office when you arrive. Sensitive therapists are aware that new clients are usually apprehensive about the first meeting and will take steps to put the client at ease. A therapist who permits new clients to sit alone in unfamiliar surroundings demonstrates a lack of sensitivity. Of course, the therapist may have an emergency which makes tardiness excusable, but he should provide you with an explanation and an apology.

There are a number of things to watch for in the initial interview. Does the therapist listen to you or does she frequently interrupt? Continual interruption indicates a lack of respect for your feelings and your judgment in deciding what is important.

An important skill taught in most graduate programs for therapists is empathic responding, which is a way of recognizing and validating your feelings. You can determine if your candidate has mastered this skill by whether the comments convey an accurate understanding of your emotions when you are telling your story and afterwards. If the therapist misinterprets your emotions several times or belittles or trivializes your pain and feelings, you will probably want to cross that person off your list.

You will want to find out whether the therapists you interview play an active or passive role in therapy. Therapists' styles range from passive to directive and confrontive. A balanced approach is generally better than either extreme; you probably don't want a therapist who does all the thinking for you, nor do you want a therapist who wastes your time by letting you flounder when you could be making progress if someone pointed out some alternatives. Studies show that therapy is not effective when the therapist only listens and does not provide any direction.

You will also want to determine whether your candidate is open-minded and flexible. Some therapists think they know everything about how to treat a problem and treat everyone the same way. Their rigidity leads them to ignore the client's individuality. If I suggest that something might be true for a client, I always qualify it by saying, "This may not be true for you. Do you think this applies? You don't have to accept it, unless you believe it fits." You want to find a therapist who is willing to listen to you and work with your individual experiences and perceptions. Ask yourself whether the therapist gave you a chance to tell your story or jumped to a conclusion before hearing all the facts.

Is the therapist warm and nonjudgmental, rather than rigid, judgmental and distant, or merely neutral? Therapy cannot be effective in an atmosphere of judgment or criticism. You must feel free to express all of your thoughts and feelings, no matter how awful you think they are, and know that your therapist will still accept you as a person. Thoughts and behaviors may be harmful to you or others, but effective therapists recognize you are doing the best you can. After all, you are in therapy to improve. I believe that characterizing feelings, thoughts, or actions as "bad" or "good" impedes healing and creates a barrier between client and therapist. People need to examine their feelings, thoughts, and behaviors in an atmosphere of acceptance in order to change.

Studies show that a warm relationship with the therapist is more important than the actual therapy. Therapists Mildred Newman and Bernard Berkowitz in a wonderful little book, *How to Be Your Own Best Friend*, advise that "One of the most important things an analyst can give is his loving interest."

Many people have never had a loving friend who would really listen to them. That experience can be one of the most powerful in the healing process. So you need to determine whether the therapist is really concerned about you—someone you feel could be a friend.

One indication of whether you like your therapist is how you *feel* at the end of your first session. Did you feel relieved, less anxious, more comfortable, or were you tense? If your body or head hurts more than when you arrived, it is usually a good indication that something is wrong. Did you feel mentally better, more aware of your feelings and behavior than before? Did you gain any new insights or information? Even in the initial session you usually can expect to learn something new or get a clearer picture of what you need to work on in therapy.

You can acquire some sense of your candidate's personality and attitudes by observing the office environment. Is the waiting room cheerful and comfortable? Are there interesting magazines to read while you are waiting? Sometimes therapists share waiting rooms, so you may have to wait until you are in a private office before you begin to appraise the therapist's taste and personality. I have been in a few therapists' offices that were decorated with dark, depressing furniture and grim, even frightening paintings. I left as quickly as possible. Studies indicate that art and art objects are extremely personal and what people select can tell a great deal about their psychological makeup and personality. Other studies show that colors and decor can have a positive or negative effect on therapy. I prefer to work on my problems in a pleasant atmosphere.

Office design and furnishings can also provide indications of the therapist's sensitivity and concern. Are the chairs comfortable? Is the office antiseptic or homey? Is the therapist barricaded behind a desk or does she or he sit facing you in a way that makes you feel you are on a fairly equal basis? Is the temperature too hot or too cold? Is Kleenex easily accessible? This may seem like a small thing, but if your therapy is effective, you will almost certainly cry, probably many times. I once commented on the fact that there was no Kleenex in a psychiatrist's office. He responded defensively, "My patients are adults. They can bring their own Kleenex!" I never returned to him.

Take a minute to look at the books in the office; they can be very revealing. How diverse are they? Are they all academic or are there some self-help books or books on holistic healing? Are there any that catch your interest? You might want to ask the therapist what he thought of one or two of these books. I strongly recommend eliminating any candidate who forbids you to read books on therapy or otherwise restricts your access to other resources.

One word of warning: if you are interviewing therapists in a public or nonprofit agency, you may not be able to rely on clues from the office environment because these therapists usually do not choose their offices or the decor. Sometimes they share offices with other therapists and may not be able to bring in personal items.

The therapist's body language can also be instructive. Body language, the meanings certain body postures and positions reveal, is a tool many therapists use to provide clues about their clients' personalities, thoughts, and feelings. You can use the same tool to learn more about your therapist.

Although covering the myriad complexities of various body postures and positions is beyond the scope of this book, there are a few revealing basics to watch for. If the therapist faces you directly without crossing either her legs or arms in front of her, this position indicates an openness to you and a willingness to listen. A closed body position (arms crossed or facing away from you) usually indicates a closed mind and a defensive attitude. That is also why therapists who are open and treat their clients as equals do not barricade themselves behind their desks.

Eye contact is also significant. Does the therapist look attentively at you, or does he avoid looking into your eyes or avert his eyes when you talk? Competent therapists derive a great deal of information from closely observing their clients because clients reveal their true thoughts and feelings through body language. A therapist who has difficulty looking directly at you is missing important clues and may have personal problems you would be better off avoiding.

You are paying for your therapist's time and attention and you are entitled to be the sole focus of that attention during your interview and your therapy sessions. A candidate who takes phone calls other than in an emergency or who permits interruptions of any kind during your session demonstrates a lack of respect for you. That person is not someone you want as your therapist. If an interruption is absolutely necessary, you are owed a brief explanation and an apology.

Ask yourself whether you feel your candidate is giving you her undivided attention. If you feel she seems bored or preoccupied, you can gain valuable information by expressing your feelings. She may explain her thoughts and you may find you misjudged her behavior. Or she may be apologetic and change her attitude. If she is willing to freely examine your feelings and her own, you have probably found someone with whom you can work out problems, a significant factor in therapy. On the other hand, if she reacts defensively or tells you it's your problem, you have a clear indication that you may have difficulty sharing your feelings and resolving conflicts with this candidate.

Openness and honesty are very important on both sides. You need to be candid about what you expect in a therapist and from therapy. If you express your expectations to your candidate and ask for his reactions to what you have said, you will acquire useful information about his attitudes. It is essential that you feel comfortable asking your therapist questions and expressing *all* expectations, feelings, and concerns you may have, no matter how embarrassing, stupid, or offensive they may seem to you. Therapy will work only if you are able to disclose things you may be reluctant to reveal, including the negative thoughts and feelings you may have at times about your therapist.

It is especially important to be able to openly discuss—and challenge—your candidate's views about theories of therapy, techniques and the type of treatment you will receive. Do not be afraid of asking as many questions as you need to fully understand your therapist's perception of your condition and what she proposes to do to help you. I cannot stress strongly enough that as a consumer, you have an absolute right to a clear understanding of what you are paying for, especially when the nature of your therapy will certainly have a much more profound impact on your life than the amount of sugar in your breakfast cereal.

There may be many things you may want to know about your candidates personally, such as their values, gender prejudices, religion, sexual orientation, politics, marital status, experience, and problems. You can learn a great deal about a candidate's philosophy of therapy simply by asking some of these questions because those who believe in an authentic equal relationship between therapist and client will be willing to answer all or some of your questions, while others who believe they must remain neutral will refuse to provide any personal information. You then have to decide what style of therapy makes you more comfortable.

Whether the therapist is responsive to your questions is more important than the answers. You can be compatible with a therapist who does not share your beliefs and experiences. The therapist's sensitivity, empathy for your feelings, and understanding of your problem are more significant than political views or identical experiences. However, if a particular philosophy or value is critical to your feelings of comfort, you should insist on a response in that area. If your candidate refuses to provide the information, you will have to decide whether or not you want to continue. The mere fact that the therapist's philosophy or values are contrary to yours may not be a valid reason for abandoning the candidate as long as the therapist is willing to thoroughly discuss your concerns and agrees not to impose his values or beliefs on you.

Some therapists may respond to general questions but refuse to share their personal experiences with you. A debate persists among psychotherapists as to the nature and extent of self-disclosure, the more recent trend being toward greater self-disclosure and openness, especially since an increasing number of people are actively seeking therapists who have successfully recovered from similar problems. I have polled clients and participants at workshops who suffered abuse as children and they unanimously expressed the belief that it was helpful and reassuring to know that a therapist had similar feelings and survived similar experiences. I agree with humanistic therapist Sidney Jourard who observed that: "Manipulation (by the therapist) begets counter-manipulation. Self-disclosure begets self-disclosure." I prefer therapists who are natural and spontaneous and not afraid to reveal their humanness.

Most therapists are aware of the importance of a good personality fit and will cooperate in your efforts to find out if the chemistry is right. A therapist who is defensive or uncooperative in an interview is probably not going to be more flexible during therapy.

Remember that making the wrong choice is not a disaster. No choice is irrevocable, you can always change your mind. You can find another therapist, go back to one you already interviewed, or switch to a group. Remember, you are totally in control of your own therapy and your therapist works for you.

✓ Interview questions

If you want to obtain more details about your therapist's response to interview questions about qualifications, you may want to include questions from the Basic Qualifications Checklist, page 54.

After telling your story, you may want to ask:

1. What are your thoughts about what I've told you?
2. Do you think I need therapy?
3. What is your diagnosis of my problem or condition?
4. How would you treat my problem?
5. What type of therapy or techniques would you use to treat my problem?
6. If you believe a certain type of therapy or technique would be particularly effective, ask whether the therapist is familiar with that theory or technique and would be willing to use it with you.
7. Express your expectations and discuss them with your candidate.
8. Do you take an active or passive role in therapy?
9. How long will my therapy take?
10. How do you feel about my reading books about psychology or therapy during the course of treatment?
11. How do you feel about my consulting other therapists or trying other therapies such as group therapy, assertiveness training courses, breath work, body work, biofeedback, or workshops during the course of treatment?
12. Can I reach you in an emergency or if I have questions between sessions?
13. What if I have to be hospitalized?
14. How much will my therapy cost?
15. Do you accept Medicare, Medicaid? Do you qualify for insurance coverage, have a sliding fee scale, etc?

Ask specific questions about your area of concern, for example:

Marital or couples therapy: See pages 203-207.

Childhood trauma, abuse, rape:

1. What do you think about dissociation?
2. How do you recover repressed memories and emotions?
3. Do you use hypnotherapy, breath work, gestalt therapy?
4. What do you think about multiple personality disorder and ego states?
5. Have you treated cases of multiple personality disorder? See pages 187-191.

Phobias: See pages 198-202.

1. Do you use desensitization?
2. How do you address the underlying cause?

Alcohol and drug abuse: See pages 161-166.

Ask any personal questions that are important to you, such as the candidate's values, religion, sexual orientation, gender prejudices, politics, marital status, and personal experience with problems such as yours.

1. What is your religion?
2. What is your belief about God?
3. What are your feelings about homosexuals?
4. Were you ever abused as a child?

(It is important to make detailed notes about your candidate's answers either during the interview or immediately afterward and to record your reactions—feelings—about the answers. Put in all the details you can so you can remember the candidate clearly later when you are making your comparisons.)

✓ Checklist for evaluating your candidates

Rating scale—Rate each candidate on each question using the following scale. Then add up the total scores. Compare *both* the totals for each candidate and the individual scores on each question in making your evaluation. Of course no candidate will receive a perfect score.

5 = excellent—I feel really good about this—everything I could hope for in this area

4 = very good—I feel good about this

3 = average—I feel O.K. about this—acceptable

2 = not very good—a few problems—I feel a little uncomfortable about this

1 = not good at all—several problems or a major problem—I don't feel comfortable about this

0 = terrible—consider eliminating this candidate

If you give a candidate more than one "0," you probably want to eliminate that one.

Do I like this person?

1. Is this person warm and nonjudgmental (or cold, judgmental or distant)?
2. Does this therapist treat me with respect?
3. Is this person sensitive to my needs and feelings?
4. Did this therapist keep me waiting before my first appointment or was he/she on time? (Evaluate apology.)
5. Did this person listen attentively to me?
6. Did this person seem to hear and understand what I said?
7. Did the therapist frequently interrupt me?
8. Did the therapist interrupt my session with phone calls or other business?
9. Was I permitted to tell my story?
10. Did the therapist make an effort to help me feel at ease?

11. Did I feel safe with this person?
12. Is this person sensitive and caring?
13. Does this person seem to understand my feelings?
14. Does this person look directly at me?
15. What does this person's body language indicate? Did this therapist sit in an open or closed position (barricaded behind desk)?
16. Is this person open-minded and flexible?
17. Is the office environment pleasant and comfortable?
18. Are the length and frequency of sessions acceptable to me? (Is this therapist willing to be flexible?)
19. Do I feel that the therapist has a clear understanding of my problem? (Does the diagnosis make sense to me?)
20. Do I feel good about the therapist's responses to my questions and concerns about my problem?
21. Does this therapist use many theories and techniques or only one or two?
22. Do I feel comfortable with the type of treatment proposed?
23. Do I feel good about the therapist's responses to my questions about theories of therapy, techniques, and the type of treatment proposed?
24. Do I feel good about this person's reactions to my expectations about therapy?
25. Do I feel this person treats me as an intelligent human being, an equal? (Does the therapist refer to me as a "client" or a "patient"?)
26. Do I feel that this candidate is condescending, arrogant, impatient, judgmental, rigid, patronizing, sarcastic, self-righteous, bored, or in any way abusive?
27. Does this therapist encourage me to ask questions and respond to them directly and openly?
28. Does this therapist encourage me to read books and utilize other therapeutic resources during my therapy?

29. Does this therapist have a sense of humor?
30. Does this therapist seem to be fairly happy, well-adjusted?
31. Did this therapist answer my questions about personal experiences, philosophy, etc.?
32. Am I satisfied/comfortable with the responses?
33. Is this therapist accessible for questions between sessions?
34. Am I comfortable with this candidate's provision for emergencies?
35. Am I comfortable with the way this therapist would help me if I needed to be hospitalized?
36. Would this therapist come to see me in the hospital?
37. Did I gain any new insights during this session?
38. How did I *feel* after my interview? Did I feel more relieved and more comfortable or more anxious and tense? How did my body feel; did I experience any aches or pains?
39. DO I LIKE THIS PERSON?

Should I choose a male or female therapist?

Whether your therapist is male or female can make a difference in some cases. The question is not one of competence but depends on your comfort level and receptiveness to working with women or men. In most cases, choosing the *person* you like most is preferable to making decisions in advance on the gender of your therapist. Interview therapists of each sex and then decide which is the best match for you.

However, in some situations the gender of the therapist may make your therapy more difficult. For example, if you are a woman and you have a tendency to enter into relationships with males who are controlling or abusive, there is a high probability that you will choose a male therapist with the same traits. You would be well advised to start with a female therapist, at least until you resolve this issue. By the same token, a man who has a domineering mother may prefer to work with a male therapist.

In cases of sexual abuse, if the sex of the therapist is the same as the victim's primary abuser, therapy may be impeded. If you are a woman who was sexually abused as a child by a man, it may be difficult for you to develop a relationship of trust with a male therapist. The same is true of adolescents and especially young children who may be intimidated by a therapist who is the same sex as their abuser. It may also be harder for women and children to ask a male therapist candid questions about what was done to them sexually and to discuss the intimate details of their abuse.

Many women who have repressed memories about their childhood sexual abuse find that they cannot recover them with a male therapist even under hypnosis and have to switch to a woman. Most women tend to be more comfortable with a female therapist and feel that their emotions are understood more fully.

This does not mean that a male therapist cannot be effective with women and children or that a man cannot understand abuse experienced by a woman. In some respects having a male therapist can be an advantage for a woman. If a woman has difficulty in relationships with men and her lack of trust stems from abuse by a male, learning to trust and work with a male therapist can be a huge step toward healing. But it may take a very long time to take that step, and most abused women are in such pain that they need to work on their abuse immediately. They can often progress faster and develop trust more quickly with a woman. Women can always work on issues of trust with a male therapist later if they need to.

The same is true for males: if they have been abused by a male, they may feel less threatened talking to a female therapist. On the other hand, Kent, a teenager, had been sodomized by a male neighbor when he was a child and was very embarrassed talking to me about what had happened. He was candid enough to say that he felt uncomfortable discussing his abuse with a woman, especially his orgasm which made him question his masculinity. I referred him to a male therapist.

Most of us have not been brought up to discuss the intimate details of our sex lives openly with anyone, let alone a member of the opposite sex. It is not easy to talk to a stranger and therapy is hard enough without adding unnecessary obstacles. You should choose a therapist with whom you can be relaxed and open; if you feel that gender makes a difference for you, follow your instincts.

In some instances, male clients, particularly adolescent boys, may need to have a masculine role model. However, if you choose someone as a role model, make sure they do not represent the worst of your abuser or someone in your family with whom you have experienced conflict. Being strong and competent does not mean being authoritarian, domineering or abusive. Well-adjusted people can be gentle and kind and still be assertive and successful.

Group Therapy

The same considerations apply to group therapy. Whether the leader is male or female or the group is mixed or limited to one gender, your first priority is to choose a group where you feel the most comfortable. Although some people are more comfortable talking about intimate matters in groups of their own sex, in a mixed group you have a chance to see how the other sex *really* thinks and to work out problems you may have in relationships with both sexes.

Your progress may be much faster in a mixed sexual abuse group than one of the same sex, even though initially you may feel awkward discussing your abuse in front of members of the opposite sex. In a mixed group you will be able to see that both sexes are equally wounded by abuse and feel the same pain. As a child, I used to envy my brother because my father did not rape him. I later read only about *female* victims of sexual abuse, so I hated being a girl because I thought it made me weak and vulnerable. Finding out that an almost equal number of boys have been sexually abused helped me discard negative feelings about being female.

Men and women are psychologically more similar than the media and some studies might make us think. Participating in a mixed group can quickly change many erroneous conclusions you may have about the opposite sex and what they think of you. By understanding more about the other sex, you will learn how to improve your relationships with them as both friends and lovers.

The gender of your therapist is far less important than whether you and you therapist have a good fit emotionally. Trust your instincts—your feelings—in deciding what works best for you. You can always try a therapist of the other sex at a later time if you choose.

Group therapy

Whether you would benefit more from individual or group therapy depends on the type of problem you are trying to resolve and your personal feelings of comfort. Each is helpful in different ways and both would be valuable if you could afford the time and money.

If you have to choose, you should probably decide in favor of individual therapy if you suspect childhood trauma or that you may have repressed memories. If you have multiple personality disorder, ego states, or any type of amnesia about your childhood or aspects of abuse, research indicates that hypnotherapy and it is usually done in individual sessions. If you have been physically, sexually or emotionally abused as a child, your first priority is to overcome the abuse because it will affect most other aspects of your life. In order to deal with childhood trauma, you have to recall it and techniques used in individual therapy are generally more effective in eliciting memories.

On the other hand, group therapy has some powerful effects: It makes you know deep down in your gut that you are not alone, that you were not picked for some terrible punishment and that you are not bad. You can tell yourself these things, you can hear them from your therapist, you can read them in this book, and sooner or later you will begin to believe them. But nothing brings those facts home as fast and convincingly as being in a group with other people who have also suffered trauma and seeing with your own eyes that they are good, nice, kind, decent people. You will quickly understand that they did not deserve their trauma and neither did you.

Groups also can help you overcome one of the most frightening of human fears—being alone. Working in a group gives you a sense of belonging and a knowledge that you are not unique in your thoughts and your feelings.

When you hear other people in a group express their feelings of rage, hatred, grief, and fear, you know that your own violent feelings are normal and that you are not crazy. By listening to others talk about their problems and fears, you can gain new insights into your own, and you will even find yourself helping other members of the group based on your own experiences. And when you help other people, you not only bring the lessons home, but you increase your feelings of self-esteem.

In general, groups have been found to be effective in cases where people have similar concerns and where continuing support is needed, such as in alcoholism, substance abuse, divorce, coping with suicide in the family, etc. Groups of special populations can also help specific age groups such as children, adolescents, college students and the elderly.

The primary drawback of group therapy is that you will not receive the individual attention you would have in private sessions and your therapy may take longer because the focus of the group will not always be on you. The group leader may sometimes cut you off before you have resolved an issue if she or he believes that the focus has remained on you too long and other members are getting restless. There may also be times when you simply do not want to raise an issue in front of a group, although in a well-run group once trust develops, members are usually able to share even their worst fears and experiences.

Another possible drawback is that some group therapists do not encourage members to let out the depth of feeling which is expected in individual therapy because they believe the group will become too unruly. This reluctance to allow members to experience emotions is one of the major defects in some groups because it deprives members of the catharsis (release of deep feelings) that they critically need. It is important to ask potential group leaders whether they encourage expression of strong feelings.

There are benefits and drawbacks to either choice. However, remember if you start with individual therapy, you can always join a group later. Many people join groups after they have been in individual therapy for a while. If you cannot afford both, you may be able to find or form a support or self-help group of people who are working on similar problems. Although you would not have the guidance of a therapist in a support group, you may not need a therapist. If a majority of the group has had some therapy, they may have sufficient experience to run an effective group themselves. You might hire a therapist to get the group started. Once groups get going, most run themselves anyway.

When you feel as though you have a handle on some of your pain and problems, you can consider trying other types of therapy. If you are pleased with your progress, stick with what you are doing. If you want to move more quickly or are not satisfied, change. At some point, for all of us, it is important to learn to work effectively with others. Therapy and support groups are powerful ways to learn group dynamics and cooperation.

Special Note for Adolescents

If you are an adolescent, group therapy will usually be the best choice for you.[1] Most adolescents are uncomfortable sitting still for an hour and talking to a strange adult about their feelings. Participating in a therapy group with others your age works better because you are in a developmental stage where the influence of your peers is exceptionally strong, and the peer pressure of a therapy group can greatly accelerate your healing.

When adolescents work together on each other's problems, they tend to stay interested and committed to the group. You can improve your self-esteem by listening to others who are your age reveal feelings about their families and perhaps their abuse, and by experiencing the acceptance of those peers when you disclose your situation. Being accepted by a group that understands what you have suffered can increase your confidence and your feelings of self-worth. And helping someone else grow can make you realize your own value.

Adolescence is a confusing and stressful time when you may make decisions that will affect your entire life. You may have issues of identity, dependence, the need for approval, rejection, and pressures to conform, as well as problems with relationships at home and at school. Participating in a group will show you that your peers also share these concerns. You can openly question your values, safely test your behavior and your limits, and learn to communicate with other people your own age.

A group can also help teenagers with behavior problems. Recent research indicates that antisocial behavior in teens, such as acting out, defiance, fighting, drug and alcohol abuse, running away, suicide, sexual promiscuity and prostitution and other criminal behavior is usually caused by childhood abuse and neglect and often by sexual abuse.[2] Abused adolescents may sometimes be labeled "ungovernable" or diagnosed as having personality or conduct disorders. But this behavior is caused by the self-hatred and anger resulting from abuse;[3] the negative labeling only damages the teenager's self-esteem further. When the underlying abuse is appropriately treated, the offensive behavior usually subsides. The label does not mean that you are hopeless or that you cannot change.

An active therapy group where teenagers confront each other and point out each other's self-defeating behavior can be more effective than individual therapy. Although teenagers often do not recognize the harmful effects of their own behavior even when a therapist tells them, they can identify those consequences when they see them in their peers. My experience in leading adolescent groups is that teenagers are quite effective in helping each other and that they become supportive and protective of group members. The group solidarity promotes rapid therapeutic progress and significant behavioral changes occur in just a few months.

If you are an adolescent, you may be afraid of joining a group because you think your situation is so terrible no one will understand. You may also fear rejection or ridicule by the group. I have never seen that happen. The group leader is responsible for ensuring that positive support is provided. I have also found that *every group member has the same fears*. Perhaps it will help you to know that you don't have to tell your story or say anything the first day or even the first weeks unless you want to. Most groups have a formal rule that you don't have to participate unless you choose to. You can just sit back and listen to the other group members talk about their experiences until you feel comfortable sharing your own.

If after a few sessions you want to leave, you can. You have the same control over your own healing and your life that adults have. But I hope you won't reject the powerful support a group can give you. I believe it's worth trying a group to see if it will help stop the pain you feel now.

Types of Groups

Therapeutic Groups—Counseling and psychotherapy groups

There are various types of groups and it is important to have a clear understanding of the group's purpose, format, and ground rules before you start. The two main types of therapeutic groups are counseling groups and psychotherapy groups, although in practice they often overlap.[4] Both groups are led by a psychotherapist and focus on individual and intrapersonal growth and problems.

A counseling group tends to focus on present problems whereas a psychotherapy group addresses both unconscious and conscious issues and past and present behavior. Counseling groups focus more on personal growth and goals. Psychotherapy groups generally deal with more severe emotional and behavioral problems and use techniques to help members reexperience traumatic events so that repressed emotions can be released. Psychotherapy groups usually last longer than counseling groups. Since, as we have seen, most problems result from childhood trauma which is often repressed, a psychotherapy group will normally be more effective than a counseling group because psychotherapy groups work at a deeper emotional level.

Encounter Groups

Encounter or personal growth groups are intense short-term experiences, usually a weekend, designed to assist people to become aware of mental blocks that prevent them from realizing their full potential and from achieving intimacy in their relationships. The aim of these groups is to create intense emotions and interaction. Encounter groups focus on expressing feelings and perceptions, and confrontations within the group are encouraged. The emphasis is on teaching people to live in the present and to develop creativity and spontaneity. These groups employ a variety of methods to foster interaction, such as massage, staring into another person's eyes, meditation, games, fantasy, and dancing, to name a few. These groups can provide valuable insights, but create a danger of evoking feelings without providing for any follow-up.

Marathon Groups

Marathon groups are even more intense than encounter groups, usually lasting for a longer time, sometimes a week or more. Most marathon groups run almost nonstop, with minimal breaks for meals and sleep; such practices are similar to those used in brainwashing. These groups have been criticized because of the stress they create for participants.

Marathon group leaders are normally unlicensed—they are not psychotherapists; most have virtually no psychological training. While many marathon groups advertise that they focus on increasing human potential and changing limiting beliefs, the techniques they use often force out deep-seated problems and traumas before the participant is ready to face them.

Beware of the quick fix. There are a number of companies which advertise instant cures and transformational miracles during marathon courses lasting a week or a weekend. Most people are struggling with many different issues which are impossible to resolve in such a short period of time. No one can wave a magic wand and heal you in a week and claims to the contrary are simply false.

These courses may actually be dangerous if you have repressed memories and emotions about traumatic events. Some of these courses use techniques similar to brainwashing—long hours, constant tension, and extreme psychological pressure to "get to your issues"—which are designed to break down your defenses and expose your problems. Your defenses are there for a purpose; you built them to protect you and if they are ripped away too violently or rapidly, you could find yourself in real trouble. A number of people who have taken these courses have had psychotic breaks and have ended up in hospitals.

Many of these courses are not run by therapists; no one does a psychological interview or evaluation of the applicants, and there is little or no follow-up. You are on your own after all of your defenses are torn away, unless, of course, you fall for the next slick pitch and sign up for another more expensive course. None of these courses have the ability to put Humpty Dumpty together again if your repressed memories are exposed too abruptly; you will need a trained therapist or a hospital for that.

Your friends may have told you how wonderful these courses are and that they "changed their lives." It is true that some people obtain helpful insights from such courses and may make changes in their lives, but your friends' problems may be ones they were consciously aware of and fully remembered. There is a big difference between "My mother loved my sister better," and being sexually abused by your mother for several years. Also, your friends may *believe* they have changed. You should watch those friends for a few months and decide if the changes are permanent. Overnight changes often last little longer than overnight.

In therapy, you take each piece of the problem only when you are ready to handle it. You have a chance to digest what you learn and assistance in adjusting to your new learning so you can incorporate it into your daily behavior.

I believe people get help in many different ways. What has worked for me may not work for you. If you really believe that you could profit from a marathon, I strongly urge you to consult a therapist first, discuss whether it would be safe for you to attend, and wait until your therapist is satisfied that you have recovered all or most of your traumatic memories and emotions. At least then you will not be in danger of having your pain exposed before you can deal with it.

Many of these courses now require that you obtain your therapist's permission if you are in therapy. This is an important recognition that the course may not be safe for people with certain problems. I hope you will follow this warning.

Lest you feel that you are being shut out of a special club, let me assure you that all of the principles that are taught in marathon courses are readily available in self-help, religious and spiritual books, from your own therapist, and a variety of other sources. Many of these marathon courses require participants to swear that they will not tell anyone what occurs, on the pretext that disclosure would ruin the experience for potential applicants. The truth is that the companies producing these courses want to create a mystique of secrecy because they don't want people to know that all of the techniques and principles have been around for a long time and can be easily discovered at your local bookstore. You can get the same information at your own pace in a safer way.

These "quick fix" courses should be distinguished from workshops, sometimes also called "marathons," conducted by licensed psychotherapists. Psychotherapists often hold therapy weekends which may cover specific issues such as coping with divorce or improving marriages. Sometimes therapists give short courses on self-help techniques, such as assertiveness training, communications skills, or mental imagery. The difference is in the expertise of the leader and the care that you will get if you need help. But most important, no legitimate workshop will claim to cure you in a week or a weekend. In a therapy workshop, you will learn some skills and techniques which may improve your life, in a way that you can safely handle and absorb, without the risk of severe emotional distress.

T-groups

T-groups, sometimes called training groups or sensitivity-training groups, focus more on group process than personal growth and are intended to improve interpersonal skills. T-groups are often used in large organizations to enhance working relationships and encourage teamwork. The goal of these groups is to help people become more aware of how their behavior affects others and to develop an understanding of group dynamics.

Self-help and support groups

Self-help or support groups are groups of people with common interests and concerns; they are sometimes known as mutual sharing groups. Although most of these groups do not have a full-time therapist to lead them, they provide members with the opportunity to interact, discuss their experiences, and help each other. Self-help and support groups may be sponsored by various religious organizations, colleges and agencies or they may be formed by people with similar interests and concerns. These groups can be extremely effective: they include Parents United, Incest Survivors Anonymous, and Alcoholics Anonymous, as well as informal local groups of people with similar problems, such as people with life-threatening diseases or families where a member has committed suicide.

Support groups are burgeoning everywhere. Although people often feel helpless in solving their own problems, they can be astonishingly effective in assisting others with the same problem. And by helping others, they help themselves. It is often easier to recognize faulty beliefs and behaviors in others than to see them in yourself. A self-help group provides an opportunity to compare your thinking and assumptions with other people.

The primary benefit of support groups is the nurturing they provide. These groups offer understanding, empathy and acceptance to people struggling with the same issues, and they develop courage and hope in their members.

Not everyone can afford therapy, and studies show that there are not enough therapists to help all the people who need it. Training people to establish effective support groups may be the answer to our country's urgent need for affordable mental health services.

Family Groups

Family groups are increasingly recognized as one of the most powerful and effective therapeutic groups. Members of a family have a tremendous influence on each other and working together in a group can very quickly bring to light destructive patterns, beliefs and relationships. In addition, the commitment to work together toward healing can improve family dynamics and bring about a greater understanding and closeness within the family unit.

Mention should be made of a new, powerful type of short-term therapy for incest families called "strategic therapy." When the abuse is recent and the perpetrator is a family member, strategic therapy has seemingly miraculous results for victims, perpetrators and the family as a whole.[5] This therapy treats the entire family over a period of six to eight weeks. Even extended family members are encouraged to participate. The perpetrator is helped to understand the seriousness of the abuse, take responsibility for it, and apologize to the victim. Other members of the family acknowledge and take responsibility for their failure to protect the victim and promise to protect her or him in the future. The emphasis is on the family unit as a whole and bringing the "secret" out into the open so that the family can break out of dysfunctional patterns to ensure that the situation cannot recur and all members can heal.

I have found this form of therapy to be exceptionally successful and have also used it with equal success for treating families where the sexual abuse occurred years before, and even in cases where the perpetrator was someone outside of the family and did not participate in therapy. I now encourage my clients in any case of abuse to bring as many family members and friends to therapy sessions as possible. For more information about strategic therapy, contact the Family Therapy Institute of Washington, D.C., in Gaithersburg, Maryland.

> ✓ **Interview questions and evaluation checklist for groups**
>
> Before making a decision to join any group you should find out exactly what to expect. It is important to interview the group leader before you sign up and obtain a clear understanding of the purpose of the group, its format and techniques. Although you may not be able to interview the leader of a weekend group, any reputable leader of a longer-term therapeutic or counseling group will require a pregroup interview before accepting you as a member. For marathon and encounter groups, try to interview someone who has participated.
>
> In self-help or support groups, members are generally free to come or go as they like, so you can visit various groups and decide whether or not you want to return.
>
> You have an absolute right to have clear answers to the following questions. If the group leader is unwilling to respond openly to these questions, find another group.

1. What is the purpose or goal of the group?
2. What is the group format?
3. How many people will be in the group?
4. How often does the group meet?
5. How long is each session?
6. How many sessions will the group have?
7. What is the composition of the group (type of problem, age, sex, education, profession, etc.)?
8. What are the ground rules for the group? (Are members permitted to socialize? Can one member attack another?)
9. Will new members be admitted after the group begins?
10. What are your professional qualifications?
11. Are you licensed by the state?
12. How many groups have you led?
13. What experience do you have in treating my problem?
14. What theories of therapy do you use?
15. What types of techniques will you use in the group?
16. Do you encourage members to express strong emotions?
17. How much will it cost to participate in this group?
18. What are the risks of being in this group? (How does the leader feel about evoking emotions, controlling abusive confrontations, keeping the group positive, handling undue group pressure on a member, etc.? Feel free to express your concerns and assess the leader's responses.)
19. What do you expect of me as a group member?
20. Will what I talk about in the group be confidential? (See the chapter on confidentiality.)
21. Will the sessions be recorded or videotaped? (No therapist has the right to record, videotape or use information from your sessions without your written permission. If you permit recording, you should find out how the material will be used.)
22. Will you be available if a crisis arises?

23. Am I free to leave the group if I wish? Are there any conditions? (You have an absolute right to leave any group at any time you want. However, most group leaders will want you to tell the group that you are leaving and why. This gives you a chance to express your feelings and to clear up any misunderstandings. Often a great deal of learning can come from these discussions.)

You should evaluate the group leader on the basis of his or her reactions, personality and behavior in the pregroup interview.

1. Is this group leader interested in finding out about my problems and concerns?
2. Will this group leader help me set personal as well as group goals?
3. Does she or he listen to me?
4. Do I feel comfortable with this person?
5. DO I LIKE THIS PERSON? (While it is important to like the group leader at least initially, it is not as important to like all or even most of the group members. Part of the learning experience is getting to know different people and becoming aware of your prejudices. One of the benefits of group interaction is that after a while you find yourself liking best some of the people you initially disliked or feared the most.)

II

Special Concerns

Will what I tell my therapist be kept confidential?

As a general rule what you tell your therapist will remain confidential, but there are exceptions. Since most people would not risk disclosing the intimate aspects of their lives if their privacy were not protected, codes of ethics for all psychotherapists and pastoral counselors require their members to keep such information confidential. Psychotherapists are subject to disciplinary action and lawsuits if they divulge information about their clients except as required by law.

Almost all states recognize the necessity for protecting the privacy of clients in psychotherapy and have laws which prevent psychotherapists from producing records and from being compelled to testify in court about the contents of therapy sessions except under certain limited conditions. In legal language, this protection is known as the "psychotherapist-patient privilege."

First, it is important to note that the legal protection applies only to psychotherapists, pastoral counselors, and mental health practitioners. If you are hospitalized in a mental health facility or ward, all of your communications and records are protected because all hospital employees are part of the mental health team. The same protection applies to communications with your psychotherapist's receptionist.

On the other hand, massage, body and breath work therapists are *not* covered by the protection, nor are hypnotists, marathon training course leaders and other unlicensed healers. These people can be subpoenaed to testify in court and you cannot prevent them from testifying as you can under most circumstances if you work with a psychotherapist. If a therapist not covered by the privilege discloses information about you outside of the courtroom, your only recourse is a civil lawsuit for damages if you can prove that you had an agreement that your communications would be kept confidential.

Even if you work with a psychotherapist, there are certain conditions where the psychotherapist-patient privilege does not apply. You have the right to waive the privilege in order to allow your records to be made available to physicians, insurance companies or whomever you choose. You can also allow your psychotherapist to testify in court. You *must* waive the privilege if you sue someone for damages that include mental distress. By bringing a lawsuit which includes a claim for mental distress, you put your mental condition at issue and therefore cannot prevent the defendant from obtaining information from your therapist to use in his defense. However, if you are sued by someone who wants your psychotherapist to testify against you, such as in a child custody case, you can still assert the privilege unless the case falls into one of the above exceptions.

A word of warning: If you tell your friends or others what happens in your therapy sessions, you destroy your patient-psychotherapist privilege, and you, your psychotherapist and those you tell can be compelled to testify about that information in court. You must treat the information as confidential in order to invoke the privilege.

In order to better serve you, your therapist may discuss your case with supervisors or consultants or at staff conferences. However, ethical rules require the therapist to inform you that such disclosures may occur and obtain your consent first. The therapist also has the responsibility to conceal your identity to the fullest extent possible when discussing your case. Discussions of your case for purposes of consultation do not affect your protection under the psychotherapist-patient privilege.

Sometimes therapists want to tape-record or videotape your sessions. You have an absolute right to refuse and to impose any conditions you choose. If you do consent, your consent should be in writing. You should find out whether the sessions are being recorded for your benefit or for that of the therapist. If you have repressed memories, it is sometimes beneficial to use records of hypnotherapy sessions to help your conscious mind accept the events you uncover during sessions. On the other hand, if your therapist wants to play the tapes or exhibit the videotapes publicly or to large groups of therapists or students, your privacy will be invaded. A psychologist I interviewed for my own treatment demanded that I consent to videotaping, insisting that "*all* his clients consented." I could see that he was much more interested in his research and making money off the videotapes of sessions than he was in helping me and I crossed him off my list.

There are two major exceptions to the general rule of confidentiality. A psychotherapist not only can but is required to disclose information if you are a danger to yourself or others. In addition, statutes in all states now require cases of suspected child abuse and neglect to be reported.

If a psychotherapist believes a client is in imminent danger of committing suicide or cannot take care of himself, the therapist is required to call the police and have the client taken to a psychiatric hospital. The client can be committed to a hospital against his will on the recommendation of his therapist for an evaluation period of 72 hours. Then the client must receive a court hearing to determine whether or not he is a danger to himself.

These exceptions are written in terms of "clear" or "imminent" danger, but there are no precise guidelines for these terms. Therapists must use sound professional judgment in determining whether or not imminent danger exists which would justify disclosure.

In the case of danger to the client, thoughts of suicide alone are generally not sufficient to come within the exception. All of my clients and I myself have had suicidal thoughts at one time or another. Suicidal thoughts may come from childhood experiences of abuse. Children who are being abused cannot escape; in most cases the people who are supposed to protect them are responsible for the abuse. Abused children reach a point where they *want* to die, they pray to die to escape from the hell they are in. When these children become adults, the old feelings of hopelessness and wanting to die reemerge, just as old feelings of fear and anger resurface. If you have these feelings, you need to keep in mind that they are usually old feelings coming from trauma and seek immediate help.

In determining if you are a clear danger to yourself, therapists weigh your mental state, how depressed and hopeless you are, whether you can take care of yourself, and if you have a concrete plan for suicide.

I have personally encountered only two cases where I seriously considered calling the police to hospitalize clients who I thought were clearly suicidal. In both cases, my clients had been sexually abused as children, were severely depressed, and had loaded guns in their possession which they threatened to use. In one case, where my client was in my office and had the gun in her car, I had her give me the gun for safekeeping and used hypnotherapy to neutralize the part of her that wanted to die.

The other case was more difficult because the woman was not a regular client. She had phoned for consultation from another city. She was a victim of child abuse, had been blinded in an automobile accident, and had just been told by the health department that her abuser had been diagnosed with AIDS. She clearly had many reasons for wanting to die and I thought about calling the police, but I knew that this woman was extremely resilient and I felt that I should do everything possible to avoid victimizing her further by involuntary hospitalization. I was able to obtain her promise to give her shotgun to a friend and to hold off committing suicide for a month. I called her back to make sure the gun was gone and also contacted a local social service agency and her church to look in on her and provide support. Although I had to disclose some basic facts in order to protect her, I was able to avoid placing her in a hospital. The choices were difficult and risky, but luckily she and I both won that time—she is still alive.

The law also requires disclosure if a client poses a threat to others. Although psychotherapists cannot be forced to divulge information about a client's past crimes, they are required to use reasonable care to protect potential victims. Some guidance was given psychotherapists in the California Supreme Court case, *Tarasoff v. Board of Education*. In that case, a college student who was a voluntary outpatient at the University of California's student counseling center told his psychotherapist that he was planning to kill his girlfriend. The therapist informed the campus police of the threat and they took the student into custody for questioning, but later released him because they found him to be "rational." The therapist sent a follow-up letter to the campus police but the therapist's supervisor asked that it be returned and that no further action be taken. Two months later, the student killed his girlfriend.

The girl's parents filed suit against the university and its therapists for failing to warn the intended victim. Although a lower court dismissed the case, the California Supreme Court found in favor of the parents, holding that failure to warn the intended victim was irresponsible and that public policy favoring protection of confidentiality must yield to protecting people from danger.

There are very strict laws requiring all citizens, not just psychotherapists, to report all cases of suspected child abuse or neglect. Failure to report even a suspicion of abuse, such as a statement without any facts, can subject a citizen to both criminal penalties and civil lawsuits years later by people abused as children. Legislators wisely believed it is better to protect children by having the police or a social service agency investigate suspected abuse cases even though some might turn out to be unsubstantiated, than to allow abuse to continue. The laws also protect citizens who report child abuse from lawsuits whether the allegations are found to be true or false.

Group therapy sessions present more complex problems regarding confidentiality. Although the psychotherapist-patient privilege applies to the psychotherapist who is leading the group, it may not apply to group members. Arguably the privilege should apply to group members because, like nurses and other assistants to psychotherapists, they are part of the therapeutic team. However, no reported court decisions have addressed this issue so far. As a practical matter, it is in the interest of all members to keep information in group sessions confidential. Group counselors almost always obtain a commitment from members to keep communications in the group private.

Although your right to confidentiality is not absolute, courts are prone to protect clients in therapy from embarrassment and humiliation. If your therapy is to be successful, you must feel free to reveal all of your thoughts and feelings to your therapist without fear of exposure.

At one time or another, almost all of us have had feelings that we don't want to live or would like to kill someone, especially if we were abused as children. Any therapist who works with techniques that elicit repressed emotions has seen murderous rage and hatred erupt from even the most mild-mannered clients. These feelings must come out if therapy is to be effective.

Therapists recognize that the real danger is not from people who express and release their feelings but from those who don't. When reporters interview the neighbors of mass murderers, the neighbors frequently describe the murderers as quiet, emotionless people who kept to themselves.

It is when we do not recognize and accept all of our feelings that we are in danger. The Chinese tell their children to "embrace the tiger" in themselves. They recognize that to be whole, we must not only acknowledge but love the savage, beastly, primitive parts of us. Only when we accept what psychiatrist Carl Jung called our "shadow side"—the dark part that we fear—are we free of its control.

The single most important thing you can do in therapy is release all of the pain, anger, grief, shame, and hatred you have stored from life's wounds. If you work with your therapist on these feelings, you will heal. If you hide them or avoid them, you won't.

There is a difference between feelings of hatred and a specific threat of violence. If you trust your therapist to help you, you also need to trust that he or she will know the difference. One of the reasons you hire a therapist is for protection, and if you are in danger of hurting yourself and others, you want to receive the best help possible, even if that means temporary hospitalization.

No one really wants to hurt anyone. People who hurt, hurt others because they want to be free of their pain and feelings of helplessness; they unconsciously feel that hurting someone will bring relief and a feeling of power. What they really want is to stop hurting. They can be free of the pain only if they express it and ask for help.

People who want to die really want help and relief from their pain. As someone who has been suicidal, I am very grateful to those who would not let me die and who helped me to heal and see the world as a different, brighter, happier place. You can break through your pain if you can be honest and talk about it. If you ask, help is available.

Can therapy make me worse?

If you have a competent psychotherapist, the answer is no. But if you have suffered trauma and repressed strong emotions, it can *seem* as though you are getting worse when you start to release those feelings. Most of us have coped with trauma by dissociating from our feelings, blocking them out of our consciousness, and are thus not accustomed to handling intense emotions.

On top of this, we have been programmed all of our lives to suppress our feelings, "keep a stiff upper lip," "smile though you feel like crying," and other similar nonsense by a culture that does not condone emotional expression.

Men have been the most harmed by a cowboy mentality that demands that they "tough it out," no matter how painful or debilitating "it" is. Little boys are brainwashed to stuff their emotions almost from birth; if they cry, they are told to act like "big boys" or are called "sissies" because "boys don't cry." Boys very quickly learn to numb their feelings and cover their pain with stony facades and macho aggressiveness. By the time they are men, they no longer know how to feel. I have spent weeks teaching my male clients how to sense and describe their own feelings. And I also have had to deal with their bewilderment and anger when toward their wives and lovers who demand that they be sensitive and share their feelings.

Our society has done a terrible disservice to men by not allowing them any outlet for their feelings except competition and aggression. If boys were allowed to express and release their natural feelings, their aggressiveness would diminish and their compassion would flourish. This is the real key to world peace.

Recently yet another pernicious element has been added to our cultural predisposition to deny feelings. Many adherents to new age spirituality, in their pursuit of unconditional love, think they can attain this state without dealing with their own hostile feelings. They believe never showing anger is equivalent to being enlightened, and are prone to ridicule anyone who exhibits anger as not being spiritual, even when their own uncaring actions would evoke rage in a saint. These are the same people who use "Have a nice day!" as a curse rather than a blessing. Because they are afraid of their own hate, they ignore the true precept of spirituality which is that we must accept and work out our negative feelings in order to experience real unconditional love. The hard part of achieving a higher level of spirituality or mental health is facing your inner demons. You cannot skip over this step.

Since most of us have been conditioned to numb ourselves, when we start to feel painful emotions during therapy we assume we must be getting worse. Actually the exact opposite is true. When you begin to allow yourself to feel the emotions you have repressed, you are getting better. In order to heal, you must be able to express and cope with your old feelings, as well as the new ones that arise on a day-to-day basis. While releasing repressed feelings may seem frightening and overwhelming at first, you will find it increasingly easy to deal with them as you become more familiar with experiencing them.

The trick is to relax and allow yourself to really feel whatever emotions are present. Take some deep breaths and become an observer of the experience: examine how your body feels, where there is tension or discomfort, how your mind feels, what you are thinking. You will find that if you do not judge or fight the emotion, it will begin to disappear. "What you resist, persists" is especially true of feelings.

It also helps to realize that there are no good or bad emotions. Feelings simply are. Hate is the most unacceptable of emotions in our society. But hate and anger are also natural emotions which are part of a genetic design to protect and heal us. They provide important defenses, giving us adrenaline to help us fight our enemies and the strength to overcome incredible obstacles. The hatred victims generate toward their abusers gives them the will to survive. Anger alerts us that something is wrong so that we can take action to change the situation. Our feelings are there for a reason; it is only when we suppress them or *act* on them in destructive ways that they become harmful. Awareness of our feelings and the ability to release them give us control over them.

There are many techniques for helping you deal with your emotions and begin to make changes in your thoughts and behavior. Some of the most important are discussed in the chapter entitled "What can I do to make my therapy easier?"

You do not have to be a basket case while you are going through therapy. If you feel out of control, cannot work, and believe your life is deteriorating, you may need to see your therapist more frequently and work on ways to bring some stability into your life. You may also need to take a break from struggling with painful issues. Your therapist should be able to help you cope with feelings that emerge so that your life is not seriously disrupted. If your therapist is unable to help you, you need to find someone who can.

Some therapists do not know how to deal with intense emotions. They may be afraid of yours because they have not worked out their own and may withdraw or try to cut your feelings off because they don't know what else to do. A competent therapist knows how to help you release emotions so that they do not immobilize you.

Therapists should prepare clients to handle strong emotions *before* they uncover them, especially if hypnotherapy is to be used. Most people have never learned mechanisms for controlling and stopping the flow of emotions, because they are used to repressing them. There are techniques which therapists can teach in advance so that clients are equipped to manage their feelings.

In addition, before exploring any traumatic issues, therapists should evaluate a client's emotional stability, state of physical health, and environmental and family situation to determine whether the client is in a position to undertake therapy. I will not use hypnotherapy or any technique that evokes strong emotions until I believe the client is strong enough physically and mentally to deal with disturbing issues. If not, we work first on strengthening the client's self-esteem and her ability to cope with stressful emotions and to resolve problems at work and at home that might interfere with therapy.

Although it is important for you to feel the painful emotions you felt as a child so you can release them, it is not necessary that you feel them all the time or every day. There is a difference between releasing emotions and wallowing in them. If you are stuck in a particularly painful feeling, your therapist should be able to help you resolve the issue that is keeping you there. You need to find ways to enjoy life and take your mind off your therapy. There are techniques that can help you focus on the present moment, which is really all any of us have. If you are paralyzed by emotions that affect your work and life for more than a couple of weeks and your therapist cannot help you find a way out, it is time to find another therapist who can.

On the other hand, as you become more aware of your feelings and behavior, you may find yourself choosing to alter circumstances in your work and relationships which may cause upheavals in your life. People are often afraid of making changes because they feel they are leaping into the unknown. They would rather stay in a painful or even abusive situation because they fear that making a change may bring something worse than what they have. I can only say from personal experiences and observing many survivors that the permanent gain far outweighs the temporary turmoil.

There are some instances in which you can actually be made worse by an incompetent or unethical therapist, although even in these instances the damage is not permanent. Our minds are very resilient and whatever harm a therapist does can be undone. This does not in any way excuse the pain and loss of time a therapist may cause, but at least you can take comfort in the fact that there will always be someone else who can help you.

A therapist can make you worse in some cases by misdiagnosing your condition and treating you for the wrong problem. Having gone for over eight years to some of the most prestigious psychiatrists in the country who never had a clue about the severe sexual abuse which caused my problems, I know how damaging and discouraging having an incorrect diagnosis can be.

Especially in cases of severe trauma, misdiagnoses are far too common. A shameful number of abuse victims have been misdiagnosed as schizophrenic, drugged and confined in inpatient facilities for the chronically ill, when they are suffering from multiple personality disorder or other dissociative disorders which could be treated on an outpatient basis without drugs.

If you, or a loved one, are ever diagnosed as being chronically mentally ill or told to take psychotropic drugs, get *at least* one other opinion. I am always amazed at the difference in knowledge among members of the mental health profession in this country, and even more surprised to find that all too frequently doctors and psychotherapists with the "best credentials" at the most prestigious institutions know the least about current diagnosis and treatment other than drugs. After training hundreds of psychotherapists, I have seen that there are many talented professionals in this country and if one, or even a dozen, are unable to help you, there are others who can. New discoveries are being made every day in the mental health field, and you should never give up searching for someone who can help you.

You may be harmed by a marriage counselor who tells you that all problems in your relationship are the fault of your spouse. You may think this is what you want to hear. The truth is that no matter how many problems your partner has, you are responsible for fifty percent of the problems in the relationship, even if yours are limited to enabling and staying with a dysfunctional person. By sanctioning your unwillingness to face your own issues, the therapist is lulling you into neglecting your own healing.

Another way you can be made worse, although only temporarily, is if your therapist forces you to go too fast. You can become overwhelmed if you are pushed to recover memories and emotions you are not ready to assimilate. I pushed myself too hard and did too much age regression under hypnosis on my own. I ended up in the hospital, where I was helped to sort things out.

If a client is not improving as rapidly as the therapist expects, some therapists who have low self-esteem may take it personally as a reflection on their competence. I had a therapist who, when I could not recover memories of my sexual abuse on his timetable, pounded on my shoulders and shouted at me that I was "Daddy's little whore" and similar epithets while I was under hypnosis. His abuse was unsuccessful in jogging my memories and was very traumatic. Although this is an extreme example of a therapist pushing too hard, it is important that your therapist respects the fact that you know best how fast you can go and will work with you at your pace.

A therapist can also harm you by making you dependent on him. One of the main goals of therapy is to empower you and help you take responsibility for yourself so you can become self-reliant. Some therapists, thankfully a small minority, have a need to control and dominate others in order to make themselves feel powerful. You can often identify these people by their need to constantly tell you how experienced, wise, and wonderful they are. Instead of letting you work out solutions to your problems, they continually give you advice and tell you what to do. And they may become angry if you don't follow their advice. Such behavior conflicts with all accepted principles of therapy. If you find your therapist running your life, leave. And if your therapist ever says, "You can't do without me" or "I am the only one who can help you," *run*, don't walk, out the door.

Many people who are in therapy are codependent and all too willing to accept a therapist who is willing to play a parental role. But by allowing the therapist to assume the role of your parent, you remain in the role of a child.

I tell my clients right from the beginning that I cannot heal them, they heal themselves. I am just a guide who can lead them to examine events in their lives, behavior patterns, and decisions they have made, and teach them certain skills. But what they choose to examine and change is up to them; they are responsible for their own healing. I constantly point out their strengths and emphasize that they don't *need* me because there will always be many other people who can help them.

One of the most important things you can learn in therapy is to accept the fact that you are responsible for what happens to you. If you are constantly asking your therapist to make decisions for you, you need to change. If your therapist constantly makes decisions for you, you need to change therapists.

The most serious way a therapist can make a client worse is by becoming involved with the client emotionally or sexually. Such actions violate the fundamental nature of the relationship and are so unethical that I have addressed them separately in the next chapter.

If you feel that you are getting worse or that your therapist is not helping you, you are probably right. An evaluation form is included on pages 111-112 to help you determine whether you would be better off changing therapists. As a general rule, trust your instincts. If you change therapists and later decide you made a mistake, you can always go back.

What if I'm sexually attracted to my therapist or my therapist makes sexual advances toward me?

If your therapist makes sexual advances towards you, the quick answer is to leave the office. When you are calmer, spend some time analyzing what happened and decide if it really was a sexual advance. If you are sure, report the therapist to your state licensing agency and the police. Unfortunately, some people do not always find it easy to protect themselves for the same reasons that motivated them to seek professional help in the first place.

A shocking number of therapists have sexual relations with their clients. In one nationwide study of 1,000 Ph.D. level licensed therapists, half male and half female, 5.5% of the males and .6% of the females reported having had sexual intercourse with clients.[1] Cases have also been reported of advances made by therapists to clients of the same sex.

Whatever the gender of the therapist, making any type of sexual overture to a client is the most egregious breach of ethics and a gross violation of the therapist's fiduciary duty to the client. People who are seeking therapy are highly vulnerable, especially after disclosing their most private thoughts to their therapists. Many of us have never had an opportunity to discuss our dreams, feelings, and fantasies with anyone, and can confuse gratitude with romantic feelings. It is very easy for a therapist to take advantage of the intimacy created in therapy, particularly since many clients are extremely codependent and unassertive.

One of the reasons people come to therapy is because they want to strengthen their defenses and break out of their patterns of victimization. When a therapist initiates or condones a sexual relationship, he not only destroys whatever trust has been established, but reinforces the client's pattern of victimization. The client then must deal not only with earlier abuse, but also with betrayal by the therapist. Even worse, the client may be so traumatized by the experience that she may never again seek the help she needs.

While it may be asking the impossible to expect therapists to never have sexual feelings towards clients, they can certainly be expected to avoid acting on those feelings.

ANY SEXUAL ACTIVITY BETWEEN THERAPIST AND CLIENT IS ALWAYS THE FAULT OF THE THERAPIST.

Some clients who have been sexually abused at an early age only know how to express their feelings in a sexual way and may make advances toward their therapists. However, even if a client strips naked and flings herself on her therapist begging him to make love to her, that is no excuse for his taking her up on it. Therapists are presumably trained to handle the irrational acts of their clients; whatever happens, they have a responsibility to act appropriately. All psychotherapists are taught that if they feel an attraction for a client, they should discuss these feelings with a supervisor or a colleague, and if they think they cannot control their feelings, they should immediately refer the client to another therapist.

Sex between a therapist and client is condemned by every major medical and psychological organization because it can be emotionally devastating to clients. Legislation in this area is very recent and at the present time only eight states have laws making it illegal for therapists to have sex with their clients. However, all states allow you to sue any therapist who makes sexual advances for unethical practice and assault. You can recover large awards or settlements, as did eight women who recently sued a psychologist for sexual misconduct in California.[2]

You should be aware of some of the ploys therapists have used to seduce their clients so you can be on guard. Therapists have told clients who have sexual problems or problems with intimacy that having sex with the therapist is part of the therapy. Not so, unless you have specifically chosen sex therapy which involves substitute sexual partners. I am skeptical about the benefits of surrogates because they dehumanize and denigrate the loving side of a sexual relationship, which is usually the part of a relationship that is missing if sex does not work. Moreover, in light of the AIDS epidemic, sex with a surrogate is unsafe because the tests are not reliable for three to six months after the last exposure.

If your therapist tells you that he simply cannot resist you and he has "never felt this way before," you should know that studies show that most therapists who seduce their clients have had relationships with *dozens* of them, so you will merely be one of many.

According to the spokesperson for California's Medical Board: "The doctor preys upon those people who are easy marks, choosing someone who isn't going to talk, someone who is needy, has low self-esteem and is looking for approval. Most women don't come forward because they think it's love; they think they are the only one."[3] Therapists who have sex with their clients are sick; they not only hurt their clients but put themselves and their careers in jeopardy.

The studies also show that relationships between therapists and their clients rarely last because of the therapist's problems and because the relationship is inherently unequal. The therapist is an authority figure, caretaker, the one who listens, and the client gets all the caring. If the relationship becomes intimate, the therapist becomes tired of doing all of the giving and the client often becomes tired of being dominated.

If your therapist makes advances towards you or has seduced you, it is important to report him or her to the licensing agency and the police. Most people are afraid of making reports because they think no one will believe them or that people will think it was their fault, so these abusive therapists are never caught and continue to harm their clients.

Since the media have devoted more attention to the subject of abuse by therapists, many new laws have been enacted and law enforcement personnel have become more sensitive to the problem. Often you will not be the first to complain about a particular therapist.

Therapists have to be very careful that their actions are not misinterpreted. Although touching can be very healing in some situations, such as holding someone's hand or even hugging them if they are crying or afraid, the therapist has to be extremely cautious not to offend or threaten the client. If a client has been sexually abused or raped, she may be terrified or repulsed by any kind of touch.

I always ask my clients whether they would like me to hold their hand, so they know that I would like to support them but respect them enough not to violate their boundaries. Being female, I rarely hug male clients and only after I know them well enough that I am sure they will not interpret the gesture as anything other than friendly concern. I know that I serve as a model for a warm, supportive, *non-sexual* relationship which may be the first that the client has ever experienced—and I do not want to do anything to impair that. As a client, you need to feel free to express your preferences to your therapist about being touched.

If a therapist suspects that the client has romantic or sexual feelings toward the therapist, the therapist should discuss these feelings openly as part of the therapy and make it clear that the therapeutic relationship is different from a love or sexual relationship and can only be one of friendship. If you feel attracted to your therapist, you should immediately tell him or her. It is common for clients to develop strong feelings for their therapists and exploring those feelings is an essential part of therapy.

A related issue is whether a therapist and client should have a social relationship outside of therapy. There are differing views on this issue, with the older and more rigid view being that therapists should not have dual relationships because their personal involvement could impair their professional objectivity. The newer more flexible view is that social relationships are permissible *unless* they might impair the therapist's professional judgment.

My personal opinion is that friendships developed in therapy should be the exception, not the rule, and that if the therapist feels that her friendship with a client will affect her judgment or interfere with therapy in any way, she should refer the client to another therapist. Friendships between therapists and former clients are difficult because true friendship implies reciprocity. Clients find it hard to break out of the pattern of treating their former therapist as a therapist and may resent listening to the therapist's personal problems. And the therapist may tire of doing therapy after office hours.

There is a reason for having a professional relationship. It allows the therapist to remain objective and concentrate fully on you. Your therapist should like you and treat you with caring and respect, but you should not expect a social relationship.

Can therapy destroy my creativity?

I felt compelled to include this chapter because I grew up around neurotic artists in the motion picture industry who were convinced that whatever they gained in mental health, they would lose in creativity. They wore their neuroses like a badge. Bizarre and even destructive behavior was not only excused but encouraged—anything was tolerated for "art's sake"—as evidenced by Hollywood's protection of Errol Flynn when he sexually abused young girls, and of other actors, writers, directors, and producers too numerous to mention who broke laws too numerous to mention and flagrantly abused alcohol and drugs. Joan Crawford lived up the street from me and I know Christina's revelations of her mother's abuse are true because I heard Joan boast openly about some of her violence toward Christina at one of my parents' cocktail parties.

Can artists be artists without being neurotic? The answer is a resounding and definitive yes. You do not have to cut off an ear to be a great painter. In fact, studies indicate that neurotic artists succeed *in spite of* their neuroses, not because of them. Neurosis does not create talent; it impedes and destroys it, as many famous people who have self-destructed illustrate. The truth is that resolving neurosis *increases* creativity and many artists are now using therapy to expand their minds and talents.

Science has conclusively demonstrated that unresolved trauma inhibits creativity because repressed memories and emotions are usually stored in the right side of our brain, the side that controls our feelings, creativity, imagination and intuition. Repressing memories and emotions takes a lot of mental energy and brain capacity. If we experience and repress enough trauma, our brains simply run out of space for creative functions, just as a computer runs out of disk space.

Once people release and resolve repressed trauma, they become *more* creative because they open up more capacity for creativity in their brains. I was able to write my first book only after I recovered and healed the memories and emotions of childhood abuse by my father. And my father, a screenwriter and novelist, did his best and most creative work after he went through a long course of hypnotherapy which prevented further abuse. Before therapy, he lost many jobs because he was full of rage and difficult to work with, traits which diminished after therapy.

If you need a list of famous and talented people who do not flaunt their neuroses, have had a reasonable number of spouses and live fairly well-adjusted lives to convince you that destructive neuroses are not a prerequisite to creativity, Paul Newman, Joanne Woodward, Steven Spielberg, Gregory Peck, Jean Claude Renoir, and Helen Hayes come immediately to mind but are only a few of thousands of examples.

Another myth is that you need to "suffer" in order to be creative. While it is true that artists need to have an understanding of the spectrum of human emotions, we all experience enough pain growing up to provide material for several lifetimes; we do not need to generate more.

Suffering does not make anyone more talented; it simply makes it harder to work productively. Some of the main symptoms of depression are loss of interest and pleasure in activities formerly enjoyed, fatigue, and inability to think and concentrate, conditions which are unlikely to result in positive creative expression. Mental problems and suffering can destroy an artistic career as actress Patty Duke so poignantly describes in her book, *A Brilliant Madness: Living with Manic Depressive Illness*.

When people attain success, they often are afraid of losing it and thus resist making any changes, even if they are in pain. Unfortunately hitting rock bottom is sometimes the only thing that forces people to face their problems. Many people believe that the pain they feel inside is normal because they have never experienced anything else. Since people don't usually talk about how they feel inside, most people don't have any idea whether or not their inner feelings are "normal," so they assume that everyone feels the way they do and continue to suffer.

A woman sexually abused and tortured for eight years as a child by her brother, said that she felt all of her life as though her insides were being torn apart by wolves. She thought her feelings were normal and that everyone felt that way until she went through therapy and her pain went away. When she described her feelings, I realized that I had felt the same way because of my abuse. I can only tell you that the way I feel inside after therapy is dramatically different and infinitely better.

Therapy can actually add to an artist's resources. The awareness you gain from therapy about your own feelings, behavior and motivations will give you a deeper understanding of human psychology which is valuable grist for any artist's mill. When you are able to fully express your own feelings, as an actor you will be able to re-create them more authentically, as a writer you will be able to describe and create characters more accurately, and as an artist you will be able to express your emotions and visions more freely.

The fable that therapy destroys creativity is perpetuated by people who are afraid to face their problems. While it is true that therapy can be unsettling and even disruptive during the first six months or year when intense emotions are being released and behavior patterns are changing, the temporary upheaval is more than outweighed by the inner peace, increased concentration, and expanded capacity for creativity, happiness and love that are the end result.

People are now seeking therapy for the sole purpose of expanding their minds and creativity. A variety of recent developments in therapy are opening up amazing new potentials, both mental and spiritual, showing us aspects of ourselves most of us have not experienced before. New techniques, such as brainwave biofeedback (page 254) and breath work (page 260), can help us increase our IQ, stimulate imagination by creating spectacular visions similar to those induced by LSD, enhance creativity, accelerate learning, induce deep relaxation, improve short-term memory, access spiritual experiences, and even increase our sexual pleasure. We can literally have it all, if we are willing to clear out the garbage and harness the incredible power of our minds.

How can I tell if I am making acceptable progress or if I should change therapists?

During the course of therapy, it is common to question whether you are making progress. There will be times when you will find yourself in the depths of depression, fearful, angry, and confused because you will be releasing and experiencing feelings that you repressed. You may become discouraged because you feel your life is not changing as quickly as you expect or desire. And there will also be occasions when you are angry at your therapist and think she has betrayed you. All of these experiences are a normal part of therapy. Progress in therapy is rarely smooth or constant.

Then how do you distinguish normal distress and difficulties from conditions which justify changing therapists? In most cases, there is no easy answer. No one can tell you conclusively whether your therapy is working or not or whether you would do better with another therapist; only you can make that determination. If your therapist's conduct is flagrantly unethical, incompetent, or damaging, you should leave. Otherwise, I can only give you some danger signals and factors to consider that may provide additional insights and help clarify your feelings. This is another area where you have to gather as much information as possible, examine the facts, and then rely on your intuition. The self-evaluation questions and checklist at the end of this chapter will provide some guidance.

There are some situations which are so potentially damaging that they warrant immediate termination. The most serious is if your therapist makes sexual advances. This intolerable and unethical conduct is discussed on pages 96-98, along with advice on how to handle sexual feelings you may have toward your therapist.

If your therapist discounts your experiences or does not believe you, you should leave. I have heard too many appalling stories of therapists who have advised victims of child abuse to "just forget it and get on with your life." This advice is not only directly contrary to psychological research, but prevents recovery by giving clients a spurious excuse to avoid facing their core issues. "Forgetting" or repressing traumatic events is what causes dysfunction; remembering and dealing with the memories, emotions and decisions about those events brings healing. Any therapist who tells you to simply forget a traumatic event is incompetent and should be avoided.

A few narrow-minded therapists still do not accept the reality that there are a large number of people who were victims of incest, sexual and physical abuse, and cult torture, despite the overwhelming evidence. Some therapists refuse to believe memories of abuse are true because they have not faced their own unresolved abuse issues. Others, primarily Freudian psychoanalysts, continue to cling to Sigmund Freud's early statements that such events are fantasies, a view which Freud himself rejected later in his life. Whatever the therapist's reasons for not recognizing the reality of child abuse, such ignorance can inflict devastating damage on an adult who is beginning to recover repressed memories or a child who is trapped in an abusive family.

A high school teacher I will call Claire began to recover memories of having been raped by her father and went to a highly recommended psychiatrist who scoffed at her memories, saying they were just delusions. She was hospitalized for two nervous breakdowns before she had the courage to leave that psychiatrist, and it was twenty painful years before she regained enough trust to try another therapist and receive the help she needed to heal.

Another all too common way some therapists discount clients is by minimizing their emotions, telling them, "Oh, you're making too much of that." One of the most important things a therapist can do is validate his client's feelings. There are no "wrong" feelings; feelings are simply the person's response to an event. The therapist's job is to accept and understand your feelings and help you explore and understand them, not to cut them off or criticize them. There is always a logical reason for emotions, although it may not be readily apparent from present circumstances, and once it is uncovered and analyzed, the emotions usually decrease.

Sometimes emotions may seem to be stronger than the present situation warrants because the situation triggers emotions stored from an earlier event. Those are the feelings you want to examine so you can release them. It is counterproductive for a therapist to cut off exploration or expression of your feelings.

Watch out for signs that you are developing an unhealthy dependence on your therapist. People who are in therapy tend to feel insecure and may not trust themselves to make decisions. Sometimes, consciously or unconsciously, they seek therapists who are strong and will tell them what to do. A primary purpose of therapy is to help you become independent by enhancing your own problem-solving skills and increasing your confidence in your ability to make decisions. A therapist who makes decisions for you is thwarting this goal and fostering feelings of helplessness.

If, after a few months of therapy, you feel that you are becoming more helpless and dependent, you need to discuss these feelings with your therapist. Sometimes old childhood feelings of helplessness may be coming out. In other cases, you may feel your therapist is too demanding or directive. Your therapist should be willing to address these feelings. If you do not receive satisfactory responses to your concerns, you may want to get a second opinion or consider finding a therapist who is able to help you become self-reliant.

Some therapists encourage dependence because they feel powerful and good about themselves only if their clients *need* them. They try to make you believe they are indispensable because of their own neurotic insecurity. If a therapist ever says: "I am the only one who can help you," "My way is the only way," or "You will fall apart without me," leave immediately. Don't ever believe that only one person can help you; there are many qualified people who can help you in many different ways.

Your relationship with your therapist has a significant impact on the success of your therapy. Studies show that a warm, supportive, friendly relationship not only makes therapy faster and more effective, but in itself may be responsible in large part for healing. It is equally true that if you do not like your therapist or he is arrogant or abusive, you will not improve and may grow worse if you start to blame yourself for your lack of progress.

Do not assume because you are going to a therapist that you must have all of the problems. There are far too many unhealed healers in all disciplines. If you frequently feel uncomfortable, intimidated, or humiliated with your therapist, you should explore these feelings with her. If these feelings persist after your discussion, interview other therapists.

Be careful, however, that you are not changing therapists in order to avoid hard issues. There is a difference between a therapist helping you face unpleasant truths or frightening experiences and humiliating or denigrating you. If you have doubts, discuss them with a friend you trust or consult another therapist.

Another way of becoming aware of your true feelings about your therapist is through your dreams. If you have nightmares about your therapist—he appears in your dreams as a spider or you want to run away from him—you probably need to think about changing.

You may also want to change therapists if yours is condescending ("I am the expert and you should just listen to what I say because I know what is best for you"), authoritarian, arrogant, impatient, sarcastic, self-righteous, or bored, unless those characteristics do not bother you. A therapist can be demanding because she cares, without being critical and making you feel inadequate.

Fancy degrees do not give anyone the right to put you down. One of the reasons I and other therapists object to calling people "patients" is because that term implies that you are sick and the therapist is well, while I believe we are equals who are equally valuable, in various stages of healing and growing. You deserve to be treated with respect, dignity and caring by your therapist, no matter what your problems.

Some therapists scream at their clients, call them names, and further destroy their self-esteem under the guise of making clients take responsibility for their actions. This type of "treatment" does not work and should not be tolerated in any setting for any reason. Healing does not take place through abuse. Research and my clinical experience confirm that if you treat people well, they will act well.

If your therapist spends considerable time telling you *her* problems, rather than simply using a few of her experiences as examples, you should leave. You should not feel in any way responsible for helping your therapist or solving her problems. She is supposed to be working for you. If you are afraid of offending or upsetting your therapist or feel that you have to comfort or reassure her, you should discuss these concerns with her.

One other practice which I consider to be unconscionable: Some psychiatrists require people for whom they prescribe medication to come for sessions once a week at a cost of $125 to $250 per session even after the dosage has been stabilized. Such sessions may not be medically necessary. Recently there has been considerable discussion and concern at psychiatric association meetings about the fact that psychiatrists are losing "patients" to other therapists because of their high fees. Some unconscionable psychiatrists are using their virtual monopoly on prescribing medication to force people into therapy with them, even though they may not have adequate counseling skills or may be a poor personality match with the patient. While there may be some circumstances which warrant weekly or monthly monitoring, most do not, and I firmly believe that people have the right to choose therapists that are best for them, who may or may not be the person prescribing medication.

If you find yourself being exploited because you need medication, you have a couple of options. It may be more cost-effective to find a psychiatrist in another city who will monitor your medication and prescribe sufficient amounts to last six months or a year. The travel costs may be far less than weekly fees. If you are taking medication for depression or other mental conditions, I believe it is essential that you also be in therapy, since medication usually acts on the symptoms, but may not relieve the underlying psychological causes. However, you should be allowed to choose another therapist with lower fees for therapy who can consult with your psychiatrist.

You may also be able to find a physician who is not a psychiatrist to monitor and prescribe your medication, so you can see the therapist of your choice. In some states, physicians and psychiatric nurse practitioners can prescribe antidepressants and other psychoactive drugs and their fees are lower than psychiatrists'. However, in complex cases, it may be preferable to have a psychiatrist who specializes in mental conditions prescribe medication. The majority of psychiatrists are ethical and will help you find both the most effective medication and therapy at the lowest cost.

Perhaps the most difficult assessment you will have to make is whether your progress is satisfactory. This determination is totally subjective and depends on an infinite variety of factors: your commitment and motivation, your relationship with your therapist, your therapist's competence and attitude, the type of techniques used, to name just a few. The checklist of questions at the end of this chapter provides a number of considerations, but you have to make the final decision about whether or not to stay with your therapist.

The hardest part is separating which problems are the therapist's and which are yours. It is very easy to blame your lack of progress on the therapist. If your pipes leak after the plumber leaves or your tooth continues to ache after your dentist fills a cavity, you can probably assume you are not the problem. But if you are not making progress with your therapist, you may be the problem.

Your progress depends to a large degree on your commitment to therapy and your willingness to perceive that you have problems and face them. We all have a natural resistance to change. Even if we are miserable, our misery is familiar. People are perversely resistant to change because they fear the unknown. Also, you may believe you are ready for therapy, but the child part of your mind, the part that has repressed memories of painful events, may still believe you will be overwhelmed if these memories are brought to consciousness and may resist your efforts.

The technical term for this almost universal phenomenon is "resistance," although many therapists dislike this word because it seems to connote a deliberate refusal to cooperate, which is not the case. Modern therapists prefer the term "ambivalence" because part of the person wants to change, while another part, usually unconscious, wants to maintain the status quo, no matter how unpleasant it may be. Whatever term you or your therapist uses, it is important for you to be aware that sometimes an unconscious part of you may be thwarting your efforts in therapy no matter how much you believe you want to change.

Ambivalence can manifest itself in many ways. You may find fault with your therapist, be frequently attracted by other types of therapy or healing techniques that you are convinced are superior to yours, change the subject to avoid exploring certain issues, or find excuses for missing appointments or being late (all of which will seem very reasonable and justified at the time). If you recognize some or all of these conditions, it is wise to thoroughly explore the possibility that you are experiencing a natural ambivalence to change before you fire your therapist.

Another psychological concept you may hear about is "transference." Transference is an unconscious process where a person shifts or transfers to the therapist fears, wishes and other feelings that are rooted in past experiences with significant people, usually parents, siblings, or parental substitutes. For example, if you were abused as a child, your basic trust was destroyed and you will probably find it difficult to trust your therapist. If a parent was rigidly authoritarian, you may perceive your therapist in that mode and rebel against him. You may *strongly believe* you have good reasons for your beliefs or feelings, but sometimes our minds unconsciously create reasons to support perceptions which come from powerful patterns of belief based on early relationships.

Whether the problem is transference or a real conflict with your therapist is one of the hardest things to sort out. It is critical for you to be able to thoroughly discuss your concerns and feelings, especially the negative ones, with your therapist because working through your transference reactions is an essential part of therapy. By becoming aware of how you perceive your therapist, you will obtain valuable information on how you view other people and the world, so that you can evaluate whether your perceptions are realistic and change them if they are not. Your feelings of transference also may help bring past painful events to consciousness so they can be resolved. Although sometimes the feelings and conflicts they cause can be painful, transference reactions are a positive part of therapy if you and your therapist use them as grist for the mill.

Lest you think you are the only one with these reactions, you should know that therapists have them too. If a therapist transfers his needs, fears and other feelings onto you, it is called "countertransference," and although therapists are trained to be aware of their feelings, they are human and may slip into their own unrealistic reactions. One of the most common countertransference reactions is when a therapist has a need for constant reinforcement and approval from clients.

If you feel your therapist is transferring his feelings onto you, you should challenge him. Good therapists are open to examining their own reactions.

Please do not misinterpret what I have said as indicating that I think all problems are due to ambivalence or transference; they are often due to actions of the therapist. Sometimes the therapist is truly incompetent. In other cases, no one is "at fault"; this particular therapist simply may not be a good personality match for you.

Sometimes, when you discuss the problem with your therapist, you may find that you are feeling fear about the therapeutic process or that you have misunderstood something your therapist said or that your therapist will be willing to change behavior you find uncomfortable. If you can work out this relationship, you will have taken a giant step toward working out problems in other relationships.

Sometimes if you are not making the progress you expect, you need to consider the possibility that you may be pushing yourself too hard and take the time you require to become more secure before you delve into a new area.

In some cases, you may simply have gone as far as you can with this particular counselor. Different therapists have different strengths and you may be able to overcome a block and reach a new level of healing by obtaining a new perspective. Ethical counselors acknowledge when they are stuck. Unfortunately some therapists have not reached a point in their own development where they feel secure admitting that they may no longer be able to help you, so you may have to make your own evaluation and decide whether you have made significant progress over three or four months.

One thing I learned from my own experience and from training other therapists: A therapist generally cannot take you any further than she has gone herself. I noticed that the more work I did on myself, the more progress my clients made, and at a faster rate. If a therapist has not dealt with her own anger, she will have difficulty helping you with yours. And a therapist who is arrogant and sarcastic will not teach you to trust. It is important to remember that your therapist's personality problems are not your fault; you did not make her that way.

Changing therapists almost always creates feelings of disappointment and failure. Even if you do not like your therapist, you have confided your most private thoughts to him and you have established a connection which, when broken, may feel like a loss. It is extremely helpful to be able to discuss these feelings with your therapist and to terminate on an amicable basis if possible. If you leave on friendly terms, you will feel better and you will also feel that you have the option of returning if you change your mind.

If you are not sure whether to stay with your therapist, you may benefit from obtaining a second or third opinion from other therapists. Consultations not only provide you with different viewpoints but also with a chance to compare the style and personality of other therapists with yours. You may find a therapist you like better, or you may conclude you are lucky to have your own. There are many excellent and ethical therapists who can help you, so there is no reason to settle for someone abusive or incompetent, or whom you don't like.

I have no hesitation about my clients working with other therapists at the same time they are working with me; in fact, I encourage them to explore other modalities. I have suggested that some of my clients try other therapists for special problems or to see if they prefer a different style. A therapist who forbids you to see other therapists while you are in therapy with him is probably someone you want to avoid.

Changing your therapist does not have to be an all-or-nothing decision. You have many options and your choice is not irrevocable. You can change therapists and go back to your original one later. You can consult and even work with other therapists while you are working with your original one. If you do see two therapists simultaneously, both therapists will be able to help you more effectively if they are aware of that fact, but if you do not want to disclose your other sessions, that is up to you. You can stop therapy altogether, and return when you feel more comfortable. Remember, you control your own therapy and have to decide what is best for you.

✓ Self-evaluation questions during therapy

It is helpful to ask yourself these questions every three or four months during therapy.

1. DO I LIKE MY THERAPIST MOST OF THE TIME? (This is the most important consideration.)
2. Do I feel comfortable with my therapist most of the time?
3. Do I feel most of the time that my therapist cares about me? (Sometimes you will feel your therapist is uncaring and even that she is betraying you. Such feelings are a normal part of transference if they are not constant and if you are able to work them through with your therapist.)
4. Does my therapist pay attention to me?
5. Does my therapist listen to me?
6. Does my therapist treat me with respect?
7. Do I feel intimidated, humiliated, inadequate or scared during many of my therapy sessions? (Spend some quiet time analyzing whether these feelings come from past events and old relationships or from your therapist's conduct. Discuss your feelings and perceptions with your therapist, and, if his responses are unsatisfactory, with a friend or another therapist.)
8. Do I feel that my therapist is condescending, arrogant, impatient, judgmental, rigid, patronizing, sarcastic, self-righteous, bored or in any way abusive?
9. Is my therapist usually late for appointments?
10. Does my therapist believe me?
11. Is my therapist sensitive to my feelings?
12. Does my therapist discount me or my feelings?
13. Does my therapist validate my feelings or try to cut them off?

14. Is my therapist willing to openly discuss negative feelings I may have about him, without being defensive?
15. Is my therapist flexible and willing to explore other options and therapies with me?
16. Is my therapist willing to let me direct my therapy? (Or even better, does my therapist encourage me to direct my own therapy?)
17. Does my therapist use a variety of theories and techniques?
18. Does my therapist emphasize my strengths and successes?
19. Do I feel I can't survive without my therapist? (If so, does he encourage feelings of dependence or does he help me to be self-reliant?)
20. Does my therapist help me analyze situations and learn to make my own decisions or does he constantly make decisions for me and tell me how to run my life? Am I responsible for putting the therapist in this position or is he fostering dependence?
21. Does my therapist encourage me to explore other ways of growing and healing, including other therapies?
22. Do I laugh with my therapist?
23. Do I feel better or have more understanding of my problems after most of my sessions with my therapist?
24. Am I making progress in attaining the goals I negotiated with my therapist?

✓ Checklist for assessing your progress in therapy

Rate your answers to these questions on a scale of one to five. Date your responses and save them to compare with future evaluations.

I feel:

5 = very much better—a really noticeable difference—I'm really getting there!

4 = much better but I have more work to do

3 = a little better

2 = not much better—I don't see many changes

1 = the same

0 = worse

(It will be helpful to discuss your evaluations with your therapist, especially any questions you answer with a 3 or less.)

1. Is my life generally working better than when I started with this therapist? (If you are uncovering repressed memories and emotions of childhood trauma, you need to allow for the fact that you may feel worse for a few months as the old emotions emerge. If you and your therapist established goals, rate your progress on each one of those goals.)
2. Are my relationships working better? (You might ask family members and close friends for their perceptions.)
3. Do I feel less pain inside?
4. Am I depressed less of the time?
5. Am I angry less of the time?
6. Am I afraid or anxious less of the time?
7. Is it easier for me to make decisions?
8. Do I feel more confident?
9. Do I have a better understanding of my feelings and behavior?

10. Do I feel as though I have more control over my life?
11. Do I feel as though I have more choices?
12. Do I take more responsibility for my feelings and behavior?
13. DO I LIKE MYSELF MORE?

What can I do to make being in therapy easier?

There are many things you can do to make therapy less disruptive and painful. The first is to develop a positive attitude. Most people think that therapy has to be painful and debilitating in order for it to work. Not so, although I went through much of my therapy believing that it had to be awful, and it was.

I suffered for years before a friend of mine who uses educational kinesiology (see page 294) suggested that learning, even in therapy, could be fun and easy. "Fun" and "easy" were words I had never associated with learning; in my family, you had to work hard and study hard, and life was definitely hard. If something was easy or enjoyable, you were cheating or goofing off. And recovering memories in therapy of being sexually abused and tortured by my father was not what I would consider amusement. My friend had to use her kinesiology techniques to reprogram my mind to accept the possibility that learning could be fun and easy.

When I began to be open to the idea that I could view therapy as an interesting learning experience, rather than another form of torture, the stress of therapy diminished and I proceeded at a much faster rate. Even when I recovered more gruesome memories and the violent emotions that went with them, I had a different perspective, more that of an observer or scientist, and I could regain my equanimity more rapidly. I even began to joke with my therapist. I realized I didn't have to take it all so seriously. After all, I was only dealing with memories—past thoughts, not present reality.

"No pain, no gain," is a fallacy created by sadists. You can heal without suffering, even though you may experience painful emotions for brief periods, and you can learn easily. The sooner your mind accepts these facts, the easier your therapy—and your life—will be.

A simple way you can reprogram your thinking is by using affirmations. Affirmations are short positive statements that are intended to replace old negative beliefs. Each statement is repeated three times, mentally or aloud as often as possible. If you think therapy and learning are hard, say to yourself, "Learning and therapy are easy and fun." You don't have to consciously believe what you are saying because affirmations work on your subconscious mind to change deep-seated beliefs.

You can also use affirmations to reprogram the basic negative beliefs most of us have about ourselves. When my clients make their first appointment, I give them three affirmations as a homework assignment. They are "I am a good person," "I am loveable," and last is whatever the client believes she needs most, usually "I am safe." If you feel that these ideas are so contrary to your reality that you cannot say them, simply add, "I choose to be a good person," or "I choose to be loveable," until you feel comfortable saying the phrase directly.

A major part of making therapy easier is keeping your life and health in balance. Many people, myself included, become so obsessed with therapy and the emerging memories that they forget to live in the present. You need to make a conscious effort to forget therapy and your problems for most of each day and engage in activities and social relationships that are pleasurable.

One day during the course of my therapy, I realized that I was in my forties, and that my father had died of a heart attack at 58. I wondered if I might die before I finished therapy, without ever having had a chance to enjoy life. That thought drastically changed my way of looking at life and therapy.

I realized that I'd better enjoy life right *now*. I started to live each day as though if I died that night, I would be able to say that I had no regrets for that day. I made a conscious effort to do things every day that I enjoyed. Therapy no longer seemed so overwhelming and my life became much happier. I still make all of my choices—about working, hiking with my dog, skiing, seeing or calling friends, cleaning house—based on the principle that I don't want to regret what I have done today—and I finally do enjoy my life.

Another way of teaching yourself to focus on the present is through a type of meditation called "mindfulness," where you concentrate on your breathing, or on the minute details of ordinary activities like eating or walking, using all of your senses.[1] We go through our lives blind and deaf to much of what is around us. Becoming mindful, consciously and acutely aware of our senses and surroundings—the laugh of a child, our friend's smile, a flower among the weeds, raindrops on the roof, the contours of a cloud—can give us a renewed sense of pleasure and aliveness. This process and other helpful techniques are described in *Reach for the Rainbow*.

An important part of achieving balance is taking care of your physical health. Regular exercise is essential if you are in therapy because you need a way to release tension. You may already be aware of the many benefits of exercise, but are you aware that exercise is recognized by therapists as being the single most effective means of combatting depression? It outperforms drugs, shock treatment and even therapy itself. The reason is that exercise causes the brain to release endorphins, hormones which make you feel euphoric, the same hormones released during lovemaking. You may have heard of "runner's high," a state of bliss runners often experience which is somewhat like a drug high. Runner's high is caused by the release of endorphins,[2] and other less painful forms of exercise have the same euphoric effect.

One of the first things I prescribe for my clients is a regular exercise program. Fast walking for forty-five minutes or an hour a day is one of the best forms of exercise. You don't need any expensive equipment. It gets you outside so that you are exposed to sunshine. New studies indicate we need at least fifteen minutes outdoors in daylight (even if it's cloudy) to maintain a minimal level of physical health. Another benefit is that you can watch other people (and perhaps meet and talk to them) and enjoy the antics of birds and other animals. I chose walking, hiking and skiing as my ways of exercising and I don't think I would have survived my own therapy without them. Again, forget the "no pain, no gain" myth. Pick a form of exercise that is pleasurable. If you hate it, you won't keep it up.

When you are in therapy, it may sometimes be difficult to direct your mind away from issues you are working on and focus on daily tasks. You may find your thoughts racing or you may feel overwhelmed by emerging emotions. The regular practice of meditation is a wonderful way of turning off your mind and obtaining inner peace.

Meditation has been around for hundreds of years, but we, in our fast-paced Western industrialized society, have ignored it until recently. The word "meditation" usually conjures up a vision of saffron-colored robes, shaved heads, crossed legs, and the slightly sickening scent of incense. Would you believe that thousands of bankers, lawyers, and corporate tycoons meditate every day in their executive chairs, while their secretaries hold their calls? Some large corporations even hold meditation breaks twice a day instead of coffee breaks. And the Seattle-Tacoma International Airport has a clearly marked "Meditation Room" for frazzled travelers!

Meditation is no longer only for the mystics. The basic principle behind meditation is to quiet your mind, to assume a passive attitude which allows your mind to take a break from its ceaseless stream of thoughts. By emptying your mind of thoughts and distractions, you can achieve a state which may be even more restful than sleep. Meditation has been found to lower your oxygen consumption, blood pressure, and heart rate as does sleep. It also produces alpha waves, slower brain waves which indicate peace and contentment and are not usually present in a sleep state. Meditation is a way to relax, find inner peace, overcome insomnia, and increase your energy and concentration.

With all that hype, you probably think meditation must be very complicated and will take you years of study. Actually meditation is a very simple, natural process which you can learn in five minutes. Don't think it must cost a lot to learn, although there are companies that will take your money to teach you to meditate if you want to pay. In fact, you can learn to meditate as I did from a wonderful book, *The Relaxation Response* by Herbert Benson, M.D., which teaches you what you need to know on two pages, from Joan Borysenko's bestseller, *Minding the Body, Mending the Mind*, or from *Reach for the Rainbow*.

Having a support network can facilitate your therapy. People in counseling often do not have encouraging or sympathetic family members or friends with whom they can talk. An important part of healing is learning to feel comfortable with people. You can begin that process right now by making a conscious effort to meet and talk to people. Introduce yourself to your neighbors, join a bridge or drama club, attend lectures and concerts, enroll in classes in your local adult education program or at a trade school or college, participate in a book discussion club. Sports enthusiasts have many options from skiing to bowling or even walking. One of the best ways to meet people is through volunteer work. There are thousands of organizations in every area of interest that need help, and helping others will make *you* feel better.

There are many other ways of making your life easier and more pleasant while you are going through therapy and you need to actively experiment until you find the ones you like best. Massage is extremely pleasurable as well as therapeutic. I have described some of the more popular types on pages 290-299. But exercise and simple meditation are essential and should become habits whatever other means you choose to use to enjoy your life in the present. While therapy should be a priority in your life, *living* should be the focus.

How do I know when I no longer need therapy?

Psychotherapy is a growth process which has no easily definable end. Healing is an ongoing process. There are always ways to improve and new things to learn about ourselves and our relationships. But we can learn and grow in many ways and few of us want to spend our lives in therapy, even if we could afford to do so.

People usually have a great deal of anxiety about terminating therapy because they may have developed some dependency on their therapist and are afraid of losing the support. They often have the mistaken notion that termination really means *the end*. But termination does not necessarily mean you are finished with therapy forever or that you will never see your therapist again. You have many options. You can stop permanently, change therapists, reduce the number and frequency of sessions, take a break and return on a set date, join a group, attend a weekend workshop, or stop for a while and see how your life works before you make a decision.

Termination may seem like a life-or-death decision but it is not. Nothing is irrevocable. You can always change your mind.

There are some practical guidelines you can use to decide whether you need or want to continue with the type of psychotherapy you have chosen. If you and your therapist established specific goals when you started therapy, you may choose to terminate when you have achieved all or most of those goals, or, if you are pleased with your therapist and believe the work has been effective, set new goals and continue.

If you did not establish specific goals, the most critical consideration is how you feel about yourself. Do you like yourself most of the time? Do you accept most of your shortcomings, weaknesses and deficiencies? Can you look in the mirror and say, without wincing, "I love *you*!" If you make a mistake, can you view it as a learning experience and go on without excoriating yourself—most of the time? Unless you can answer "yes" to these questions, you probably need to continue with therapy.

The other major consideration is whether you are satisfied with the way your life is working. Do not expect perfection. Neither you nor your life will ever be perfect because we live in an imperfect world. No matter how long you work in therapy, you will never be free of problems and challenges.

The real issue is not whether your life is free of problems, but whether you can cope with your problems. If you can handle most problems satisfactorily, you probably no longer need therapy. One enormous advantage you have already gained from being in therapy is the knowledge that help is always available and that if you encounter a problem you cannot handle alone, you can find someone to help you.

Another question you need to ask yourself is how you feel inside. Are you relatively free of tension, anxiety, fear, depression, and anger most of the time? No one, NO ONE, feels happy all the time. Pain and discomfort are part of being human and are responsible for much of our psychological and spiritual growth.

You can reasonably expect to be content and free from uncomfortable emotions more than half of the time. If, most of the time, you no longer react with anger, fear, depression or anxiety to things that used to trigger intense feelings, you probably have released enough of your repressed emotions to stop therapy.

The same general criteria apply to your relationships. Are most of them satisfactory most of the time? It is unreasonable to demand that your marriage, friendships, and work associations be totally free from conflict. The measure of your success in therapy is how well you resolve those conflicts when they arise.

If you and your partner or spouse are in couples therapy, it is preferable for you both to agree on whether you have made sufficient progress to stop.

Forgiveness is an essential element of psychological healing. If you are still harboring hatred or resentment toward people who have hurt you, your healing is not complete. It is especially important to forgive your parents, not for moral reasons, but for practical ones. Your parents and the people who raised you have a powerful influence on your life. Your relationships with them form patterns that can last a lifetime unless you work them out. If you have not reached some kind of inner peace with respect to your relationship with your parents or caretakers, you will continue to have problems in other relationships.

Most people have a grave misconception about forgiveness. It does not mean that you condone or overlook the hurtful things that were done to you. Abuse is never "all right." Nor can you forget what you have suffered; those events are part of your history and have affected your life.

The true meaning of forgiveness is "letting go." You can let go of what happened by letting go of your feelings of bitterness, resentment and hatred toward those who hurt you—*without condoning what they did*. Forgiveness is for you, not for the person you forgive. If you hang on to your destructive feelings, they will ruin your life. And by holding on to your bitterness and thoughts of revenge, you are holding on to your abuser and giving him continued power over you. Letting go means that you release the energy that keeps you tied to your abuser and the abuse, so that you are free.

In order to reach the stage where you can truly forgive and let go, you must first recognize and release the depth of hatred and rage you have stored toward those who hurt you. You cannot skip over this step. If you think you do not have any stored anger, I can only tell you that I have never found a single case where this is true.

Being hurt especially by those we love naturally engenders anger and hatred. These emotions are the most frightening and unacceptable in our culture, and we tend to repress them because they are the hardest to face. But you cannot forgive or heal until you confront and release them. I urge you to stay in therapy until you can accept and release your rage and forgive those who have hurt you.

As a general rule, if you look forward to most days when you get up in the morning, you have probably outgrown the need for therapy. In deciding when to stop therapy, it is important to use your common sense and trust your feelings. It is your life and there are no "shoulds" here.

A word of warning: If you suspect that you are thinking of leaving therapy because you do not want to face some difficult memories or issues, discuss this suspicion thoroughly with your therapist before you quit. Usually if you have such a suspicion, it is because your mind is telling you that you have more work to complete. Sometimes we may think we have made substantial progress and that our lives are working well, but the improvement may be only temporary, a kind of recess before we go on to deeper work. I thought—and hoped—that I had finished recovering traumatic memories of my abuse many times during the course of my therapy, but I kept finding more memories and deeper levels of repressed emotion.

I actually did not discover the core of my uncontrollable anger until long after I had stopped psychotherapy, when I tried conscious connected breathing to test whether I wanted to use it with clients. Only then was I able to reach and release the intense hatred I had for people in general because no one had helped me during the years I was being abused as a child. I knew then that I was finally done because I could *feel* it in my body. I felt lighter, free of pain and tension. And events that used to trigger rage no longer bothered me.

One benefit of being in therapy is that you do not have to make the decision about whether to terminate by yourself. You should discuss feelings about wanting to terminate with your therapist because he may have useful insights that will make your decision easier.

Termination is a critical stage of therapy. The way you conclude your therapy has a strong influence on your progress and growth after you stop. Leaving therapy almost always causes turmoil and mixed feelings which need to be resolved with the therapist. If you omit this stage or cut it short, you will deprive yourself of a valuable part of the therapy process and you may be left with loose ends that will haunt you later.[1]

Termination is a time for evaluating, consolidating and reinforcing what you have learned so that you can make the most effective use of your new knowledge in the outside world and not revert to old dysfunctional patterns. You will want to assess what you have learned, what was the most valuable, how you can put what you learned into practice, how you will handle problems that arise, and what you will want to focus on to continue your growth on your own.

As part of your termination discussions, you and your therapist need to be careful not to overlook any unfinished business that may haunt you when you stop therapy. The act of terminating is itself a significant event that can trigger old feelings of loss and abandonment which need to be addressed. Take the time you need to insure that you have closure with your therapist; don't leave any uncomfortable feelings hanging.

Therapists also have feelings of sadness when a client terminates and these mutual feelings of loss need to be shared. If you are able to terminate your relationship with your therapist in a positive way, that achievement can be a useful model for dealing successfully with future partings and losses.

The termination stage in group therapy is even more crucial than in individual counseling. In fact, most leaders of psychotherapy groups believe the termination stage is the most decisive part of the entire process; if this stage is omitted or not handled properly, the benefits members obtain from the group experience can be greatly reduced.[2]

When a group leader asks you to make a commitment to complete all of the sessions, there is a good reason as I learned from personal experience. I had to catch a plane the day before the end of a week-long workshop because of a speaking commitment and missed not only the joyous culmination ceremony the leader had planned, but the chance to express and work out the feelings of loss and separation I had about saying goodbye to people I had grown close to and cared for. I was left with a negative, incomplete feeling that was very much in contrast to the positive feelings experienced by group members who stayed until the end.

Effective group termination allows members to express their feelings and concern about separation, and to mourn the loss. It also provides an opportunity for members to discuss ways to integrate the group experience into their daily lives. Often members are encouraged to provide feedback to each other about strengths and weaknesses. Termination is a time where members can help each other summarize what they have learned and analyze interactions and conflicts within the group that might reflect patterns of interaction in their families. It is an experience that should not be missed.

What if you believe that you should fire your therapist? If your therapist is making sexual advances toward you, of course you need to leave immediately. (See pages 96-99.) But in most other cases, it will be more helpful to discuss the reasons why you are leaving with your therapist. If your perceptions of the problem are accurate, it is important for you to tell the therapist what is wrong so that he can become aware of his actions and hopefully correct them. Discussion of the problem may clarify the issue; you may find that you have misunderstood what your therapist said or his motivations. This discovery will provide you with a model for working out misunderstandings in the future.

Whether you want to leave individual or group therapy, it is important to be able to listen to other opinions and reactions, even if you do not agree with them. *You do not have to accept those opinions;* simply consider them and use what has value for you. It is healthier to leave after making sure you have done everything you can to understand and reconcile the situation, because you will then leave with a sense of calm certainty about your decision, rather than with feelings of betrayal and anger.

You will benefit from taking advantage of any follow-up sessions. The better group leaders usually conduct a group follow-up session about a month after the group ends.[3] Inpatient programs may also provide for some type of follow-up within a few weeks or months after a patient is discharged.

If your therapist does not schedule any follow-up sessions, you may elect to go back occasionally for a mental health checkup, the same way you monitor your physical health. I do not believe an annual checkup is necessary, but keep in the back of your mind the fact that you have created a support system which you can use whenever you feel overwhelmed or stressed-out.

Therapy is not just for dealing with traumatic events and crises that have already occurred, it is also for preventing such crises from happening. One session can prevent a problem from developing that might take many sessions to resolve later.

If you decide to go back into therapy but want to try something different, you now have experience and will know what to look for. You will be more aware of the issues you want to resolve and better able to find a therapist to help you.

Termination is not the end of growth; it merely gives you the opportunity to put into practice the new skills and attitudes you have learned—and to live your life to the fullest.

What if I need to be hospitalized?

In most cases, you will not need to go to a hospital. However, there may be circumstances when a hospital is the safest place to be. This chapter will help you choose whether to go to a hospital and how to select a hospital or other facility where you will obtain appropriate care. As with therapists, many hospitals are excellent, but others, even in large cities, may be way behind the times in the treatment of childhood trauma and other mental conditions. The appalling fact is that there are far too many people in hospitals, drugged to the point of somnambulism, who do not need to be there at all.

When is hospitalization appropriate? To protect the individual and obtain intensive treatment. If someone is clearly in danger of hurting himself or others or cannot take care of himself, he needs to be hospitalized. Laws in all states provide that people can be hospitalized involuntarily for evaluation and treatment under such circumstances. In the case of abuse survivors, self-mutilation and the danger of suicide are the most common grounds for hospitalization.

Therapists, whatever their academic degrees, are schooled in recognizing the symptoms of severe depression and are trained to hospitalize people who have suicidal thoughts, a plan for killing themselves, and the present means to carry through the plan. Although the principles seem simple, their application is often difficult. There is a delicate balance between protecting a client's life and requiring her to be hospitalized against her will which takes away her right to choose for herself, may make her feel more depressed and hopeless, and may destroy the relationship of trust which has been built between therapist and client. Many people think of suicide more than once. Certainly not all need to be hospitalized.

Involuntary hospitalization is a last resort. I have found that hospitalization can often be avoided if the question of suicide is addressed directly and hypnotherapy is used to determine where the feelings are coming from so that they can be released and the negative thoughts reframed. I usually deal with suicidal thoughts in the first session, explaining that these thoughts are often old ones coming from feelings of hopelessness as a child when there was no way to escape the abuser.

If a client is severely depressed and has present thoughts of suicide, I work with the client, sometimes using hypnotherapy, to reveal the basis for those thoughts and neutralize them. I also obtain an agreement from my client consciously, and from any parts or personalities that are suicidal, that the thoughts will not be acted upon.

In one case, Jennifer, a survivor of sexual abuse, told me that she often thought of suicide and had purchased a gun which she kept under the seat of her car so she could find it easily if her mental pain became too great. It is hard not to panic when you know someone has a loaded gun in her car parked in your driveway. I seriously considered calling the police and told her so. However, Jennifer was willing to work on recovering the memories which were triggering her suicidal feelings. At the end of a three-hour session, I asked her to give me the gun for safekeeping and a commitment that she would not hurt herself while we worked together. She gave me her promise and the gun and did not attempt suicide.

Far too many people with multiple personality disorder are needlessly hospitalized. Richard Kluft, M.D., one of the foremost authorities, says that in most cases hospitalization is unnecessary. He recognizes that survivors of such extreme abuse have the power to protect themselves and not allow destructive parts to take over. Kluft also believes that hospitalization may teach people to become more dysfunctional because it leads them to believe they are unable to take care of themselves.

If I feel someone needs hospitalization, I say so. But unless that person is in immediate danger, I let him make the decision because I believe we all know when we need help. Violet had been brutally abused by her father and was feeling anxious and depressed as she recovered gruesome memories. When she did not appear for her regular appointment, I telephoned her home. Her phone had been disconnected. She was a schoolteacher, but had not gone to work for a week. I became concerned and asked the police to check her apartment. I learned that Violet was ill and that her abusive husband had disconnected the phone and had been holding her incommunicado, cutting her off from all communication with the outside world. Violet's condition deteriorated over the couple of weeks to the point where she was not eating, sleeping or taking care of herself. She began to sound very confused.

Violet and I discussed whether she should go into the hospital. I told her I would not put her there without her consent, but because of her husband's abusive behavior and her deteriorating condition,

I thought it would be a good idea for her to be in a safe place where she would have the care she needed. We knew that she had more memories to uncover and that the hospital would be a safe place for this work.

Violet decided that she wanted to go into a hospital. Since it was her choice, she did not feel that she was crazy; she knew that she had made a sensible decision and was taking care of herself. Away from the influence of her husband and family, Violet began to have flashbacks about having been abused in a cult where her father had taken her. She regained her physical and mental strength in the hospital and made substantial progress in therapy during the month she was there. She also decided to leave her husband.

Some people choose to use hospitals as a safe haven for recovering memories. A respected local therapist discovered she had been violently raped when she was five by a man who broke into her home on Christmas and again the night after. She checked herself into a hospital because she decided it would be easier for her to uncover her repressed memories in a place where she felt safe.

It is important to choose a hospital carefully. Some hospitals rely almost totally on drugs and do not provide much support or therapy. And a few hospitals have practices which are so outdated they are harmful. Because I train therapists throughout the country, I have become aware of instances where victims of sexual abuse have been treated in a cruel, archaic manner. For example, one therapist's client who had been severely physically and sexually abused was placed by her parents in a well-established hospital. This woman has multiple personality disorder, but apparently this hospital did not recognize this disorder and punished her for switching personalities. Each time it occurred, she was placed in isolation and *restraints*. Not only did the hospital fail to give her supportive and caring treatment, it invalidated her and punished her for what she was experiencing. Needless to say, this woman's condition worsened.

When you choose a hospital, it is important to thoroughly investigate the hospital's beliefs, policies and methods of treatment. You want to take care to select a hospital which emphasizes psychotherapy rather than drug therapy and has a specific program designed to treat your problem. Your therapist is the best person to advise you. If you do not have a therapist, you or a supportive friend or family member should obtain references and information about local hospitals and then check them out.

Psychiatric hospitals, clinics, residential treatment centers, and general hospitals with psychiatric wards provide treatment for mental conditions. As a rule, psychiatric hospitals, specialized clinics, and residential treatment centers tend to have the most specific programs for most mental health conditions and the most enlightened therapeutic techniques, but this is not always true. Some psychiatric hospitals are merely expensive. It is wise to get referrals for hospitals from your therapist and others, and, if possible, talk to a couple of people who have been treated in the hospital you are considering.

An important consideration is whether the hospital or other facility will permit your therapist to work with you during your stay. Most enlightened hospitals encourage this practice, knowing that your therapist has established a relationship with you and that your therapist's presence can expedite treatment. These hospitals recognize that the client needs continuity and support and that the therapist needs to know how the client is progressing so that treatment will continue smoothly when the client leaves the hospital. Unfortunately, not all hospitals are enlightened and staff members may take the position that they do not want an "outsider" meddling in their work. They may use licensing or insurance "requirements" as an excuse. These institutions are to be avoided.

Some hospitals are primarily research institutions, frequently those connected to universities, and may place an undue emphasis on psychotropic drugs for treatment. Many of these institutions receive substantial funding for testing experimental drugs. Psychotropic drugs have damaging side effects some of which may not disappear for a year, if ever. In most cases, people on these drugs are so doped up that they cannot think clearly and certainly cannot participate in any meaningful therapy. Such drugs should only be used when all other options have failed, but sometimes hospital staffs do not take the time to try other options. If medication is necessary, the lowest effective dose should be prescribed for the shortest period of time and only in conjunction with therapy.

Unfortunately, some hospitals do not adequately evaluate new patients and may hand out drugs based on erroneous diagnoses. Misdiagnoses occur far too frequently. Some symptoms of severe trauma overlap with symptoms of other mental conditions and can be misinterpreted. For example, victims of trauma, especially those with ego states and multiple personalities, sometimes hear voices, which is also a symptom of schizophrenia. A few months ago, I was talking on the telephone with a psychologist friend of mine in San Francisco, a man who has been a therapist for many more years than I have. He sounded very tired and depressed and I asked him what was wrong. He said he was working in an inpatient psychiatric facility for patients who were considered to have chronic and incurable mental illnesses and that one of his women patients, a ten-year resident, had cut herself all over her body the night before and he had been up all night with her. I remarked that she must have been sexually abused.

My friend was astonished. He said he had learned only that night that she *had* been sexually abused and asked how I could possibly have known. I told him that self-mutilation is a recognized symptom of sexual abuse and began to ask about this woman who had been diagnosed as an incurable schizophrenic. It quickly became clear to me that she had classic multiple personality disorder, was not receiving any therapy, and had been drugged for ten years on Thorazine which she did not need. Such ten-year "mistakes" make me livid.

The sad fact is that some doctors and hospital staff members do not *listen* to their patients. Once a patient is diagnosed with a "chronic" illness, he is warehoused. Staff members tend to ignore patients they believe are psychotic and incurable. Some doctors who do not want to believe that children could be subjected to brutal and bizarre abuse tend to discount what their patients are saying as "delusions," and cease their investigations.

It is time for hospitals and doctors to start healing people instead of labeling and sedating them. Doctors and staff members also need to become more aware of their own problems and feelings so they do not become overwhelmed by the confusing emotions and images pouring out of their patients. It is easier to dismiss someone as "crazy" and prescribe drugs rather than to take the time to listen and decipher what the person is trying to disclose. Drugged patients are tractable and placid. When the hospital releases them, other therapists are left to deal with the aftermath.

Researchers are beginning to discover what clinicians have known for some time: what comes from people's minds is the result of traumatic experiences. The most bizarre thoughts and behaviors make sense once we know what they suffered. The most important thing doctors and hospital personnel can do is to listen to what the individual is telling them and work with the memories and the fears. Doctors should assume that all patients can heal and look for ways to help them.

I do not believe any mental condition is incurable unless major parts of the brain have been destroyed. Researchers are finding that even when the brain is physically injured, it creates new pathways through other areas to compensate. Do not believe anyone who tells you that your condition is hopeless or incurable; it simply means *that person* does not have the skills to help you. You need to look elsewhere.

There are certainly circumstances where drugs are necessary to diminish racing thoughts, hallucinations and extreme depression. However, drugs are prescribed too frequently and unnecessarily. Only if all other options have been exhausted, a thorough evaluation has been made, and, ideally, more than one medical opinion has been obtained, should drugs be used.

Before you enter a hospital, you should first make certain that you will not be given any drugs without your permission or the permission of a family member or representative. Moreover, you should not be given drugs without talking to your own therapist first. Be sure to obtain information about the type of drug and its side effects before you take it.

You also have the right to be informed of the nature of your condition and an absolute right to seek other opinions and change hospitals if you choose.

I strongly recommend that you evaluate hospitals in advance. Obtain recommendations and interview the admissions person of several hospitals even if you think you will never need one. It is better to be prepared. If you are unable to do so, arrange with a trusted friend, family member, physician or lawyer to watch over you. Make sure that your advocate is willing and able to stand up to doctors and hospital administrators if necessary. Give this person the authority, written if possible, to have you transferred to another hospital or examined by psychiatrists not connected with the hospital for additional independent opinions. Give yourself a way out.

Interviews with personnel at prospective hospitals are as important as those with individual therapists. Usually you will be able to talk to someone in the admissions office, but it is also advisable to talk to the head of the unit where you would stay. If you encounter any reluctance on the part of the hospital to answer your questions specifically and completely, find another hospital. Competition among psychiatric hospitals for patients is intense these days and the more reputable ones will be candid and helpful in responding to your concerns.

I am aware of one psychiatric hospital, with inferior treatment programs, that pays therapists who visit their clients in the hospital higher than normal fees in order to obtain referrals to the hospital. Avoid hospitals with policies that make kickbacks to therapists.

On important issues, get the information *in writing*. Lest you think I am unduly suspicious, I can only say that several clients and even therapists have encountered situations at hospitals where they have been told one thing by the admissions office and later found that the doctors or billing office did something else. I had a personal experience where the admissions person quoted a daily rate and the hospital later charged almost *triple* the amount. Hospital treatment is extremely expensive, even if you have insurance. You need to find out the daily rate as well as all the extra charges that hospitals impose. One in Salt Lake City charges several dollars for one tampon—and the cost of tampons and other "extras" is not covered by insurance.

In dealing with hospitals these days, it is important that the hospital administrators and staff know that you can take care of yourself and that someone is looking out for you. Have your therapist or your personal physician call the hospital every couple of days to check on your progress. If you have a friend who is a therapist, doctor or lawyer, give her name to the hospital as someone who is to receive information about you and have that person call the hospital and the therapist in charge of your case, and call you directly every couple of days to find out how you are doing.

Do not hesitate to let the hospital know that you understand your rights and that you will file a lawsuit if necessary. If you are afraid that hospital personnel will not treat you well if you assert your rights, let me assure you that the opposite is true; they will respect you. Yale Medical School surgeon Dr. Bernie Siegal, author of *Love, Medicine and Miracles*, counsels patients to be assertive. He says studies show that difficult patients seem to heal faster. Thankfully Dr. Siegal's statements are having an effect on the medical profession, persuading doctors and hospitals to be more responsive to people's needs.

I urge you to explore residential treatment centers as an alternative to hospitals. Many are much less expensive and may provide superior therapy because they specialize in treating a particular problem, hiring experts and training their staff members in that area. These programs are more like halfway houses with no security or surgical facilities, but staff members are on duty 24 hours and counseling is always available. The ones I am aware of have psychiatrists either on staff or on call so you can obtain medication if necessary. The cost of treatment at a center for survivors of sexual abuse in Santa Fe, New Mexico is $6,000 per month compared to a Utah hospital's basic monthly charges of $20,000. I consider the methods of treatment and supportive atmosphere of some centers to be better than those in any hospital I have seen.

Unless you have a serious medical condition, you may not need the facilities of a hospital. If you simply feel you need support or to be in a safe place for a while to recover memories or you want intensive therapy for a short time, a residential center may be right for you. It is worth investigating to find out if there is a residential center in your state or elsewhere which specializes in the type of problem you want to resolve. Since the cost of treatment at a residential center is so much less than a hospital, the travel costs will be more than outweighed by the savings and you may get the additional benefit of a vacation in a lovely location. Of course you will want to evaluate residential treatment centers as thoroughly as you would hospitals.

✓ Questions to ask before going to the hospital

The following are questions you may want to ask in interviewing hospital personnel and forms you can ask them to sign:

1. Do you have a unit or special program that deals with *your problem* (childhood abuse, multiple personality disorder, drug or alcohol abuse, eating disorders, etc.)? In the case of substance abuse and eating disorders, find out if the underlying causes are recognized and treated. In the case of multiple personality disorder, find out if that condition is recognized by the hospital and the staff and what their feelings are about the condition and its treatment.

2. Is the emphasis of your program primarily drug therapy or psychotherapy?

3. What types of therapy are used in your program?
4. How often will I meet with a therapist for individual psychotherapy? Group psychotherapy? (Do not confuse groups where you play ball or make ceramics with psychotherapy groups. Get the specifics.)
5. Will my private therapist be permitted to see me for at least two hours a week? (Be sure to get this commitment in writing. See the form at the end of these questions.)
6. Will I be released when I decide I want to leave? (If your hospitalization is voluntary, you should be able to leave at any time unless you are a clear danger to yourself or others. Some hospitals try to keep you until your insurance is used up. Make sure you have an agreement with the hospital and your doctor that you can leave when you want to and get this commitment in writing. See form.)
7. How much will hospitalization and my treatment cost? (Get fees in writing. See form at end of questions.)
8. Are there any other expenses I will have to pay? What are they? (Get this in writing. See form.)
9. Will you obtain my consent before giving me any medication? Do I have the right to refuse medication? (See form.)

Be very careful to *read* what you sign at the time of admittance to the hospital, or have someone do it for you. Just because something is on a printed form does not mean you cannot change it the way you want. I always write on the hospital form at the time of admittance that I or my client have the right to leave and the right to refuse medication. I always cross out anything that says that the hospital or the doctor can do whatever they want with respect to medicine, surgery or anything else, and I have never been turned away.

✓ Hospitalization forms for your protection

These forms may be photocopied for your use. They state your legal rights and hospitals should be willing to acknowledge these rights in writing. If not you may want to select another hospital. These forms may be consolidated into one document. If possible have someone outside of the hospital keep the signed copies for you.

Consent to have information provided

I request that information about my condition and treatment

be given to _____
Insert name of therapist, friend, doctor, lawyer

upon their or my request.

_____   ____/____/____
Your signature   Date

Voluntary hospitalization

_____ acknowledges that _____
Insert name of hospital   Insert your name

has voluntarily admitted herself or himself for treatment.

Hospital represents and promises that _____
                                                                                    Insert your name

will not be kept in the hospital without her or his consent and

is free to discontinue hospitalization at any time. Hospital

understands that _____ would not consent
                              Insert your name

to be admitted to this hospital without this agreement and is

agreeing to enter this hospital in reliance on this agreement.

_____   ____/____/____
Signature of hospital official   Date

The hospital may want you to add a sentence allowing you to be kept involuntarily if you are a clear danger to yourself or others. This is the law and would override any agreement. Your best protection is to thoroughly check the reputation of the hospital.

Hospital consent to treatment by personal therapist

_____ hereby agrees that _____
<u>Insert name of hospital</u>   <u>Insert name of therapist</u>

may visit and provide psychotherapeutic treatment in person

and by telephone to _____ for two hours per
                         <u>Insert your name</u>

_____ . Hospital understands that _____
<u>Day or week</u>   <u>Insert your name</u>

would not consent to be admitted to this hospital without

this agreement and is agreeing to enter this hospital in

reliance on this agreement.

_____   ____/____/____
Signature of hospital official   Date

Right to refuse medication

_____ agrees that _____ has the right
Name of Hospital   Your name

to consent to taking any medication, to be informed of the

risks of all medication, and to refuse any and all medication.

Hospital understands that _____ would not
Insert your name

consent to be admitted to this hospital without this agree-

ment and is agreeing to enter this hospital in reliance on this

agreement.

_____   ___/___/___
Signature of hospital official   Date

If you are not able to make these decisions, delegate them in writing to your therapist, a family member, your physician, or a friend.

Cost of hospitalization

_____ represents that the costs of psychiatric
Name of Hospital

hospitalization are as follows:

1. Daily rate _____ . This rate includes (does not include) all fees for doctors, therapists, and staff provided by hospital.
2. Fees for individual therapy _____
3. Fees for group therapy _____
4. Fees for psychological tests _____
5. Fees for medical examinations _____
6. Fees for special activities _____
7. Fees for medication _____
8. Fees for blood and other medical tests _____
10. Fees for supplies _____
11. Any and all other fees not covered by the daily rate or not specified above.

_____

_____

_____

_____

Hospital understands that _____ would not
                                         Insert your name

consent to be admitted to this hospital without this agreement and is agreeing to enter this hospital in reliance on this agreement.

_____   ____/____/____
Signature of hospital official   Date

How can I help a loved one who needs therapy?

Helping someone recognize the need for therapy is a difficult task and takes almost superhuman tact and sensitivity. No matter how loving you intend your suggestion to be, it may be construed as rejection and criticism. When you say someone needs therapy, the implication is that something is wrong with him.

The best way to encourage loved ones to try therapy is to ask them to help *you* by participating in *your* therapy. When my clients—usually women because they tend to be more open than men to seeking help for their problems—are unable to persuade their spouses to attend therapy sessions, I recommend that the wives ask their husbands to come one time in order to *help their wives*, not because the wives think their husbands need therapy. Once the reluctant spouse or partner attends a session and sees that the therapist is non-judgmental and will not blame him or gang up on him, he is usually willing to participate and attend more sessions. An honest appeal for help also works to induce other family members to join in your therapy.

If you are a family member or partner and your loved one's behavior is affecting the relationship, you might propose that the two of you try therapy together to improve the relationship. That way your loved one will see that you are taking some of the responsibility for problems and will not feel as though you are placing all the blame on him or her.

If your loved one's dysfunctional behavior is hurting herself or others and she is not in therapy, direct intervention may be warranted. As a first step, you might give her a book or article about recognizing and recovering from the problem. The most effective way to get results is to say as little as possible. "I care about you and thought you might be interested in this," is all that is needed. If you try to force her to read what you give her, she will probably rebel and take your advice as criticism. If reading material does not motivate your loved one to seek help, stronger measures may be necessary.

You may want to consult with a therapist about your loved one's problems, not only to help you understand them better but to help you deal with your own frustration and feelings about the situation. Sometimes changing your responses to a loved one's actions will change their behavior.

If these measures do not work, you might try an "intervention process" to convince your loved one to accept help. The intervention process was originally used in cases of alcohol and drug addiction where addicts refused to admit they had a problem. Family and friends gathered together to describe how they perceived the addict was hurting them and himself and to persuade the addict to acknowledge the existence of a problem and accept help. In a case that made international headlines, former President Gerald Ford and his family successfully used the intervention process to help Betty Ford face her drug and alcohol addiction. Such interventions have an 85% success rate.

A similar intervention process can be successful for a loved one who refuses to get help for emotional problems. Although therapists used to believe that therapy would not work unless it was voluntary, experience has proven otherwise. Even if people come to the first session reluctantly, a good therapist can put them at ease and help them see the benefits of therapy and the support it provides. I have treated teenagers who were dragged in by their parents or ordered to come by juvenile court. My experience is that they are so miserable and terrified despite their bravado, their defenses quickly break down and they become committed to healing.

If you decide to use the intervention process to encourage your loved one to seek help, you should first obtain the assistance of a counselor who can prepare you and tell you what to say. Then gather together as many supportive friends and relatives as possible who are aware of your loved one's problem and sincerely want to participate. It is helpful to have someone present who has recovered from a similar problem to talk about his healing even if that person is an outsider. You may also want to employ a therapist to facilitate the intervention and inform your loved one about the therapy process. Often misunderstandings about what happens in therapy keep people from obtaining help.

During the intervention, participants acknowledge their concern for their loved one and describe how the loved one's behavior is hurting them and others. Interventions are usually successful because recipients feel the genuine concern of people who care about them and are dismayed to learn that their actions have been causing others distress. Typically they are experiencing such intense inner pain that they welcome being offered a way out.

But sometimes, nothing works. If your loved one is an adult, there may be nothing else you can do unless she is a clear and immediate danger to herself or others and fits the legal definition for involuntary commitment to a psychiatric hospital. Such criteria are difficult to prove, and in most states the legal process requires evaluation by two psychiatrists and a court hearing. Involuntary commitment is a drastic step and should only be used as a last resort after all other options have been exhausted.

Sometimes people have to hit bottom before they seek help. If your loved one is a spouse or partner who refuses to get help, you may have to decide whether you want to continue the relationship or find a more fulfilling one. This choice must be based on your own needs. You do not deserve to suffer and if you think your loved one cannot survive without you, you are mistaken. Sometimes staying with a dysfunctional person or addict can actually impede healing; you may be enabling your loved one's destructive behavior by actions which reinforce that behavior. Losing someone important sometimes motivates people to finally seek the help they need. And when they are forced to take care of themselves, they may shed their codependency.

Of course, if your loved one is a family member, you will want to continue to provide love and emotional support. Sometimes giving unconditional love and acceptance, without condemning or pushing someone to change, can work miracles. But you must let go to the extent that you refuse to allow even someone you love to ruin your life. You may need help to accept the fact that your loved one is responsible for his own life and healing and has to find his own path in his own way.

Of course where your children are concerned, you cannot give them a choice about whether or not to see a therapist. If they need help, you must make the decision for them and take them, no matter how much they protest.

If you are worried about a child who is not your own, your options are more limited unless you can enlist the support of the child's parents or guardian. Thankfully our laws have become more protective of children so there are now ways of getting help for minors even if their parents refuse to do so. Failure of a parent or guardian to provide a child with needed medical help, including psychotherapy, constitutes criminal neglect. Although you can make a report to the police or your local social or family service agency, it may be difficult to convince a prosecuting attorney to take action because in most states such cases require proof beyond a reasonable doubt.

A more practical alternative, if you are the noncustodial parent of the child or a relative, is to bring a civil action to obtain custody of the child or a court order to force the custodian to provide the necessary therapy. In custody proceedings, the primary consideration is what is in the best interests of the child.

If you suspect a child is being physically, sexually, or emotionally abused or neglected, the law *requires* you to report your suspicion to the police or your local social service or family assistance agency. All states have laws which impose criminal penalties on people who know about child abuse but fail to report it. These laws also give the abused child the right to sue in a civil action anyone who fails to report the abuse. The child can recover damages resulting from the failure to report the abuse even into adulthood.

These child protection laws protect people who make reports by mandating that the report and the name of the person be kept strictly confidential and by preventing suits against people who make reports even if the charges are not correct.

If the system works properly, and unfortunately this is not always the case, your allegations will be investigated and the child will receive protection and therapy. In more enlightened states, such as Wisconsin, cases of intrafamilial abuse are treated as civil, rather than criminal, matters and the entire family receives therapy.

You should never hesitate to report child abuse. The effects of abuse are devastating and can ruin the victim's life. Do not assume that "things will get better"; studies show that abuse almost always gets worse. If you stop the abuse and the victim gets therapy, you not only will have spared the child years of anguish, but you may have also prevented the child from abusing a future generation.

If you are reading this chapter, you are a very caring person and your loved one is lucky to have a friend or relative like you. Although you should not let your loved one's problems destroy your happiness, you should know that people can change and that love really does heal. Your friendship and support can make a difference.

How can I help a loved one who is in therapy?

If your loved one is a member of your family or a partner, the best way you can help is to participate in their therapy. Most therapists now recognize the powerful influence of family dynamics on emotional and behavioral problems and treat not only the individual client but as many family members as possible. Joint therapy is easier, faster and more effective for all participants and ensures that changes will be permanent.

Sharing self-exploration in therapy will help you grow closer to your loved one, and, if you are a spouse or partner, preserve your relationship. The fact that you are willing to support your loved one by participating in her therapy unequivocally demonstrates your love in a tangible way. You will gain a much greater understanding of your loved one's problems and actions when you hear her inner thoughts verbalized and see her real feelings expressed. You will also have the chance to examine your own thoughts and feelings. Honest and open communication almost always increases love and intimacy. And working on your own problems in therapy will increase your capacity to love.

Having a family member or partner in therapy places a strain on relationships because of changes that inevitably occur. You will adapt more easily to the changes if you have the support of a therapist and the increased understanding of your loved one and yourself that therapy can provide.

Even more important, you will have a chance to face your own issues and problems. If you are thinking, "I don't have any," I assure you this is not the case. Dysfunction, trauma and abuse run in families. Since abuse, especially sexual abuse, is passed down in families, if your loved one is a family member, it is highly likely that you were also abused. In cases of incest, if one sibling was abused, the others usually have been too, regardless of sex. And studies indicate that the parents of abused children have generally been abused themselves in childhood.

Even if you escaped actual abuse, you did not escape the harmful effects of having a member of your family abused. The pernicious ripples from abuse affect everyone close to the victim. If you truly want to help your loved one, the best thing you can do is heal yourself.

Birds of a feather really do flock together. We seem to have a kind of unconscious radar which attracts us to people who have similar problems. If you are close to someone who suffered child abuse, the chances are very great that you too have been abused, if not physically or sexually, then emotionally.

If your partner was abused, the chances are high that you were unconsciously attracted to each other because of your mutual problems. My clients' partners often reject this idea initially. Carter, an outwardly congenial man, came to a session with his sexually abused wife and announced firmly that he had had a "storybook" childhood and had no issues to discuss. A bit of probing revealed that both of his parents were in the military and strict disciplinarians; his father beat him regularly and his mother hit him with a ruler every time he made a mistake reading aloud.

Although Carter felt he had little in common with his wife, we quickly uncovered a dynamic basic to both partners: both had several siblings and felt rejected by their parents. It was this desperate need for attention that had made the wife vulnerable to victimization by a neighborhood molester. And this same unrecognized mutual need was causing their marital problems.

Therapy will change your relationship with your loved one because therapy generates growth. If you are both in therapy, both of you will grow. But if only your partner goes through therapy, she may outgrow you.

You may be experiencing these fears about your loved one's therapy and be unconsciously impeding your loved one's progress because you are afraid of being abandoned when your loved one heals. You may be concerned that if your loved one becomes more secure and independent, she may not *need* you anymore. That is a definite possibility. But a healthy relationship is not based on need, it is based on love and respect. Love and respect grow out of shared experiences and facing challenges together as equals. I have found that couples who heal together stay together. When one heals and the other does not, the relationship often dissolves.

I believe that participating in joint sessions and having individual sessions with the same therapist is the most effective way of healing individually and in the relationship. However, if you and your loved one cannot find a therapist with whom you both feel comfortable, you can still benefit from working with different therapists. You can arrange some sessions where you and your loved one work together with *both* of your therapists present, so that no one feels at a disadvantage. It is difficult for a therapist to understand the dynamics of a relationship without observing how the members interact. Family therapy sessions I have held with therapists of partners and other family members have been very successful.

Supporting someone you love through therapy can be exhausting, confusing and frightening. It is helpful and comforting to understand as much about the process of therapy and your own feelings as possible. Even in the unlikely event that you have not been abused or have dealt with all of your own significant issues, the support you can get from a therapist or a group while your loved one is going through the process will be worthwhile.

There are other ways you can help a loved one who is in therapy; an essential one is changing your own attitude about your role. Watching a loved one suffer from emotional problems is intensely painful. We want to help, to stop the pain, to *fix it*. But often nothing we do seems to work and we feel helpless. Men become especially frustrated because they have been taught to take charge and to protect their families. They feel worthless if they cannot *do* something to fix the situation.

If you want to help a loved one, you must begin by accepting one basic truth: *you cannot fix anyone.* Unless your loved one is a child, you are not responsible for their healing. Adults are responsible for their own healing and heal at their own pace.

The Adult Children of Alcoholics have a motto which is particularly applicable to the spouses and partners of people in therapy: "You didn't cause it and you can't cure it." It is a reality you must accept.

The sad fact is that there is very little you can *do*. You can't take your loved one's pain away. Even if you could, you would do great damage. Victims of childhood trauma need to feel and express their pain, including all of the violent feelings of rage, grief, hatred, shame, and fear that they have repressed for so long. If you try to discourage those feelings or cut them off, you are preventing healing.

Individuals heal at their own rates and need to progress through certain stages in order to accept the truth of their abuse and release their feelings without becoming overwhelmed by them. Pushing someone to heal faster than is right for them can force them into denial or psychosis.

Some people who are in therapy have been healing themselves unconsciously for a long time and seem to heal faster. Others seem to be stuck in their anger or depression. There is no "right" or "wrong" about the amount of time necessary for people to deal with their pain. As a general rule, people have an uncanny way of knowing exactly how to heal themselves.

So how can you help? The best thing you can do is LISTEN and give your unconditional love and support. Most of the time, your loved one will not expect you to *do* anything except listen and love them. Isn't that what we all really want?

People who have been abused, abandoned or unloved as children have a deep and sometimes unconscious belief that they are bad and that somehow they caused their fate. Especially if they have been sexually abused, they are often terrified that if anyone knows the truth, they will be shunned and rejected. Some have been told by their abusers that they have been ruined forever and that no decent person will ever want to be around them. Even if they have not been told this, most abuse survivors believe it. What loved ones want most is to know you love and accept them no matter what happened to them. They also need to know that you love them in spite of what they see as their unacceptable feelings of rage, hate, shame, depression and worthlessness.

Part of accepting your loved one is accepting what happened to him. Your loved one may tell you such bizarre and horrible things that you may have great difficulty believing they are true. Our minds often reject facts that are too painful to assimilate. Clinical experience indicates that memories recovered by abuse victims are usually true. Even the most gruesome types of abuse have now been documented by hospitals and law enforcement and social service agencies. See chapter on sexual and physical abuse, pages 167-182.

When your loved one begins to recover memories of her abuse, she may have difficulty believing them because part of her mind is afraid of being overwhelmed as she was when the events occurred. Just as your survivor needs time to accept the terrible truth, so do you. Always be honest with your loved one; she has had enough lies. Tell her you are having a hard time believing such awful things could happen, but that you believe *her* and will explore it with her. Keep an open mind and give your mind time to process what your loved one remembers. Learn as much as you can about child abuse before coming to any conclusions.

When someone you love is in pain, the most effective response is to simply hold them and listen. Tell them you love them and don't assume because you told them last month, last week or even earlier that day, they are convinced. People who have been abused believe they are inherently unlovable. The negative programming they have carried with them for many years cannot be erased by a day or even a year of reassurance. It takes a long time to reestablish trust.

The way to show loved ones you are listening is by validating their emotions. Allow them to feel whatever they are feeling. Don't try to shut off the feelings because they are painful to you. People in distress want to know that what they are feeling is O.K.—that they are entitled to feel what they feel. We are all entitled to our feelings. Sometimes our feelings may seem unreasonable to others, but that is how we *feel*. Arguing about what someone feels is futile. There are no "shoulds" or "shouldn'ts"; feelings simply *are*.

The most effective verbal response to your loved one's pain is to reflect back what you think they are *feeling*: "That must have been terribly painful (frightening, humiliating)." "You sound very angry (scared, sad)." People need to have their feelings validated. They often fear they are crazy because they do not understand what is going on inside them. By confirming what they feel, you affirm their sanity. They want you to understand and accept their feelings because that means you understand and accept *them*.

If you don't know what your loved one is feeling, ask. "It sounds as if you are confused, are you?" "I am not sure what you are feeling, and I want to understand. Please help me." You do not have to interpret your loved one's emotions exactly; your desire to understand is the most important factor.

Sometimes when feelings have been suppressed for years, your loved one may find it difficult to express what he is feeling because he may be completely out of touch with his own emotions. By asking him to explain how he *feels*, you can encourage him to get back in touch with his emotions and help him heal.

Don't be afraid to be honest about *your* feelings. If something was terrible, say so: "That was really terrible." "That must have been horrible for you." "How awful!" Put the blame where it belongs—on the abuser: "What a dreadful thing to do to you." "She hurt you so much." Express your outrage, anger and grief.

Take every opportunity to point out how strong and intelligent your loved one is. "It's amazing that you survived. How strong you must have been to live through that." You never have to lie; the fact is that your loved one *has* survived and had to be exceptionally strong to do so. Reassure her that she is safe now—she doesn't live there anymore. By affirming her strengths and ability to help herself, you help her see the truth about herself instead of reinforcing her false image of helplessness.

One of the worst things you can do is to give advice or offer solutions. No matter how obvious or effective your solution is, if it is unsolicited, it will usually be rejected. Advice is extremely difficult to accept from a loved one because recipients tend to hear criticism even when it is not intended. They infer that you think they are stupid or at fault, so they shut you out. You've probably heard many times, "I can't do that. I've tried that, it doesn't work. You don't understand." It is difficult not to become very impatient with the constant negativity and resistance of people in pain. It becomes easier when you realize that what they really want is *validation of their feelings*, not solutions.

If you feel your loved one is acting unreasonably in a certain situation, trying to convince him to act differently is usually futile. The problem is generally *not* the present situation but is caused by feelings coming from childhood pain. You are dealing with a wounded child and no rational argument will help. The best way to deal with the situation is simply to listen and love. Do your best to make your loved one feel safe and that you love him or her no matter what. Find ways to tell your loved one that you will always be there and compliment him or her on qualities, personal traits that you admire, rather than achievements.

Advice is more readily accepted from a professional and that is one of the reasons why therapy is recommended. A therapist is not personally involved and when she gives advice it is viewed as more neutral and less threatening than advice from a loved one. We also perversely believe something is more valuable if we pay for it.

Another pitfall about advising a loved one is that if your advice is followed, you may be blamed if it fails. And people can be very creative about making unwanted solutions fail.

But the greatest flaw in giving advice is that it may reinforce your loved one's feelings of incompetence and dependence. When you give advice, you are implying that the recipient does not have the ability to make his own decisions. I believe we each have the answers to all of our problems inside us. And deep down inside, we know this truth. We resent others assuming they know what is best for us. That is why unsolicited advice is rarely accepted, while advice which is requested usually is followed.

People in pain tend to feel very isolated. They think they are the only ones who have ever been through such agony. They lose sight of the fact that others are also in pain. This isolation is reinforced when friends and family members shield them from problems because of the fear of further burdening them. You may think: "They have enough to deal with," or "My problems are minor compared to theirs." But by sheltering loved ones from your problems, you are reinforcing their feelings that they are alone and that no one understands them because they believe everyone else is perfect and has no problems. They feel worse about themselves because they think they are the only ones who feel overwhelmed and out of control. If they are allowed to focus on someone else's problems, they start to see that pain and problems are universal and stop feeling so abnormal and alone.

We often think that if someone is in severe distress, we would be selfish to burden them with our problems. But the reality is quite different. People in distress are drowning in their own pain. One way of pulling them out is to make them feel needed. They feel guilty for burdening *you* with their problems and making you unhappy. When they are allowed to help others, they begin to feel useful and valuable. Most of the time, they will be relieved to focus on someone else's troubles for a while.

Supporting someone through therapy takes infinite patience. Most people cannot sustain the kind of continual attention and patience demanded during this process. Even therapists find their patience stretched at times. It is far more difficult for someone who is personally involved and cannot take a break at the end of a session.

YOU MUST TAKE CARE OF YOUR OWN NEEDS. If you are to help your loved one, you must accept and follow this principle. You simply cannot be there all the time for someone. The fact is that it is not healthy for you to be available every minute your loved one thinks he or she needs you. You will burn yourself out. You cannot help anyone else if you don't help yourself first. The Bible says "Love thy neighbor *as* thyself," not more than yourself. Unless you take care of yourself, you can't take care of anyone else.

Our survival instinct is the most basic instinct we were given; it supersedes all other instincts. We do not do anyone a favor when we force ourselves to neglect our own needs to take care of someone else. If we ignore our primary survival instinct, we are overwhelmed with stress and become ill or so filled with resentment toward those we are trying to help that we blow up at them or find little passive-aggressive ways to get back at them.

If you are always at the beck and call of your loved one, you are fostering dependence, the exact opposite of what she needs. It is sometimes difficult to strike a balance between giving people needed support and promoting unhealthy dependence by reinforcing their fears that they can't survive alone. If you are always there to assist them, they will assume you think they are incompetent and their illusion of helplessness will be sustained. Your goal is to help them recognize that they can take care of themselves.

You need to set some boundaries for yourself and your loved one. If you can't take any more, say so. When you reach that point, *be honest*. Tell your partner you love him, but that you are feeling too much pain or exhaustion and have to take a break.

If your loved one has been abused as a child, there are times when she may take her pain out on you. This is one of the most frustrating and bewildering experiences for partners, friends and family. You are doing your best to be supportive and loving and all of a sudden you are seen as the bad guy. No matter what you do to help, you get a negative response, even extreme rage and wild accusations.

When someone is screaming at you or accusing you, it is difficult not to take it personally. But you are not the target. Abuse victims have stored tremendous rage and hatred toward their abusers and all the people who did not help them when they were being abused. When something triggers their old memories and feelings, they revert to their childhood patterns and react to today's events as though they are experiencing their past abuse. In their minds, they may see you as their abuser or as someone else who betrayed them.

When they are caught in these old emotions, people are not conscious of what is happening to them. The child part of them is in control. It usually does no good to point this out or to try to reason with someone in this state because you are dealing with a very wounded child. The best you can do is tell them you love them but that you cannot deal with them now and, if it is necessary, leave the room or the house.

Because your loved one was betrayed as a child by people he loved and trusted, he expects betrayal. He will test you over and over again to see if you can be trusted. He will see you as betraying him when you are not and will even try to force you into betrayal. Point it out when it happens but don't buy into it. Tell your partner directly that you know he has difficulty trusting anyone, that you love him, that you will always love him, but that you will not let him hurt you or push you away. Don't get into an argument about who is right. Tell your loved one you are leaving the room or the house for a short time and will be available when he is ready to accept your friendship. We can't fight with someone who does not fight back.

THE FACT THAT A LOVED ONE WAS ABUSED OR IS IN PAIN IS *NEVER* A JUSTIFICATION FOR ABUSING YOU. You do not have to tolerate any kind of abuse, verbal or physical, from someone you love. Tell your loved one that you understand that she is in pain, but that you will not allow her to take it out on you. If you make it clear that you will not permit yourself to be abused, you will be surprised how quickly it will stop.

Your life does not have to cease because someone you love is in therapy. Both of you need to have some fun and relaxation every day if possible. You can help your loved one by scheduling fun things to do together. Both of you are under stress and need regular exercise. Exercise together, join support groups, take classes. Find ways of getting away from the introspection and problems.

My general rule is to limit clients working on their problems to one or two hours a day at most, with exceptions of course, and I encourage them to live as fulfilling a life as possible the rest of the time. There may be some days when your loved one is struggling with particularly intense emotions and may not feel like having fun. If this happens more than once a week, your loved one is focusing too much on the past and should be encouraged to get out and do something or get additional help from the therapist.

Even if your loved one is unwilling to make time for fun, *you* need to do it for yourself. Just because your survivor is in pain does not mean you cannot enjoy life. I know you are thinking, "How can I possibly enjoy myself when someone I love is in pain? That's unfeeling and selfish." The fact is that your loved one is not being abused now. Your self-sacrifice and suffering will not help; your martyrdom will only make your loved one feel more unhappy and guilty because he sees the negative effect he is having on your life. Making yourself miserable will not relieve your loved one's pain.

There are times when you must actively intervene to help someone in therapy. IF YOUR LOVED ONE EXPRESSES SUICIDAL

THOUGHTS OR FEELINGS OR EXTREME DEPRESSION, YOU SHOULD CONTACT A THERAPIST IMMEDIATELY.

There is a high risk of suicide among people who were seriously abused as children because they wanted to die when they were being abused and these old feelings can reemerge and overwhelm them. Work out a plan with your loved one for handling suicidal feelings if they arise. If you feel uncomfortable coping alone, arrange NOW for a therapist, hospital or friend to assist you if necessary.

As a general rule, you should avoid criticizing or second-guessing your loved one's therapist because you will just provoke a defensive reaction. However, if it becomes clear to you that your loved one is not making any progress or seems to be getting worse, you may have to intervene. Sometimes people idealize their therapists and become dependent on them, leading them to unrealistically blame themselves for lack of progress. Lack of progress may be due to your loved one's need for a break to assimilate and adjust to what she has learned, but it can also be due to the incompetence of the therapist. Get as many facts as you can and use your common sense in evaluating the situation. It is sometimes easier for an outsider to perceive that a therapist is not effective. If you are concerned, ask to speak to the therapist or encourage your loved one to seek a second opinion.

If you and your loved one are both in therapy, sometimes one of you will be more needy than the other. You will each have to honestly express your needs. I believe your commitment will be well worth the effort and you will find that sharing your feelings and your therapy will help you achieve a truly loving, lasting relationship.

III

Specific Problems

Depression—Therapy and the use of drugs

Many people suffer unnecessarily from debilitating clinical depression when they could get relief from therapy and antidepressant drugs. Sometimes we may not even be aware that we are in trouble because the symptoms creep up on us gradually, and we fail to notice the changes. Although depression is one of the most common and treatable of all mental illnesses, it is often the most difficult to detect.

According to the American Psychiatric Association, one in four women and one in ten men can expect to become severely depressed during their lifetimes—and the symptoms can appear at any age. Yet people may attribute the physical symptoms of depression to the flu, sleeping and eating problems to stress, and emotional problems to lack of sleep or improper eating. Or they may deny the existence of depression by saying things like, "She has a right to be depressed! Look at what she's gone through." Although sadness over the loss of a loved one or a divorce is normal, sometimes such losses can trigger a depressive episode. In fact, many kinds of major life changes, even if positive such as moving or getting a better job, can create stress leading to major depression.

How do you tell if you fall into this common category? People suffering from depression almost always feel sad and may also feel anxious, helpless, hopeless, "empty," and irritable. The National Institute of Mental Health recommends that you seek professional help if you have had four or more of the following symptoms continually for more than two weeks:

1. Noticeable change of appetite, with either significant weight loss without dieting or weight gain.
2. Noticeable change in sleeping patterns, such as fitful sleep, inability to sleep, early morning awakening, or sleeping too much.
3. Loss of interest and pleasure in activities you used to enjoy.
4. Loss of energy, fatigue.

5. Feelings of worthlessness.
6. Persistent feelings of hopelessness.
7. Feelings of inappropriate guilt.
8. Recurring thoughts of death or suicide, wishing to die, or attempting suicide.
9. Overwhelming feelings of sadness and grief, accompanied by waking at least two hours earlier than normal in the morning, feeling more depressed in the morning, and moving more slowly.
10. Disturbed thinking, having beliefs not based in reality about illness, sinfulness or poverty.
11. Physical symptoms, such as headaches or stomachaches.[1]

If you fit the four-symptom profile, you need professional help to relieve your feelings of depression, understand the reasons for your feelings, and learn coping skills that can help you avoid depression in the future.

Whatever you do to relieve the symptoms, it is essential for you to explore and resolve the *reason* for your depression.

DEPRESSION IS NOT A DISEASE YOU CATCH LIKE A COLD. THERE IS ALWAYS A REASON FOR DEPRESSION.

If a doctor tells you that depression is just chemical and you can be cured by simply popping some pills, get another opinion. Remember, many M.D.s choose physical medicine because they do not want to deal with or even acknowledge psychological factors. You may have physical symptoms or a chemical imbalance in your body when you are clinically depressed, but these physical symptoms and chemical changes may be the result of some kind of serious mental stress in your life. Stress causes chemical changes and imbalances.[2] Thus, while antidepressant drugs may temporarily relieve the physical symptoms and correct the chemical imbalance, they do not cure the cause that created your depression in the first place.

You may say, "Well, if drugs make me feel better and I'm no longer depressed, who cares?" If you don't mind being on drugs for the rest of your life—drugs which cost $60 to $120 per month and have unknown, long-term side effects—and you are willing to take the risk that the stressor which is causing your depression will pop out in some other dysfunctional behavior or in a more serious form such as a fatal disease, then you may not want to examine the underlying cause of your depression.

You should be aware, however, that antidepressant drugs have side effects, the most common short-term effects being sleep disturbances, headaches, nausea and dry mouth. In many cases, people adjust to the drugs after a period of time and these symptoms disappear. The more important fact is that no one knows the long-term effects of any of these drugs. The oldest of the commonly prescribed antidepressant drugs, Prozac, has only been widely used for about seven years; long-term effects of drugs are generally studied for a minimum of fifteen to twenty years. As the book, *Listening to Prozac*, states, people have had some very unpleasant experiences with that drug, although it is not entirely clear whether these symptoms are due to the drug or the underlying cause of the depression. Several other authors have approached me with manuscripts of books about the adverse effects of Prozac, so users clearly have a perception that problems exist.

Zoloft, Paxil and Effexor have been sold for far shorter periods of time than Prozac and we know even less about their long-term effects. They appear to have fewer short-term side effects than Prozac. If you decide to take these drugs, you should be aware that Zoloft is the cheapest. If you take 50 milligrams a day, you can break the 100-milligram pills in half and use them for two months, as I did.

In general, I have serious concerns about drugs that artificially affect brain and neurotransmitter functions as these drugs do, and greater concern about their long-term use. We simply do not know enough about brain chemistry to be able to change it in a cavalier fashion.

You should also know the following facts. Studies indicate that psychotherapy is as effective as medication in treating depression without the physical side effects of drugs. And Seymour Fisher, a psychologist in the department of psychiatry and professor at the State University of New York Health Center in Syracuse and the author of *The Limits of Biological Treatments for Psychological Distress*, analyzed more than 250 clinical trials on antidepressants and found that drugs are only fifteen to twenty percent more effective than inactive placebos. Other studies show that the attention and concern of the doctor who prescribes medication are responsible for beneficial results rather than the medication.

Most important, you need to know that if you stay on antidepressant drugs for a long time, sooner or later other symptoms of the real reason for your depression will reappear. If we ignore the warning signals our bodies give us, our bodies will produce stronger and increasingly unpleasant signals until we heed the message and deal with our problems.

Most people now recognize that headaches, chest pains, shortness of breath, and feelings of stress precede heart attacks and that victims of heart attacks often ignore these early warning signs. I and many of my colleagues believe that depression is caused by suppressed anger which if not resolved can lead to fatal diseases such as cancer, multiple sclerosis, and other "inexplicable" diseases. If you want to reach an optimal state of physical and mental health, you must clear out the mental stressors that are preventing you from reaching that state. There is a growing recognition that our minds control our bodies, including our physical and mental health. Therefore, it does not make sense to inject a physical substance into our bodies while ignoring what our minds are creating.

I do not believe that masking symptoms is the best way of treating a condition. Does that mean I do not believe anyone should ever use antidepressant drugs? Of course not.

I believe you should take advantage of anything that will help you. If you are so depressed that you cannot get out of bed and your depression makes it difficult for you to participate in therapy, you should take antidepressant drugs until you are able to function. I have taken them myself for several months under those conditions. Luckily I had a doctor who would prescribe drugs only for a short time and insisted that I go out and exercise for an hour every day. He knew what most doctors now acknowledge: exercise is the most effective antidepressant known. Daily regular exercise can cure depression more effectively than drugs. But you may need drugs for a short time while you work up to a daily exercise schedule.

Although the actual benefits of antidepressant drugs are questionable, some people do feel better when they start taking them and are therefore able to get their lives back on track. I believe drugs should be prescribed only as a last resort, in the lowest dose possible for the shortest time, and in conjunction with therapy which addresses the underlying cause of the depression and teaches skills to deal with the unavoidable losses and setbacks in life.

The most important step is to start some kind of therapy to find out why you became depressed in the first place. Sometimes the cause can be a recent event such as the death of a loved one. But since most people can go through bereavement without becoming clinically depressed, there are usually other causes. Sometimes it is an earlier, unresolved loss or childhood trauma. Many of us were hurt as children and the feelings of depression we felt when we were helpless and could not escape can recur when we are adults.[3] In other instances the depression may result from suppressing our feelings and needs and trying too hard to please everyone. The suppressed anger and resentment we feel from denying our needs can push us into clinical depression. Or we may receive a promotion or a wonderful new job but become depressed because we feel unworthy or suffer from happiness anxiety. There are many reasons for feelings of stress and depression.

So how do we find the causes of our depression and how do we know what therapies will work? Studies show that the old "talk" therapies are not effective in resolving depression because they take such a long time to uncover the cause, if they ever do, and are not designed to provide for the release of suppressed feelings. Modern therapies are faster and reach the emotional level more effectively.

Given today's choices, I would try brainwave biofeedback, breath work, hypnotherapy if I suspected that I had repressed childhood memories, and body work. Brainwave biofeedback seems to be particularly effective for depression where the therapist also helps the client uncover feelings causing the depression. Biofeedback also appears to cure chronic fatigue and migraine headaches. (Please see the sections on brainwave biofeedback—page 254, breath work—page 260, hypnotherapy—page 246, and body work—page 289.) In any case, I would use a therapeutic technique which releases the stored emotions causing the depression so that it does not recur.

Alcohol and drug addiction treatment programs

The most important first step in any alcohol or substance addiction program is to get you off alcohol and drugs. Alcoholism is a progressive disorder that eventually results in death if not treated. Detoxification—the process of removing the intoxicating or addictive substance from your system—usually has to take place before other forms of treatment can proceed.

A revolutionary new method for treating alcohol and drug addiction, brainwave biofeedback, has been developed. I suggest that you read the section on page 254 now. I have included the other more traditional ways of addressing addiction in this book for your information, but frankly, if I had an addiction problem and wanted to recover, I would *run* to the nearest biofeedback center.

Of course no one method will solve all of your problems, so I also recommend that, in addition to therapy, you join a support group and other programs which can help you understand your problem and feelings, change your destructive patterns of behavior, and teach you basic living skills.

Once you are free of addictive substances, have started the recovery process, and your living situation has stabilized, then it is time for more intensive therapy to uncover and resolve the cause of your addiction. Although alcoholism has been characterized as a "disease," new research has uncovered a link between alcoholism and child sexual abuse. Clinicians have long been aware that the feelings of anxiety, helplessness and hopelessness which motivate people to escape with drugs and alcohol are often the result of similar feelings repressed during abuse, and research now supports this observation.[1] While support groups can help you stay away from alcohol and drugs through peer pressure and support, they usually will not help you release the painful stored emotions that are the root of your addiction problem.

Twelve-step programs

The twelve-step programs started by Alcoholics Anonymous are perhaps the best known and most established examples of a mixture of spiritual and psychological principles. These programs have demonstrated their effectiveness not only for alcoholics, their families (Al-Anon), and the adult children of alcoholics (ACOA), but have expanded to include substance abuse (Narcotics Anonymous and Cocaine Anonymous) and anyone from a dysfunctional family. New groups have been developed expressly for survivors of sexual abuse, since most victims come from severely dysfunctional families.

The twelve-step formula of sharing experiences, group support, recognizing present defects, forgiveness, and turning over one's life to God or a higher power have had beneficial effects on thousands of people. The first step alone, admitting addiction, is a powerful agent for change: "We admitted we were powerless over alcohol (drugs), that our lives had become unmanageable." A major advantage is that these programs are free, nondenominational and available in most communities.

A major drawback is that no trained therapist is present to help if you are severely distressed or recover a particularly unpleasant memory. The absence of a therapist also means that the meetings may lack direction. Another weakness is that twelve-step programs do not provide for releasing emotions. Some groups are very formal, following the rigid rules of Alcoholics Anonymous which do not permit group members to comment on each other's statements or confront each other. Other groups are conducted like group therapy sessions, permitting members to point out each other's self-defeating behavior in supportive ways. Sponsors may provide support but in some cases may not have dealt with their own problems and may not be much help.

In general, while twelve-step groups for alcoholics have been successful—in fact Alcoholics Anonymous has been until recently *the* most successful program for keeping alcoholics sober—they fail to address effectively underlying trauma. Moreover, some groups of AA promote dependency on the group for life. Traditional programs for alcohol addiction, including AA, have a sixty to eighty percent relapse rate. The best twelve-step groups acknowledge their limitations and once participants are stable, encourage them to seek counseling to resolve underlying causes of addiction. Other groups unfortunately encourage dependence and become almost like cults.

Most groups for adult children of alcoholics and survivors of sexual abuse have the same defects as AA. However, all of the twelve-step programs provide powerful support systems combined with spiritual principles that make a significant contribution to the healing process. Since twelve-step programs are free and clearly beneficial, you have nothing to lose by trying them. You can choose individual therapy, brainwave biofeedback, and join a twelve-step program. I believe in trying *everything* until you find what works best for you.

Rational Recovery

Rational Recovery, a fairly recent alternative to Alcoholics Anonymous and other twelve-step programs, is described in its brochure as a "national self-help support program for chemically dependent and food-abusing people." Support group meetings are free and are usually held twice a week.

The most significant difference between Rational Recovery ("RR") and the twelve-step programs is one of philosophy; RR does not have a spiritual component nor does it espouse a belief that participants have to attend meetings for the rest of their lives. RR is based on rational-emotive therapy (see 241). As the RR brochure states: "Since our main goal in RR is to help people attain self-reliance, we first teach people how to let go of their dependence on drugs/alcohol or food, and then from the need of support groups.... Also, there are no absolute steps, public prayers, labels, sponsors, or moral inventories."

Studies are being conducted on the effectiveness of this program. RR, like AA, does not adequately provide for emotional release and does not delve into the underlying causes for the addiction. Until there is more definitive research on the long-term results of various addiction recovery programs, I can recommend only that you try both the twelve-step and RR programs and decide which works best for you. In either case, you should use these support groups as a foundation for more intensive psychotherapy so that the real reasons for your addiction can be put to rest for good.

Other outpatient programs

A wide variety of private, public and employer-sponsored outpatient programs and groups, with widely differing degrees of effectiveness, have been developed for the treatment of drug and alcohol abuse. They typically include education on the nature and effects of addiction, methods for achieving and maintaining a new way of living, family counseling, group and individual therapy, and help in developing self-esteem and living and interpersonal skills. The better programs include aftercare and encourage psychotherapy to address underlying and related problems and change dysfunctional ways of thinking, acting and behaving.

Recently some health insurance programs have begun to cover addiction treatment and many organizations have created programs to take advantage of these payments. Some are trying to confuse the public using names like "AAA" for hotlines and facilities which appear to be connected with Alcoholics Anonymous but are not. These programs need to be carefully screened, using the techniques outlined in this book. It is essential to obtain at least one recommendation from someone who has participated in the program, interview key personnel because the competence of the counselors is often the major factor in a program's success, and observe sessions or activities in progress before making a decision.

Inpatient or outpatient programs which use a punitive or judgmental approach toward addiction or addicts are generally not as effective as more supportive programs. Addicts already have poor self-esteem; tearing them down further is counterproductive. There is a big difference between helping someone recognize a problem and humiliating someone in distress or making them feel guilty or inferior. Pick a program that makes you feel better about yourself. Rehabilitation and recovery programs can be confrontational and still treat people with dignity and respect.

Inpatient treatment programs

There are many inpatient programs for the treatment of substance addiction too numerous to mention here. Some hospitals have their own inpatient and outpatient programs designed by the director and staff. The number of independent inpatient and outpatient programs has proliferated. Most inpatient programs are expensive and not all are covered by insurance; check your insurance plan before you check into a hospital or inpatient facility.

In general, inpatient programs are useful for detoxification (drying out) and providing a safe place while your body goes through withdrawal from chemical dependency. Inpatient programs can last from four weeks to six months or more. Most experts believe four weeks is just a start and that such programs are too brief to provide enough support. You need enough time to change your habits, learn to eat properly, take care of yourself, and function effectively on a day-to-day basis. Many people who started drinking or taking drugs as teenagers or even preteens may have never learned such routine skills as cooking or doing the dishes and laundry. Good inpatient programs train people in living skills and provide support so they can develop healthier behavior patterns.

If you are paying the high cost of an inpatient program, you should also expect to receive intensive group and individual counseling. You should make sure that the inpatient program you choose is aware of the link between alcohol and substance abuse and childhood trauma and has therapists who can help you with your underlying issues. Many alcohol and drug abuse treatment centers have counselors and even groups which address sexual abuse issues, but it is important to obtain the specifics about what type of therapy will be offered *before* you check in.

It is also important to obtain specific information in writing about *all* of the hospital's costs before you check in. Some hospitals charge a daily fee and then add additional charges for the services of therapists, doctors, medication and activities. Make sure you are aware of all of the possible charges. See "Hospital forms for your protection," pages 135-139.

While most inpatient programs are effective for detoxification, many experts prefer programs at residential treatment centers and halfway houses over those at hospitals. However, if you feel more comfortable going through withdrawal in a hospital, you can still use a residential center or halfway house for longer-term care and support. Most states now have several such facilities and some even provide care for mothers and their infant children in the same program.

Another important consideration if you choose a hospital is whether follow-up treatment and counseling are provided. People who suffer from alcohol and chemical dependency almost always require several months or even a couple of years of support and treatment before they feel confident about being able to avoid the temptation to relapse.

Whether the hospital provides counseling for family members is also a significant consideration. Studies indicate that therapy is more effective and relapses are less frequent when families are treated together.[2]

Check with a national organization as well as local and state organizations before making a decision on an inpatient program. If possible, it is also useful to attend a couple of twelve-step or RR group meetings and to ask participants for their recommendations before you commit yourself to any long-term, expensive program. You will usually find people in these groups who have stayed at the facilities in your area and their input can be invaluable. Additional suggestions about investigating and evaluating hospitals can be found on pages 128-133.

Sexual and physical abuse

If you were sexually or physically abused as a child, you have suffered overwhelming pain and intense emotions. Whether or not you recall all or a portion of your abuse consciously, the abuse has seriously affected your life in many ways and will continue to cause you pain until you deal with it. However, the good news is that if you are reading this book, you have almost certainly survived the worst thing you will ever go through in your life, and you did it when you were only a child without the knowledge, resources or ability you have now. You survived when you had no one to help you but yourself, so you can get through anything. You are truly a survivor and nothing will ever be that bad again.

You can heal, no matter how severe or prolonged your abuse. I personally know several people including myself who have healed despite years of the most violent and brutal sexual abuse and torture by family members or in cults. I also have met many people who were so severely abused they protected themselves by creating a number of separate personalities. They too have healed and are living happy fulfilling lives.[1]

Childhood abuse affects more than half of the population. The conservative statistics are that one in every three or four people has been sexually abused under the age of 18. That means that **over 50 million people** in the United States have been sexually abused as children. Other studies put the numbers even higher.[2] Similar figures are coming out of Canada, England, Australia and France. In fact, one out of every five trials in France, in the Cours d'Assises, involves incest.[3]

Studies in the United States indicate that eighty percent of sexual abuse is committed by a person in the family or known to the family; most sexual abuse is incest. So if you were sexually abused by someone in your family, you are not alone, and you were not singled out for any special punishment.

The figures on the incidence of sexual abuse include only acts which fall into the legal definition. They do not include sexually suggestive acts or the threat of sexual abuse even though clinical evidence indicates that an adult acting seductively can have the same devastating long-term effects on a child as actual rape.

If physical abuse and neglect are added to the figures for sexual abuse, the conservative estimate of the number of people who have been abused as children according to the limited legal definition exceeds half of the population.

The most damaging effect of child abuse is that it destroys self-esteem. Some people think that all victims of child abuse drop out, go on welfare, abuse alcohol or drugs, or engage in crime or delinquency. Unfortunately many do. But just as many victims of abuse go to the other extreme and compensate for their low self-esteem by *over*achieving. My career illustrates this sometimes overlooked symptom of abuse. I felt so bad about myself and so worthless, I thought the only way I could prove I was worth anything was to earn another A, or another degree, or another award. But whatever I achieved was never enough to make me feel good about myself.

Another myth of abuse, especially sexual abuse, is that it occurs only among families in the lower socioeconomic scale. The fact is that abuse is not confined to any class or any ethnic or religious group. Just as many victims and abusers can be found among therapists, doctors, lawyers, policemen, judges, priests, ministers, rabbis, professors, politicians, and celebrities as among people who are uneducated or poor. My abusive father was an award-winning screenwriter and novelist.

In addition to destroying self-esteem, all forms of child abuse and particularly sexual abuse have many long-lasting effects on behavior, emotions and personality. Such abuse produces a wide variety of psychological and physical symptoms. The effects of abuse do not usually disappear on their own—children do not "just grow out of them." In fact the opposite is true; the effects of abuse generally grow worse as the victims grow older. Abuse establishes patterns of victimization which may be repeated in relationships, employment situations and other circumstances which severely affect the victim's ability to live a satisfying life.[4]

Many survivors of abuse wonder if their own memories of abuse are true or if they are making them up. We would all like to believe abuse does not occur, but the sad truth is that it does—far too frequently.

The overwhelming majority of therapists, whether social workers, psychiatrists, or psychologists, now recognize that child abuse is a reality and that people rarely make up stories of abuse. In fact, many children and adults do just the opposite, denying or minimizing their abuse, or even lying to cover it up out of fear of their abusers or misplaced loyalty to family members. Adults who begin to recover memories of abuse, especially incest, are horrified and want desperately to believe their memories are not true. Often there is corroboration from a family member, but usually the victims' own violent feelings which accompany the memories convince them. No one who has seen an abuse victim relive an episode of abuse during a flashback or under hypnosis can doubt the veracity of these memories; the emotions are far too intense to be feigned or imagined.

If studies in the United States, England, Canada, Australia and France report that one out of every three or four adults has been sexually abused in childhood, is it possible that all of these people are making up their abuse or that they are suffering from mass hysteria or psychosis? The answer is a clear "No." There are too many documented cases of sexual abuse, including thousands where abusers were caught in the act or confess. Police stations, hospitals and social service agencies throughout the world have thousands of hideous photographs of children with torn vaginas and ruptured rectums.

In light of the media attention given to the unfounded and misleading information being spread by a small group calling themselves "The False Memory Foundation," I feel compelled to clear up some misconceptions they have created.

First of all, there is no such thing as a "false memory syndrome." This term was made up by the "false memory" groups who put together psychological words to mislead people into believing that there is a condition of false memory in people who are the victims of abuse. No such "syndrome" exists.

Attempts by "false memory" groups to make people believe that such a syndrome exists are doomed to failure because the only way to test such a theory is to have people who claim their memories are false subject themselves to hypnosis or some other method that can reliably determine if their memories are false. The fact is that many people recant accusations of abuse because they cannot face the pain of bringing repressed memories of abuse to consciousness, or because of pressure from their abusers.

Does this mean that no one ever fabricates a claim of abuse or becomes confused about childhood events? Of course not, but these cases are rare. The probability of someone lying about abuse is extremely small because of the embarrassment and shame attached to having been sexually abused. When I lead workshops to train therapists in the treatment of child abuse, I always ask whether they know of any false claims of abuse. The few incidents I have heard of involve child custody cases where one parent coaches the child to accuse the other parent of abuse, usually in custody battles. However, competent therapists can easily distinguish between true cases and false ones on the basis of the child's emotions and other factors. I personally know of one case where a sophisticated 14-year-old male runaway picked up a developmentally disabled 18-year-old male and accused him of sexual assault in order to avoid vagrancy charges. I am not aware of any cases of adults having "false memories" and in almost all of the cases I have seen there has been clear corroboration of the abuse.

The problem is that the "false memory" groups are asking us to doubt all reports of abuse, when only one reported case in ten thousand or more may be false. I do not believe that these groups are interested in protecting children or healing adults who have been abused. Members of these groups are attempting to intimidate therapists who treat abuse victims by sending them death threats and picketing their offices wearing paper bags over their heads, screaming profanities. To this date, these groups have supported only adults accused of child abuse. Right now one of these groups is supporting a Utah father who has been charged with sexual abuse by his children who are in a foster home. Even though the genitals of these children show physical evidence of sexual abuse, this group is claiming no abuse occurred. How can this group know the children are lying when they have not talked to the children or examined them— and before any court hearing has taken place?

"False memory syndrome" does not have legitimate scientific or academic support. Its proponents distort studies, taking them out of context. They rely heavily on studies of Dr. Elizabeth Loftis in Washington, who is not a clinical psychologist and does not treat victims of trauma. Her studies do not deal with childhood trauma or any other directly inflicted trauma. Loftis' subjects are shown movies or videos of trauma *experienced by other people*, such as scenes of airplane crashes. Her subjects do not experience trauma personally; they merely see disasters happening to someone else, something we all see every day on the local news and in disaster movies. Loftis' subjects sit safely in a laboratory. Since her subjects do not experience personal trauma, these studies are not relevant to determining the reliability of traumatic memories.

We do not need experts to tell us that there is a huge difference between experiencing trauma yourself and watching pictures of someone else's trauma. Neurobiological and psychological studies at Harvard Medical School show that *ordinary non-traumatic* experiences are processed by a part of the brain that judges, analyzes, and rearranges ordinary memories and that these memories can become distorted. The neurobiological research demonstrates that *traumatic events bypass* the part of the brain that processes and analyzes events, and are imprinted on an entirely separate part of the brain *exactly as they occur* with information from all five senses and with the emotions intact.[5] Traumatic memories remain in our minds without distortion and can be recalled in detail far more accurately than ordinary memories because they are not processed or analyzed and thus are not distorted.

Studies have been conducted on children to test the reliability of their memories and specifically to determine if they could be induced by therapists to make false accusations of sexual abuse. Dr. Gail Goodman, a psychologist at the University of California at Davis, and her colleagues studied four- and seven-year-olds to evaluate the reliability of children's memories and how they responded to leading or strongly suggestive questions designed to elicit false accusations of sexual abuse. The scenes acted out in the Goodman studies were based on actual child abuse cases.

One study created a stressful situation where children were taken into a dilapidated trailer and a strange man talked to them using hand puppets. He put on a mask and played a game of Simon Says where he touched the children on the knees. He photographed the children and tickled them. The researchers videotaped everything through a one-way mirror to insure they had a precise record of what happened.

Ten to twelve days later, the children were interviewed about the events and asked many leading questions of the type that some people might think would elicit a charge of sexual abuse, such as, "He took your clothes off, right?" Even though the psychologists deliberately tried to induce the children to make false accusations, the children's reports were almost completely accurate.[6] In another study, Goodman also noted that the children who were the most stressed remembered best and in greatest detail.

There is a great deal of confusion about a recent California lawsuit brought by a father whose adult daughter accused him of having raped her a number of times as a child against therapists who treated his daughter as an adult. The notorious *Ramona* case was also the subject of an episode of *Dateline NBC*.

Gary Ramona was a wealthy vice president of the Robert Mondavi Winery, with a "multimillion-dollar home and a $400,000 a year income," according to the *Dateline* show. He and his family lived what he described as the "American dream." But when his daughter, Holly Ramona, left for college, she was severely depressed, bulimic and in therapy, although she had no memories of the sexual abuse at that time. Holly began to have flashbacks of incest with her father and asked her therapist to give her sodium amytal because she wanted confirmation of the abuse. The memories Holly recovered under sodium amytal confirmed the abuse and Holly and her mother confronted Mr. Ramona the following day.

Mr. Ramona denied abusing his daughter. His wife, who believed her daughter and had her own memories of circumstances that supported the charges, divorced her husband. Holly and her sister left their father and he lost his job. Holly's mother and sister testified in support of Holly.

Holly sued her father for abusing her. Mr. Ramona sued Holly's therapists for $8 million for malpractice claiming that they "planted" the idea of sexual abuse in Holly's and Mrs. Ramona's heads. The jury found one of the therapists negligent in treating Holly because they thought the therapist did not sufficiently challenge Holly's recollections, and awarded Ramona, who spent over $1 million fighting the therapist, $500,000 for lost wages, but nothing for mental and emotional distress. The case was appealed and later settled, for less than the amount awarded by the jury. It thus has no value as a precedent.

So what did this highly publicized lawsuit prove? First of all, it is important to realize that the "whole truth and nothing but the truth" rarely comes out in court. Anyone who has been in court or watched courtroom dramas on television is aware of how various rules of evidence and court procedures limit, conceal and distort facts presented to the jury—and witnesses lie. It is not possible to present accurately all of the events in the limited time allotted for a trial, especially a case such as *Ramona*, where events took place over a period of almost twenty years.

Second, Mr. Ramona publicly announced that he was exonerated, that the jury found that he was not an abuser. Not true; the jury did not decide this issue. The question of whether or not a therapist was negligent is completely separate from the issue of whether or not Ramona abused his daughter. In fact, Tom Dudam, a juror interviewed on *Dateline NBC*, when asked if the jurors intended to clear

Ramona, stated: "That's not what we said. That's certainly not what we said. And...that was probably the only reason that compelled me to even want to talk about it because I didn't want it...to look like we said, hey, the guy is innocent, he never did anything." According to this juror, the message the jury sent was: "That everybody has to be a little bit more careful about how their therapy affects that individual."

When asked if he thought Holly's father sexually abused her, Dudam stated:

"I think there's a possibility that he did. From Holly's standpoint, certainly everybody believed that she believed what she was saying. I think that was probably the most believable thing.... We believed that maybe she had this mental thought. As to whether it was a memory, a fantasy, it was difficult for the jurors to agree that...this could happen to one person over the course of many, many years, and for her just to completely suppress it."

For the Ramona jury, the question of whether or not someone could suppress memories of childhood abuse was confusing and the answer was left unresolved. Apparently the jury was not sufficiently informed about how common repression of traumatic memories is. Perhaps the lawyers were not able to bring in enough information to educate the jury on such a complex subject in the short time allotted for a trial. Or perhaps the natural tendency to deny the psychological existence of repression overrode information presented to the jury. It is difficult to understand why the jury did not give more weight to the fact that Holly was depressed, bulimic and had dreams of abuse, *before* she ever saw a therapist.

The truth is that the Ramona case did not exonerate Gary Ramona nor did it prove memories of abuse are false. Even if the jury had specifically found that such memories are false, which it did not, such a finding would simply demonstrate that juries and judges can be wrong. Several older California Supreme Court cases state that the Chinese are not human but animals, which proves that even the loftiest courts can be grossly misguided.

Who are the members of the False Memory Foundation? One of the original founders, Dr. Ralph Underwager, recently revealed his true views when he stated that pedophilia is a "responsible" choice in an interview in *The Journal of Paedophilia*.[7] (Webster's Dictionary defines pedophilia as "sexual perversion in which children are the preferred sex object.") Underwager is quoted as saying: "Paedophiles need to become more positive and make the claim that paedophilia is an acceptable expression of God's will for love and unity among human beings ...What I think is that paedophiles can make the assertion that the pursuit of love and intimacy is what they choose. With boldness they can say, 'I believe this is in fact part of God's will'."

Much of the publicity garnered by the False Memory Foundation has been due to the unrelenting efforts and the celebrity status of its main spokespeople—the parents of Roseanne Barr Arnold. Roseanne has accused her parents of brutal physical and sexual abuse, which her parents deny. However, Roseanne has multiple personality disorder which results from severe and prolonged childhood physical and sexual abuse. Her anger and bizarre behavior are also symptoms of abuse, but ones which some people regard as "crazy," making her unbelievable.

Because many of us are impressed by academic degrees, some people find more credible the paper released by Dr. Jennifer Freyd, a psychologist and professor in the Department of Psychology at the University of Oregon, who was publicly attacked by her mother, Dr. Pamela Freyd, a cofounder and Executive Director of the False Memory Foundation. After these attacks, Jennifer Freyd issued the paper[8] announcing that she had been sexually abused by her father, that her mother was aware of some of her father's sexual acts, and that her father had discussed his own childhood sexual abuse.

The False Memory Foundation has done tremendous harm to the effort to stop the cycle of child abuse by confusing the public and professional organizations with media propaganda to make us believe that there is such a thing as "false memory syndrome," a "syndrome" which did not exist before such groups were formed. Prosecutors and judges have been swayed by distorted television shows and news articles and are sending abused children back into abusive homes. Some therapists are now refusing to take cases of sexual or cult abuse and are afraid to use hypnotherapy because of the Foundation's intimidation tactics, and so people who need help are being turned away. The Foundation is attracting thousands of dollars, because if twenty million people, or even a tenth of that number, are abusers, many are willing to pay large sums of money to ensure that their victims will be discredited. The Foundation and its members are funding the defense of many accused perpetrators, as well as filing intimidation lawsuits against authors of books on sexual abuse, such as *The Courage to Heal*, making the totally unfounded claim that books can induce "false memories."

In the long run groups such as these cannot possibly succeed in their attempts to cover up the truth about childhood abuse. It is impossible for anyone to cover up millions of documented cases of abuse throughout the world and overwhelming evidence, like photographs, witnesses who have caught perpetrators in the act, and the innumerable confessions of perpetrators themselves.

A group such as the "False Memory Foundation" was bound to spring up to prey on our natural desire to deny the existence and magnitude of the pernicious problem of child abuse. We want to believe that incest and cult abuse are not occurring. We would all like to deny the national and international statistics that show that more than a quarter of the world's children are sexually abused and that more than half of all children are abused or neglected to an extent that constitutes criminal child abuse.

Our natural instinct is to deny the truth when we are faced with something shocking and horrible, just as most people initially deny being told by a doctor that they are dying. It is simply too painful to accept immediately. In addition, many of us have not dealt with our own childhood abuse and some of us are still repressing the fact that it occurred to us, which may bring up frightening feelings when we hear about abuse, and even more strongly evoke our defense of denial.

Did you know doctors were still denying that children were being *physically* abused by their parents only thirty years ago? Despite being presented with overwhelming physical evidence of children with broken bones, bruises, and lacerations, most physicians in the 1950s denied that parents were battering their children. Radiologists who had taken x-rays of battered children had to join with the Humane Society which decided children should have the same protection as animals to convince the medical profession and the public that a problem existed. The battered-child syndrome was not officially recognized until *1962*.

Rich perpetrators hire lawyers who can easily confuse abused children and make them look like liars on the witness stand. Lawyers also use the dysfunctional behavior of adults molested as children to destroy their credibility. In our society, we admire people who control and repress their emotions, so juries tend to believe perpetrators who show little feeling and testify coldly and "rationally," over the testimony of children and adults who have been traumatized and are distraught because of the abuse.

What makes abuse cases even more difficult to prove is the fact that when some perpetrators deny the accusations of their victims, they may actually believe that they are telling the truth. They may not be *consciously* lying; they may have totally blocked out their acts of abuse, as well as their own earlier victimization. Many perpetrators learned to dissociate and block their feelings as children when they were being abused and as adults continue to dissociate when they act out the role of the abuser. Perpetrators have an even greater reason than abused children to suppress their memories because they not only have to contend with their own childhood trauma, but also the terrible guilt of having inflicted the same pain on someone else, usually a family member. How many of us could easily face such a reality?

We cannot possibly put all of the abusers in our country in jail; we have to find another solution for the problem. I believe we need to address the abuse epidemic in our society from a place of compassion rather than retribution.

We need to focus our energy on healing the problem of child abuse and helping *all* of the victims and victim-perpetrators. You may be surprised to learn that, as a victim of incest, I do not believe that perpetrators should be criminally prosecuted. I believe we should adopt the system used in Wisconsin and Belgium where incest is treated as a civil matter and the family is provided with therapy for as long as necessary. Perpetrators are placed in halfway houses and closely monitored rather than imprisoned and are allowed to continue to work to support their families, so their families do not have to go on welfare. The state is spared the cost of lengthy trials, incarceration and family support. The perpetrator receives treatment to prevent recidivism. This procedure ensures healing of all family members and avoids the unjust result under our criminal system where perpetrators go free because the strict "beyond a reasonable doubt" standard in criminal cases is so difficult to prove, or because juries and judges believe mandatory minimum sentences for abuse are too harsh.

The programs in Wisconsin and Belgium recognize that perpetrators are driven by unconscious compulsions resulting from their own abuse. Perhaps I can see the need for compassion because I have memories of my father's remorse over what he did to me, as well as my experience in treating adolescent perpetrators who repeated the abuse they had suffered on children younger than themselves. It is far easier to have compassion for a fourteen-year-old girl who, after being brutally sexually and physically abused by her stepfather, sexually abuses a five-year-old, than to have compassion for a forty-year-old adult who abuses a five-year-old. But their motivations and their pain are the same.

Sexual abuse and rape are not crimes of lust; they are crimes of violence. When perpetrators begin to feel helpless and out of control, those feelings trigger repressed memories of the helplessness, pain, and lack of power they felt when they were being abused as children. In order to rid themselves of the terrifying feelings of helplessness, they repeat behavior they learned as children and take on the role of the abuser, the person with power.

Please do not misinterpret what I am saying as excusing child abuse. Child abuse is never excusable. But I would prefer to concentrate on healing the abuse epidemic rather than simply punishing perpetrators. Experience has amply demonstrated that putting people in jail does not solve the problem—the high recidivism rates have proven that fact.

I believe that all people can be healed. In training therapists throughout the country, I have become aware of the many effective new techniques for healing which have been developed by therapists and are being used with amazing success. Although a few therapists say some criminals, perpetrators and pedophiles cannot be healed, other therapists are successfully healing these people. Our focus needs to be on finding ways to heal, rather than on denying that a problem exists or by simply disposing of wounded human beings. We need to recognize that *all* people are valuable and that each of us has something unique to contribute.

If you were abused as a child, you probably blocked out all or part of your memories of your abuse. So how do you know if you were abused and need therapy?

Gaps in your childhood memories may indicate abuse. If you find yourself exploding in uncontrollable anger, or hitting people, children or pets, you are probably reacting to stress in ways you were taught and need to work on the underlying feelings that are causing you to lose control. You may have nightmares or flashbacks of your abuse. You may begin to notice destructive patterns of behavior or a string of abusive relationships. Or you may find yourself drawn to books, articles and television shows about abuse.

Psychiatrists at Harvard Medical School and clinicians have compiled a list of symptoms for a condition which they call "Complex

Post-Traumatic Stress Disorder," which covers most of the symptoms of child abuse:

1. A history of subjection to totalitarian control over a prolonged period (months to years). Examples include hostages, prisoners of war, concentration-camp survivors, and survivors of some religious cults. Examples also include those subjected to totalitarian systems in sexual and domestic life, including survivors of domestic battering, childhood physical or sexual abuse, and organized sexual exploitation.
2. Alterations in affect regulation [emotions], including
   - persistent dysphoria [depression]
   - chronic suicidal preoccupation
   - self-injury
   - explosive or extremely inhibited anger (may alternate)
   - compulsive or extremely inhibited sexuality (may alternate)
3. Alterations in consciousness, including
   - amnesia or hypermnesia for traumatic events
   - transient dissociative episodes
   - depersonalization/derealization
   - reliving experiences, either in the form of intrusive post-traumatic stress disorder symptoms [nightmares or flashbacks], or in the form of ruminative preoccupation
4. Alterations in self-perception, including
   - sense of helplessness or paralysis of initiative
   - shame, guilt, and self-blame
   - sense of defilement or stigma
   - sense of complete difference from others (may include sense of specialness, utter aloneness, belief no other person can understand, or nonhuman identity)
5. Alterations in perception of perpetrator, including
   - preoccupation with relationship with perpetrator (includes preoccupation with revenge)
   - unrealistic attribution of total power to perpetrator
   - idealization or paradoxical gratitude
   - sense of special or supernatural relationship
   - acceptance of belief system or rationalizations of perpetrator
6. Alterations in relations with others, including
   - isolation and withdrawal
   - disruptions in intimate relationships
   - repeated search for rescuer (may alternate with isolation and withdrawal)
   - persistent distrust
   - repeated failures for self-protection
7. Alterations in systems of meaning
   - loss of sustaining faith
   - sense of hopelessness and despair.[9]

Recent studies have linked childhood sexual abuse to depression, obesity and other eating disorders such as anorexia nervosa and bulimia; premenstrual syndrome; pain with intercourse which cannot be medically explained; conduct disorders; somatization disorder; personality disorders such as borderline, antisocial and histrionic disorders; alcohol and drug abuse; promiscuity and prostitution; panic disorders; and a variety of unexplained pains, gastrointestinal disturbances, and hysterical conversion symptoms such as unexplained paralysis.[10]

If you see yourself in several of these symptoms, it would be wise to seek therapy to determine the cause—and to improve the quality of your life. My life has changed dramatically for the better since I discovered and resolved my own childhood abuse with the help of several therapists. If you do not like yourself or are not happy or contented most of the time, you will benefit from therapy even if it turns out you were not abused as a child.

The most effective treatments for sexual and physical abuse are the ones described in Part III and in my earlier book *Reach for the Rainbow: Advanced Healing for Survivors of Sexual Abuse*.

Four basic goals of effective therapy for childhood trauma:

1. **Recovery of sufficient memories of your abuse to understand your behavior.** There are several therapies now available to help in recovering memories: hypnotherapy, brainwave biofeedback, breath work and body work. Memories can also be recovered in group therapy, and through various Gestalt and writing techniques which are designed to access repressed memories, but these processes usually take longer.

2. **Release of emotions.** This appears to be the most important step, one that most people cannot jump over, even though they would like to avoid painful feelings. Healing comes primarily from releasing emotions, and hypnotherapy and breath work appear to be the most effective means of releasing emotions at a deep level. Biofeedback and body work, and other techniques such as Gestalt and mindfulness meditation may also sometimes be helpful in releasing suppressed emotions.

   AS A GENERAL RULE, IF THE THERAPY YOU CHOOSE DOES NOT ENABLE YOU TO FEEL POWERFUL EMOTIONS, IT WILL PROBABLY NOT RESOLVE YOUR PROBLEMS AND WILL NOT HEAL CHILDHOOD TRAUMA.

3. **Recall decisions you may made about yourself, others, and your life as a result of the traumatic events and replace harmful decisions with helpful ones.** Abused children usually make many erroneous decisions about themselves, other people and the universe, and many of these decisions are unconscious. The most damaging effect of childhood trauma is the destruction of the child's self-esteem. Whether a child is physically, sexually, or emotionally abused or neglected, the child almost always believes he deserved such treatment.

   Young children are at a developmental stage where they think the world revolves around them, that they cause everything that happens to them. Abuse seems like a punishment, so children conclude that they have done something bad. When they are unable to pinpoint what they have done, they conclude that they must be inherently bad or flawed in some way. Children usually generalize their experience even further. In our society, children hear that God loves and protects "good little children." If they are not being loved and protected, they assume that even God must be punishing them.

   In order to heal, you need to uncover all of your destructive decisions and change them at *both* an emotional and intellectual level. The most effective way I have found to uncover damaging decisions is through hypnotherapy, but you can uncover such decisions using other methods, such as rapid eye movement desensitization. It is important to change your decisions while experiencing the emotions you felt when the decision was first made.

4. **Develop positive self-esteem, and establish healthy communications, relationship and living skills, and positive patterns of behavior.** It is not enough just to eliminate negative emotions, thoughts, and behaviors. They must be replaced with something positive. People who have been abused as children usually come from dysfunctional families and need to retrain themselves into healthier patterns of interaction and behavior. You need a therapist who can help you think and behave in functional ways and teach you skills for creating healthy relationships.

You may need to see more than one therapist in order to achieve all of these goals. Your first priority should be to deal with your present harmful behavior. In choosing a therapist to help you overcome childhood trauma, you need to make sure that your candidates are familiar with post-traumatic stress disorder. If you have been sexually abused, you will of course want to find a therapist who is experienced in that field and who has treated several abuse victims to a successful conclusion.

If you know or suspect that you have repressed all or part of your memories of the abuse, I strongly recommend that you find a therapist who has had experience with multiple personality disorder (MPD) and hypnotherapy. This does not mean that because you have repressed some memories you have multiple personality disorder. But certain types of repression, such as ego states, resemble some of the features of MPD and if your therapist is familiar with the more severe cases of MPD, she or he will certainly have the skills to help with less complex symptoms.

The techniques which are the most effective with MPD and other types of amnesia are highly specialized and demand that the therapist have adequate training and experience. Hypnotherapy is now recognized as the treatment of choice for MPD and other amnesia states.[11] (Hypnotherapy is covered on page 246.) Common sense leads to the conclusion that forgotten memories generally cannot be restored by just talking, and yet that is what some uninformed therapists attempt to do. How can you talk about something that you cannot remember?

If you suspect that you may have forgotten events or portions of memories having to do with your abuse, or if you find out during therapy that this is the case, your therapy will proceed faster and more effectively if you find a therapist who has the ability to use hypnotherapy, breath work (page 260), or brainwave biofeedback (page 254), so that you can access your memories, feelings, and decisions as quickly and safely as possible. Some therapists who use biofeedback also use hypnotherapy.

If you have abused a child or are doing so now, you can also be helped—and you can heal. Although some therapists say that some perpetrators cannot be healed, I know dozens of therapists who are successfully treating perpetrators of all kinds, not by behavioral techniques but by the methods described above for victims. Studies show that almost all people who abuse children sexually have themselves been sexually abused as children.[12] The same is true of people who physically abuse children; they are typically repeating what has been done to them.

New research shows that most of us have repressed all or part of events which were traumatic to us as children.[13] In order for your treatment to be effective, you must deal with *both* your adult actions and the trauma of your own childhood abuse. You must recover and release the painful emotions you felt when you were being abused as a child if you want to feel peaceful and ensure that you will never feel compelled to abuse anyone again. Behavioral therapies which deal only with your adult acts and change only your present behavior will not resolve the underlying childhood trauma or eliminate the emotions that are causing you to abuse.

Whether you are a victim or a victim-perpetrator, you must resolve your underlying trauma in order to be free and find inner peace.

Rape and domestic violence

If you are in an abusive relationship, you first need help and support to get out of that relationship. Your best initial step is to contact a shelter for victims of domestic violence because these shelters offer vital assistance and provide twenty-four hour help—for free. Even if you do not want to stay in a shelter overnight, these shelters generally have the most effective programs for victims of spouse abuse, including support groups, and are excellent referral resources for obtaining additional help.

For rape victims, the local rape crisis center is the first place to contact. The staffs there will be sensitive to your problem—they are familiar with the pain rape victims suffer. Many are themselves rape victims. They are trained to help you deal with the emotional effects of the rape as well as supporting you through the criminal process if necessary.

Since the trauma is usually very recent in cases of rape and spouse abuse, your first priority should be to deal with your present feelings—or the lack of them if you are numb from the shock. Group programs in rape crisis centers and shelters provide much-needed support during the recovery process and can be extremely effective in helping you recognize that you are not alone and your feelings are not unique.

Research indicates that talking about your experience and expressing your emotions as soon as possible are the primary keys to recovery. The worst thing you can do if you have been raped or battered is to keep it secret and try to "live with it." Although you may think you can get through it by yourself, you will suffer the effects for many years unless you can talk about what happened and ask for help. The sooner you get help, the quicker and easier your recovery will be.

Once you have dealt with your immediate experience and are more stable, you need to take the next step and explore whether experiences in your childhood may have contributed to your rape or battering. Current research reveals that victims of childhood sexual and physical abuse are subject to revictimization as adults.[1] These studies indicate that the risk of rape, sexual harassment, and battering for victims of childhood sexual abuse are double that of the general population. One study of incest victims found that two-thirds were subsequently raped.[2] Of course, these figures include only rape victims who consciously remember their childhood experiences; it does not include the many victims who answer "no" to questions about childhood abuse when polled because their memories of childhood abuse have been repressed. A majority of victims of violence in adult relationships were also victims of physical and/or sexual abuse as children.

For those of you who have been raped or beaten, I want to emphasize that you did not cause these things to happen to you. You are not in any way at fault. Earlier abuse often establishes subtle behavior patterns of victimization which are unconsciously recognizable by victimizers, and these patterns may subject you to a greater risk of revictimization. To ensure that you will be safe from future revictimization, it is extremely important for you to deal with any issues you may have involving childhood abuse.

The patterns of revictimization were first brought home to me dramatically by the experience of Rachel, the mother of a friend. When Rachel, a Jew, was only seven years old, she was imprisoned in Auschwitz, a Nazi death camp. Her entire family perished in the concentration camp, and Rachel was used as a camp prostitute for any Nazi guard or soldier who wanted her. When the Americans liberated Auschwitz, Rachel was nine years old. She had no family and was sent to New York where her body was healed. But no therapy was available to heal her mental wounds.

Rachel was intelligent, excelled in school, and graduated from an American university. She married a wealthy man, gave birth to my friend and another child, and lived a life of seeming normality. She never talked about her experiences in Auschwitz. As an adult, she has been raped *five* times.

In my own clinical practice and workshops, I have found that more than half of my clients who were sexually abused as children were also later raped as adults. One of my clients, whom I will call Christie, was an extraordinarily talented teacher, who worked her way up to a position as an administrator at the Lansing Community College in Michigan by the time she was forty. She was raped several times over a period of months by a science department chairman.

Christie's husband, a lawyer, could not understand why Christie did not tell him about the rapes until they were moving out of the state; he had tremendous difficulty accepting the fact that Christie could not prevent her repeated rapes. However, he wanted to support her and filed a lawsuit against the chairman and the university.[3]

Christie was also bewildered by her inability to stop the rapes. The fact that she had no conscious recollection of being abused as a child increased her sense of guilt over her inability to ask for help to stop the rapes.

Christie started therapy with me to find out why she could not protect herself and because she suspected the reason was that she had been sexually abused. She had no memories of the abuse or the identity of her abuser, but she was very angry with her rigid, perfectionist father and thought he might be the abuser.

We were both surprised when memories emerged under hypnosis of her prolonged sexual abuse and torture by an older neighborhood bully. The bully had totally intimidated Christie from the time she was four until she was seven and her family moved away. He punished her violently if she tried to resist his abuse. As an adult, Christie was unable to stop the chairman from raping her or even tell anyone about them because of the unconscious pattern of fear and submission established by her abuse as a child.

Lawyers for the college and the department chairman argued that Christie merely had an affair which she concealed from her husband. However, current research on the existence of unconscious patterns of revictimization convinced Christie's rapist and the college to pay her a substantial settlement. Judgment was entered against the chairman, but the college pressed to have a gag order imposed which would have forced Christie to remain silent about the settlement and the rapes. Christie and her husband refused to allow the cover-up and insisted that the record be made public in order to prevent this type of abuse from continuing.

Survivors of abuse have to be constantly vigilant to the danger of becoming involved in threatening situations, or of freezing when they should run or fight. Self-defense courses can be effective in helping abuse and rape survivors overcome old patterns of victimization and learn new ways to protect themselves.

Research shows that victims of rape and battering suffer from the same psychological syndrome as survivors of war and torture—post-traumatic stress disorder.[4] (See the discussion of this disorder starting on page 13.) In order to heal from the effects of trauma and diminish the possibility that you may be raped or involved in an abusive relationship again, you need to find a therapist who can help you overcome the effects of post-traumatic stress disorder as well as the effects of any earlier abuse.

Multiple personality disorder and ego states

Multiple personality disorder has been found to be more common than was previously recognized. In the past, when someone exhibited signs of multiple personality disorder, their friends and relatives would say things like, "Oh, Aunt Tillie is having one of her spells," or "Joe is just not himself today." Despite its frequency, this disorder is frequently misdiagnosed because some therapists are unfamiliar with its symptoms which may be mistaken for the delusions or hallucinations of schizophrenia or a mood disorder with psychotic features.

People with multiple personality disorder have two or more distinct personalities or personality states, and in some cases may have over a hundred. In classic cases, each personality has unique memories, behavior patterns, and social relationships. Different personalities may take full control of the person's behavior at various times and can switch within seconds or minutes. Generally personalities are unaware of the existence of other personalities.[1]

People suffering from multiple personality disorder may have periods of amnesia or blackouts where they "awaken" to find themselves in strange surroundings or they may be aware of lapses in time for which they cannot account. They think they must be "crazy" because they hear voices of other personalities, have flashbacks (waking visions of traumatic events), or feel that they are "possessed" by another person, spirit or entity.[2]

"In the case of multiple personality disorder the etiological role of severe childhood trauma has been firmly established," according to Judith Herman, M.D., a psychiatrist on the faculty at Harvard Medical School, in her outstanding book, *Trauma and Recovery*.[3]

This disorder is typically caused by repeated physical and sexual abuse in childhood. A child who is being abused cannot escape. The child cannot control the abuse and does not know when or if it will stop. Children cannot comprehend what is happening and are overwhelmed by violent conflicting emotions and unremitting pain.

The intolerable stress causes the mind to cut itself off from what is occurring. Dissociation is the psychological term for the process by which we insulate ourselves from too much mental pain; our minds protect us by blocking out emotions and memories which are so horrible we are unable to mentally process them.

The process of dissociation has recently been confirmed by neurobiological research documenting the brain functions which record traumatic experiences in a separate part of our brains from other memories. Traumatic events are imprinted exactly as they occurred with the intense emotions, without analysis or comprehension. Our memories of these events remain hidden from consciousness until our minds determine that we are able to begin to deal with them.[4] We then begin to receive hints—often through nightmares or flashbacks, or through an increased awareness of the existence of other personalities—that we have repressed memories we need to address.

Abused children can respond to severe abuse in three ways: they can die, and many children in our country die of abuse every year—an average of three a day.[5] A second response is to become psychotic and dysfunctional. The third is to dissociate from the anguish and repress the trauma in order to function and survive. Some children block out the events from their conscious minds, storing them in separate pockets of memory which contain events and/or emotions, sometimes called ego states. Others create distinct personalities to deal with the abuse and to cope with various life situations.

Therapists are finding that most people who have been abused more than once as young children have ego states created by trauma. These are like personality states because they contain memories and emotions sealed off from consciousness, but they do not take complete control of the person's actions. One ego state may contain the child's memories of the first abuse. Another ego state may contain memories of abuse at later times or by other abusers. Some ego states may store particular emotions. Existence of these ego states is consistent with neurobiological research that traumatic memories remain imprinted in our brains.

The mechanisms of dissociation and repression, including ego states and multiple personality disorder, are obviously the healthiest response to trauma, and the children who subconsciously choose these responses are intelligent and creative. They divide their minds into various personalities or ego states to deal with the continuing horror. Each personality or ego state seals off memories and feelings in neat little packages so that the child does not have to deal with too much pain at once. The child is insulated from the pain and unbearable feelings and remembers nothing at the conscious level. In the case of multiple personality disorder, one or more personalities deal with the abuse and protect the other personalities from knowledge of the abuse so that the child can continue to perform daily activities.

Children who are being terribly abused appear to unconsciously conclude that the personalities they are developing are inadequate because they cannot protect themselves from abuse. Since they do not receive any positive reinforcement for their original developing personality traits and behavior, these children create new ones in their desperation to cope with trauma and obtain love. Their feelings are so overwhelming that children place them somewhere else—in another personality. One woman recalled being a small child sitting on her grandfather's lap, chatting in his native language, when he suddenly died of a heart attack and fell on her. She split off a personality that spoke his native language and grieved his loss. As an adult, she was treated unsuccessfully with drugs for depression and even electric shock treatment. When her multiple personality disorder was discovered and the grieving personality treated, she made a "full and lasting recovery."[6]

Depending on the severity of abuse and how long it continues, a child may create from two to over 100 or more distinct personalities. Studies have shown that these personalities may be of different ages, different sexes, and may even respond differently to psychological tests. What is more amazing is that the personalities may have different physical characteristics, such as eyeglass prescriptions, allergies and IQs.[7] In a recent case, one of a woman's personalities had diabetes, while the others were healthy.

Although having multiple personality disorder can be agonizingly disruptive, it has some positive aspects. The fact that people are able to create a variety of traits in separate personalities has some staggering implications for us all. If people with multiple personality disorder have the capacity to develop totally different physical and psychological traits, we may all have the ability to create ourselves as we want to be. This disorder also seems to indicate that our minds control "diseases" and physical conditions to a greater extent than we presently acknowledge. I tell clients with this disorder that they already know how to create what they want, they have only to use the ability they have already demonstrated.

Researchers believe that infants naturally have a number of states of consciousness. If an infant is abused, a portion of his consciousness may be isolated from the whole, walled off to protect the greater consciousness from something it is too immature to process. Recent research indicates that integrating personalities or states of consciousness may be a developmental task which children who have not been abused perform when they are approximately eight years old. These researchers speculate that trauma causes barriers to be formed around states of consciousness which prevent integration from occurring at the normal age. Other researchers assert that we all have various states of consciousness and personalities which exist throughout our lives. Trauma merely exaggerates these natural states, making them more dramatic and pronounced.

When a personality takes full control of a person's consciousness, especially those created to deal with the abuse, the person may experience periods of amnesia and not consciously know what happened during the intervals of blackout. Usually intense headaches accompany changes from one personality to another. For many clinicians, these symptoms indicate classic multiple personality disorder.

If you are experiencing these symptoms, it is important to immediately consult a therapist experienced in treating multiple personality disorder because you may be doing things that are embarrassing or harmful to you during the blackout periods. I strongly recommend that you select only therapists who have successfully treated cases of this disorder and are trained in hypnotherapy. Research has shown that the personalities and ego states are created by trauma through a process of self-hypnosis and that is why hypnosis is necessary for uncovering those states and bringing the memories to consciousness.[8]

Multiple personality disorder is completely curable in a couple of years if you have a competent therapist. If any therapist you interview expresses shock, disbelief, or any negative reaction to your condition, leave at once. Some therapists who are uninformed and untrained may be overwhelmed by this disorder; a few may deny that it exists at all.

You need to question your candidates very carefully about their knowledge of multiple personality disorder and its treatment. Treating someone with this disorder is like treating a family; each part must be treated individually and helped to cooperate with and contribute to the whole. The various personalities need to be brought to consciousness so they can release their repressed memories and emotions to become healthy, helpful parts of the individual.

Each personality must be treated with kindness and respect because each contributed to the person's survival. There is almost always one personality that has acted as the protector or caretaker and this personality can assist other personalities in becoming healthy and functional. Each personality is usually frozen at the age and emotional development when it was created. Therapists must keep in mind that they are dealing with a number of very wounded children, some of whom may be repositories of intense hostility, rage and hatred.

Although some personalities may appear to be destructive or hostile, experienced therapists know that these personalities are important. They have contributed to the person's survival by providing a way to fight back and by giving the person the strength to endure the trauma. These personalities have to be reeducated to use their characteristics in positive ways to support the individual.

Your therapist should know how to help you select those aspects of various personalities you want to strengthen and retain and those you wish to channel into other directions. You can negotiate with your personalities and decide what is best for you and for them.

You need to remember that your mind created your personalities and ego states and your mind knows exactly how to heal you. You have the keys to unravel your own mental puzzle and you need to trust your instincts, both in choosing your therapist and in directing your healing.

When you select a therapist, one effective technique is to consciously call out that part of you that is an adult and can make the best decisions for you. If you have created various parts of yourself, you have the ability to use them to help you. Never make decisions in an emotional state. Take some deep breaths and use a relaxation technique to clear your mind. Then simply tell yourself mentally that you want to make a decision which will help all parts of you and that you want the adult part of you that can make the best decision to come out and take over. Assure all your parts that they will be treated gently and ask their help in choosing a therapist who will treat you with kindness and respect. You were able to create personalities and ego states to protect you, and you have the ability to use them now to help you choose a therapist and heal.

Eating disorders

The most common eating disorders are anorexia nervosa, bulimia and obesity. According to Anorexia Nervosa and Related Eating Disorders, Inc. ("ANRED"), anorexia nervosa is a life-threatening disorder of deliberate self-starvation with wide-ranging physical and psychological components. People suffering from this disorder usually have an intense fear of gaining weight or becoming fat; they often have a distorted perception of their bodies and see themselves as fat even when they are emaciated. Many anorexic girls and women lose so much weight that they develop amenorrhea—loss of menstrual periods.[1]

Weight loss is usually achieved by drastic dieting, often combined with excessive exercising. People with anorexia nervosa frequently make elaborate meals for others, but limit themselves to a narrow selection of low-calorie foods. They also may hoard, conceal, or throw away food. Physical symptoms may include constipation, loss of hair, growth of fine body hair, intolerance of cold and low pulse rate.

Psychological changes often appear as the illness progresses including depression, irritability, indecisiveness, stubbornness, social isolation, and dislike of change. Anorexics usually have low self-esteem, a perfectionist attitude about weight and appearance, and a tendency to be nonassertive in dealing with people. They are typically depressive, obsessional, hysterical and phobic. Most anorexics withdraw, deny that a problem exists, and seldom seek help.

According to ANRED, eating disorders affect as many as twenty percent of young women between the ages of twelve and thirty. Anorexics used to be found almost exclusively among young white women from upper- and upper-middle-class families. Today, young women between twelve and sixteen are still a high risk group, but researchers find self-starvation in women and men of all ages, religious and ethnic backgrounds, and socioeconomic groups. Between five percent and eighteen percent of anorexics die from the effects of this disorder.

Bulimia is related to anorexia nervosa and is characterized by binge eating and purging. For some bulimics, a binge is six cookies after a diet meal. For others, a binge is 50,000 calories gobbled down in one or two hours. Most bulimics purge by making themselves vomit as soon as they have eaten. Many overexercise to burn calories. Food is usually eaten as inconspicuously as possible or secretly.

Bulimics have self-esteem problems, an unhealthy concern about weight and appearance, an obsession with food and a distorted body image. Bulimia often follows periods of unsuccessful dieting. Eating becomes a way of coping with other problems, resulting in secretive binges, which in turn cause increased feelings of guilt. And that leads to the purge part of the cycle, with self-induced vomiting, fasting, and often abuse of laxatives, diuretics and diet pills. This disorder commonly begins in adolescence or early adult life.

Many health problems can result from bulimia and extreme cases can lead to weakness and dehydration, heart and kidney damage, stomach ruptures, seizures, tooth and gum disease, and even death.

Although some people suffering from bulimia deny that they have a problem, others recognize that something is wrong but may not know how to get help or are afraid to ask because of what others might think.

Obesity, or being over the normal maximum weight for your age and height, may be due to a physical problem and you should have a medical examination that includes a hormonal analysis before you start psychotherapy. However, obesity is more frequently due to compulsive overeating resulting from low self-esteem, anxiety and depression which are usually caused by trauma. Once physical causes have been eliminated, psychological causes should be explored.

Earlier studies of anorexia nervosa and bulimia were unable to explain the origin of these disorders, and theories ranging from a disease of the pituitary gland to the stresses of adolescence and the cultural emphasis on thinness have all been discredited. Recent studies have linked anorexia nervosa, bulimia, and obesity to childhood sexual abuse which confirms what therapists have been discovering for years in clinical practice.[2] It is significant that the symptoms of people with eating disorders are almost identical to symptoms of abuse victims as well as the criteria for post-traumatic stress disorder. While not all cases of eating disorders have been traced to sexual abuse, the correlation between these disorders and sexual abuse is high. The remaining cases usually involve low self-esteem due to physical and/or emotional child abuse.

There is a reason for eating disorders and they can be cured when the cause is uncovered and resolved. Experts in the field recognize that if the underlying issues are not addressed, eating disorders will recur.

Eating and sex are basic needs and the words used to describe them are often identical. Since our minds make an unconscious association between eating and sexual acts, it is not difficult to understand how victims of sexual abuse who have suppressed their trauma would displace their repressed feelings onto food.

Psychotherapists are able to regress clients under hypnosis to traumatic events which resulted in an unconscious decision about weight causing the disorder; some clients consciously remember the decisions they made without hypnosis. Gwen, a brilliant college professor and the victim of sexual abuse and torture by her father, was fully conscious of the reasons for her anorexia. She said she starved herself so that she "would not be a sexual being." By starving herself she kept her body childlike, without breasts or periods, to avoid appearing sexually attractive. Gwen also blamed herself for wanting love from her father and said she thought that if she could remain a child, she could deny her sexual feelings and convince herself that she was not at fault for the abuse. Once she realized the connection between her anorexia and her father's abuse, and placed the responsibility for her abuse on her father instead of herself, she was able to maintain a normal weight.

Bulimia is often a reaction to having a penis forced into one's mouth, although the purging may be related to other types of sexual abuse. Children who felt as though they were going to throw up while being abused or had semen in their mouths may reenact how they felt through bulimia. Purging may also be a symbolic attempt to cleanse oneself from rape or other sexual abuse. Bulimia can be an outlet for anger in a current abusive relationship; the bulimic transfers her intense rage towards her abuser to her body. Bulimia is also a way to cope with stress and relieve tension.

Obesity tends to be a protective reaction to sexual abuse. Victims conclude that if they are fat, they will be sexually unattractive and safe from sexual harassment. One client of mine who had been sexually abused found under hypnosis that she had also concluded that if she were heavier, she would be bigger and stronger and thus would be better able to physically defend herself from assault.

I have not found anyone who was more than fifty pounds overweight who did not have some repressed sexual issue that made it difficult to lose weight. In some cases, the traumatic event was not even physical, but merely involved the *threat* of sexual abuse. In a couple of cases, seductive or negative comments made by the mother or father about the person's body or sexuality appeared to be the underlying cause of obesity. In all cases, the victims concluded that it was wrong or unsafe to be physically attractive and reacted by becoming obese. My experience and that of other therapists is that once the repressed traumatic events are brought to light, the emotions released and the decisions reevaluated, weight is lost *without any drastic dieting*.

In my own case, I was about ten pounds overweight for most of my life, despite frequent dieting. After helping so many clients lose hundreds of pounds by uncovering their unconscious decisions about weight, I decided to hypnotize myself and find out why I couldn't lose a mere ten pounds. The answer came quickly: when I was being sexually abused by my father with my mother's knowledge, both my parents were skinny, so skinny they were probably anorexic. My father was six feet tall and weighed 125 pounds. They both gained weight after the abuse stopped. So my child mind concluded that thin people were mean and abusive. I did not want to be mean and abusive like my parents, so I would not allow myself to become thin. I had to convince my child mind that being slim would not make me a monster by consciously focusing on kind people who were thin and fat people who were mean. After I reprogrammed my thoughts, the ten pounds dropped away without my having to diet.

The first step for treating any eating disorder is to evaluate the necessity for hospitalization or placement in an inpatient program. Depending on the client's physical condition, hospitalization may be necessary to prevent starvation and ensure adequate nutritional intake. For children and adolescents with extreme cases of anorexia, bulimia or obesity, an inpatient treatment program may be the most effective treatment option because the child can be removed from an abusive situation and may feel freer to disclose any abuse and receive therapy.

Children and adolescents often have a great deal of resistance to treatment; eating disorders are a psychological defense, a way of avoiding awareness of other serious problems. When they are with their peers who have similar problems, they begin to accept the fact that they have a problem and become more amenable to treatment.

Until recently, inpatient treatment was the treatment of choice, but success was limited because the underlying cause of eating disorders remained a mystery. Today therapists should be cautious about hospitalization for adults who have been physically or sexually abused unless the condition is life-threatening because hospitalization could further damage self-esteem and increase feelings of victimization and helplessness. Some people may want to face their problems in a safe environment, but others may feel a damaging loss of control. Treatment in an inpatient setting may intensify the client's belief that she is "crazy" (a belief that is often instilled by the abuser and echoed by other family members).

Most experts agree that if the client is medically stable and not suicidal, outpatient individual therapy should be tried first. If you are an adult, you should first obtain a medical opinion about your physical condition and then use your best judgment about whether inpatient or outpatient treatment is best for you.

Many hospitals and inpatient programs still follow models of treatment for eating disorders based on outdated behavioral chemical dependency programs and Alcoholics Anonymous. They may cure the eating disorder, but since the eating disorder is merely a symptom of a deeper trauma, the problem will remain and manifest in other harmful ways. If you are considering hospitalization or an inpatient program, be sure that the institution recognizes the link between eating disorders and sexual abuse and that its program provides psychotherapy as well as medical and nutritional treatment. The better programs have follow-up counseling to keep people on the road to recovery. (For more information about evaluating hospitals see pages 128-133.)

Most of the theories of therapy have been tried for eating disorders, from psychoanalytic to cognitive to behavioral. The psychodynamic therapists fail to address weight and nutritional problems and the behaviorists and physicians overlook emotional and family issues. Eclectic therapists who treat the underlying trauma and resulting unconscious conclusions as well as addressing nutritional issues and eating habits are the most successful. Since hypnotherapy is the acknowledged treatment of choice for cases of abuse involving repression or dissociation, hypnotherapy should be seriously considered in cases of eating disorders. In some cases, other methods of releasing memories can be used, such as Gestalt techniques, brainwave biofeedback, conscious connected breathing, journaling, right-hand/left-hand writing, or participation in sexual abuse groups.

My preference is for hypnotherapy because it is the quickest way of getting to the underlying trauma; the therapist can simply ask the client to take his mind back to the reason for the eating disorder and immediately pinpoint the traumatic memory and the decisions about weight based on it. Whatever method you choose, you can be helped if you face your underlying problems and learn to love yourself.

Anxiety disorders—
Panic attacks and phobias

Although everyone feels anxiety or panic at some time in their lives, for people suffering from anxiety disorders these feelings are overwhelming and persistent, often drastically interfering with daily life. Anxiety disorders fall into five broad categories—panic disorders, phobias, obsessive-compulsive disorders, generalized anxiety disorder, and post-traumatic stress disorder.[1]

A panic disorder is characterized by four or more panic attacks in a month, or one or more panic attacks followed by persistent fear of another. A panic attack is a period of intense anxiety and unprovoked fear that one is dying or going crazy. Panic attacks typically begin with intense fear, at times sheer terror. Among the somatic symptoms that follow are shortness of breath, dizziness, heart palpitations, chest pain, choking and smothering sensations, nausea, trembling or shaking, sweating, hot flashes and chills. Emotional symptoms include depersonalization, feelings of impending doom and fear of dying, going crazy or losing control.

A phobia is an involuntary fear reaction that is inappropriate to the situation. It involves a sense of dread so intense that individuals do everything possible to avoid the source of their fear, even if it means radically curtailing their lives. Phobias may begin as a reaction to a panic attack and the fear that it may recur. A simple or single phobia is marked by dread or avoidance of a specific object or situation, such as heights (acrophobia), witnessing blood or tissue injury, flying, animals or closed spaces (claustrophobia).

Social phobia is distinguished by extreme anxiety about being judged by others or behaving in a way that will lead to embarrassment or ridicule. People with social phobia may be unable to speak, eat or write a check in public or use public restrooms. A vicious cycle may be created in which anxiety impairs performance and poor performance fuels the fear.

Agoraphobia is a complex set of fears and avoidance behaviors associated with being alone or feeling trapped in a public place. It may occur in combination with panic disorder and can cause some people to become terrified of the prospect of going to a shopping mall, a party, or, in extreme cases, even leaving their homes.

Panic disorders and phobias affect approximately 8.3% of the population—over 14 million Americans[2]—and, although these disorders are among the most common and treatable, only one out of five people suffering from such disorders receives adequate treatment.

Obsessive-compulsive disorder is characterized by recurrent and persistent thoughts or obsessions about disturbing situations such as contamination, violence to the person or loved ones, or self-doubt. Usually, but not always, people with obsessive-compulsive disorder feel compelled to perform some routine or ritual (compulsion) that helps relieve the intense anxiety brought on by the obsession. The routine is usually time-consuming enough to interfere significantly with normal functioning. The most common compulsions are cleaning and checking if doors are closed, gas turned off; others include hoarding, counting, and repeating.

People experiencing high levels of unrealistic anxiety for more than six months concerning two or more personal life situations—such as health and finances—may suffer from generalized anxiety disorder. This disorder manifests itself both psychologically and physically in many ways, ranging from uneasy edgy feelings and chronic restlessness, to stomach trouble, sexual problems, or insomnia.

Post-traumatic stress disorder ("PTSD") can affect people who have survived severe mental and physical trauma, such as childhood physical, sexual and emotional abuse and neglect; rape; war; kidnap; torture; and disasters such as fires, floods, or plane crashes. This condition is discussed in more detail starting on page 13.

Until recently anxiety disorders were treated primarily with behavior therapy and medication, but neither brought permanent relief. While asserting that medication may provide temporary relief from panic attacks and phobias, Dennis J. Munjack, M.D., Director of the Anxiety Disorders Clinic at the Los Angeles County-University of Southern California Medical Center and a member of the Phobia Society of America's Board of Directors, warns that "to this 'positive' must be added the 'negatives' of the often laborious process of drug trials, possible side effects, withdrawal problems, and so on. And medicines don't 'cure' anybody, *per se*. Relapse rates for patients treated with medication alone are very high, and may exceed the relapse rate with behavior therapy treatment. The question of comparative relapse rates is an important one. More research is critically needed here."

Although millions of dollars have been spent on research to determine the cause of phobias and panic disorders, no definitive cause has been found. It has been hypothesized that these disorders are genetic because studies indicate that they tend to run in families; however, no evidence to support a genetic cause has been found despite intensive research. And while researchers at the National Institute of Mental Health (NIMH) have discovered chemical abnormalities in people with panic disorders and phobias, other studies indicate that the extreme stress of abuse and trauma can cause similar abnormalities.[3] Until children are studied from infancy to adulthood, we will not have a conclusive answer to this issue.

Newer studies and clinical experience point to a different cause: childhood trauma which generates such intense terror that memories of the event and feelings are blocked from consciousness.[4] Later events that remind the person of the repressed incident trigger the old feelings of fear which may be intensified by fear of exposing the old trauma. People do not "catch" phobias like a cold; this debilitating condition is the result of a severely stressful and frightening past experience.

Clinical experience indicates that dysfunctional behavior almost always has a very logical explanation, one which is generally traceable to childhood trauma. A few days before I wrote this chapter, a young man I treated a few years ago at an adolescent unit, whom I will call Jimmy, telephoned to tell me he was changing jobs because he worked making laundry bags in a small room and felt very uncomfortable and scared in such places. I knew Jimmy had been severely physically and sexually abused from infancy until he was six years old and asked if he wanted to explore the cause of his fears so he could be free of them. Jimmy insisted that the cause was simply being confined in a small space but agreed to look further.

I asked him to close his eyes, take several deep breaths and then think of a time in his childhood when he had felt the same way.

Jimmy immediately remembered being locked by his mother in a tiny dark closet as a very young child and feeling the same way he did at his job. His mother and her boyfriend had abused him, and he did not know what would happen when he was released from the closet. I had him picture himself as vividly as possible as a small child in the closet and feel how alone and afraid he was.

Jimmy had a great deal of courage and stayed with his fear for several minutes until he began to feel it decrease. I then had him imagine growing up to his full present height, about six feet, while still in the closet and breaking the door open so that it could never be locked again. The relief in Jimmy's voice confirmed his statement that he felt "much better."

I have had dozens of similar dramatic revelations in my own practice when I explore the reasons behind clients' fears and phobias. I have uncovered phobias resulting from deaths or illnesses in the family during childhood as well as from abuse. In one case, a very intelligent woman was terrified of leaving her house because she felt people were watching her. She said she *knew* that her fears were irrational, but she could not overcome them. She had been a victim of cult abuse, and her fear was explained by a memory of lying on the floor naked when she was four years old while robed men danced around her in a circle before raping her. Once this memory and the emotions surrounding it were released, her fear of being watched disappeared. I have yet to find a case where there was no rational explanation for a seemingly "illogical" fear, nor have the hundreds of therapists I have polled during my workshops.

An increasing number of researchers and clinicians are coming to the realization that panic disorders, phobias and obsessive-compulsive disorders may be symptoms of post-traumatic stress disorder, usually resulting from childhood trauma.[5] An NIMH study recently linked alcoholism with panic disorders and phobias. New information also links anxiety disorders with suicide attempts.[6] Significantly *both* alcoholism and suicidal thoughts have now been linked to childhood sexual abuse.

Recent neurobiological studies reveal that chemical changes occur during the severe stress of childhood trauma, and these changes are consistent with findings of chemical abnormalities in people with phobias. The fact that panic disorders and phobias seem to run in families can be explained by the fact that child abuse, especially sexual abuse, is passed down from generation to generation through behavior, rather than defective genes.

Medication and behavioral therapy have not been successful in providing a permanent cure for anxiety disorders because they address only the *symptoms* of the problem, neglecting the underlying cause. Therapists, including psychiatrists, appear to agree that medication should only be used for phobias as a last resort, after therapy or if therapy cannot proceed because the person is so immobilized by anxiety.

Based on the new studies, the most effective treatment appears to be a combination of behavior therapy and psychotherapy which delves into the underlying cause of the problem—such as hypnotherapy, Gestalt techniques, breath work, or other methods that uncover and address the core fear triggering the panic attacks or phobia.

The national nonprofit organizations, such as the Anxiety Disorders Association of America, which provide a clearinghouse for information and lobby for funding for the cure of anxiety disorders, are beginning to acknowledge the relationship between such disorders and past trauma, but discovery of this link is still new and you may have to do some searching to find a therapist who is up-to-date and uses techniques which can evoke the cause as well as treat the symptoms.

Many people feel embarrassed by their fears and think that their problems are unique. These feelings constrain them to suffer in silence and to delay seeking treatment for years. It is important to get help as quickly as possible because untreated anxiety disorders usually get worse. Victorians called panic disorders "the vapours," and there are still a few uninformed therapists who may trivialize your disorder or misdiagnose you as being a "bundle of nerves" and prescribe a tranquilizer. If so, it is time to find another therapist.

Relationship problems— Couples and marital therapy

The new theory of psychotherapy based on resolving childhood trauma is increasingly being used in marital and couples counseling, as more therapists recognize that patterns established in childhood have a powerful impact on relationships. Our choice of partners, as well as our interaction with them, generally mirrors our early relationships with parents and caretakers, especially if those relationships were painful. Marriage and family counselors have found that it is not enough to work on problems between partners; they must also deal with traumatic events in each individual's past.

Generally, couples therapy is more effective than treating the individuals separately. Even before the advent of trauma therapy, marital counseling was found to be successful approximately 75% of the time where couples were seen together, but was only successful in about 50% of the cases where partners were treated separately.[1] Experience has shown that family dynamics exert a potent influence on us and that when more family members join together in therapy, faster and more effective healing takes place.

Although there may be times where circumstances require separate sessions, most marriage and family counselors believe that treating partners together is best because it increases communication and understanding. Seeing partners separately often increases conflict because the individuals may become suspicious of what is taking place between their partner and the therapist in their absence and accuse the therapist of favoritism.

A variety of theories and techniques are useful in couples therapy, just as they are in individual therapy. Thus an understanding of the basic theories described in Part V is helpful in choosing a counselor for couples. However, there are some theories and techniques that are especially suited to couples therapy.

Almost all couples can benefit from learning to communicate more effectively. Effective communication is critical not only in personal relationships but in all human interaction, but unfortunately these skills are not part of our basic education. Simply teaching partners to listen to each other, to verify their understanding of what their loved one is saying, and to respond in a positive, empathic way which indicates understanding and a desire to resolve a problem to the mutual satisfaction of both parties can dramatically improve the relationship. Enhancing communication is an essential part of all couples therapy.

Another important part of therapy is exploring each partner's expectations of the relationship. Very often people mistakenly assume that their partner wants them to act a certain way or expects something from the relationship. Simply having couples list and discuss their expectations, needs and desires can quickly rectify misunderstandings.

Although behavioral techniques can change dysfunctional patterns of communication and eliminate basic misunderstandings, they fail to address the underlying emotional problems. Emotional reactions caused by past trauma have a more powerful influence on outward behavior than any learned skills and can easily overwhelm any teachings that are purely intellectual. For example, most people know intellectually that it is wrong to hit their spouse. And yet, when they feel overwhelmed by feelings of helplessness and anger, they resort to physical violence, reverting to patterns of behavior they learned in their own childhoods. Behavioral and cognitive therapies reach only the surface of our minds. If behavioral changes are not felt at an emotional level but are merely accepted intellectually, they cannot withstand the force of repressed emotions. When those emotions are triggered, people revert back to their old patterns which are imprinted at a deeper level in their minds.

Effective couples therapy deals both with problems in the relationship and individual problems, including those due to unconscious reactions to childhood trauma. Experts in the field of couples therapy, Gay Hendricks, Ph.D., and Kathlyn Hendricks, Ph.D., have written an excellent self-help book entitled *Conscious Loving: The Journey to Cocommitment*, to help partners become more aware of unconscious patterns of behavior. This book also includes exercises to show partners how to help each other change those patterns.

These submerged patterns of behavior and emotions must be brought to consciousness and transformed if permanent change is to take place. Although a variety of techniques can help bring repressed trauma to consciousness, research indicates that hypnotherapy is the treatment of choice.[2]

Most therapists see couples jointly but use hypnotherapy only in individual sessions. I used to limit hypnotherapy to individual sessions until one of my clients wanted her husband to be present for support, and he clearly wanted to attend. After making sure both understood that strong emotions could come out and that her husband had to remain very quiet no matter what happened, I agreed that he could stay.

Because she felt safe with her husband beside her, this woman was able to recover a memory of being raped as a child by a neighbor. She experienced all of the violent emotions she had felt. It was very hard for her husband to witness this outpouring of anguish, especially since he wanted to comfort her and stop the process. But he knew that she needed to get her feelings out and that he would thwart her healing by interrupting.

After almost an hour, her emotions subsided and we were able to uncover the decisions she had made as a child, decisions which had a striking influence on her reactions towards her husband. He saw how some of his actions reminded her unconsciously of the childhood abuse and caused her to react violently. For the first time he really understood the pain his wife had suppressed. He had assumed that she did not love him and even at times hated him, but attending this session enabled him to see clearly that she was reacting to something for which he was not responsible.

His wife realized for the first time that she had been unconsciously identifying her husband with her abuser. When she became aware under hypnosis of how certain of her husband's behaviors reminded her of her abuser, she was able to separate the two in her mind.

This couple's relationship immediately improved due to his increased understanding, her expanded awareness, and the support she felt from his presence at the session. Their experience taught me the incalculable benefits of doing hypnotherapy with partners and other family members present.

There are so many false assumptions and misunderstandings in relationships. We have been taught to hide our pain and our true feelings from each other. When our defensive veils are lifted and our loved ones can see into our hearts, an immediate closeness develops and healing occurs. Love blossoms through understanding. I am still amazed by the reaction of empathy and protectiveness that results when people understand the pain their loved ones have endured.

Since healing past trauma may require many sessions, I do not encourage partners or family members to attend all or even most of their loved ones' hypnotherapy sessions because they can become burned out. They have their own problems. But I encourage each person in a relationship to attend enough of the other's sessions so that each can clearly understand the basic cause of problems in the relationship and develop a real feeling for the deep pain the other has suffered. The results are dramatic, far beyond anything I have seen achieved in individual hypnotherapy sessions.

The considerations for choosing a couples therapist are similar to those for selecting any other psychotherapist, except that you will also want to ascertain whether the therapist has had experience and success in helping couples. Although some therapists who specialize in treating families and couples are licensed as marriage and family counselors, you do not have to limit your search solely to people with this license; other therapists are also trained to deal with problems in relationships. It is important to inquire into your candidate's experience and interest in dealing with relationships such as yours and to check references carefully to determine the therapist's success in couples counseling.

While you and your partner should of course interview therapists together, you should each rate candidates separately and compare your ratings. Each partner should fill out the checklists on page 66. If there is a large disparity between the two ratings, continue to interview candidates until you are both reasonably happy with your choice. You should both feel that most of the time the therapist supports and treats you equally. If one of you does not trust the therapist or thinks the therapist is consistently taking the side of your partner, the therapy will not be effective. As in individual therapy, the nature of your relationship with your counselor is important and will have a significant impact on your progress.

The best way to determine if the two of you have chosen the right therapist is whether your relationship improves. If you do not see any improvement or have a significantly clearer understanding of issues by the third or fourth session, you should start to question your choice. Discuss the lack of progress with your partner and with your therapist. If necessary, obtain an opinion from another therapist, but do not be afraid to make a change. Remember, your counselor works for you and should be judged on results.

Often simply the commitment of partners to work together in therapy to improve the relationship will create an immediate improvement. A commitment to making the relationship grow is an essential element of a lasting relationship. Even couples who have a generally healthy relationship can strengthen and renew their feelings for each other by using therapy to explore ways to become closer or by participating in other self-development and spiritual programs and groups.

IV

Therapy for Children

How do I find a good therapist for my child?

Therapy can be helpful for children of all ages. The earlier a problem is recognized and a child receives help, the more effective therapy will be—and the child will have fewer problems later in life. Some therapists even treat infants. One psychiatrist limits his practice to babies six months and younger.

You may be wondering what problems an infant could have that would warrant therapy. The violence of the birth process and the way a baby is handled after birth can be traumatic and establish damaging mental and behavioral patterns that may last throughout the child's life. Researchers have found that separating babies from their mothers even briefly, in incubators or for other reasons, affects the bonding process and this trauma may cripple the child's relationships unless it is resolved. There are reasons why some babies cry constantly or refuse to nurse or cuddle. These symptoms should not be ignored. It is better to have a baby examined by a pediatrician and a therapist immediately to determine what is wrong than to watch your child suffer the effects throughout his or her life.

Selecting a psychotherapist for your child may be more stressful and bewildering than choosing one for yourself. The field of child therapy presents a conflicting array of theories, techniques and approaches, and if you consult three therapists, you are likely to get three totally different opinions. So given the confusing multiplicity of choices, how do you select a therapist for your child?

I interviewed several respected child therapists and asked them what they would look for if they had to choose a therapist to help their own children. Although some of their approaches differed, the qualifications were remarkably consistent.

How to find candidates to interview

Almost all of the experts immediately warned me never to choose a therapist from the Yellow Pages. Although you may have a sense of urgency, especially if your child has been traumatized by abuse or is acting out, it is better to take the time to do a thorough selection and find someone who is both competent and compatible rather than grab the first therapist who has an available hour. You may waste a great deal of time and money on the wrong therapist and later *still* have to find one who can help your child.

Your first step is to obtain referrals from people you know and trust. The referral checklist on page 42 can also be used for evaluating candidates for child therapy. Your pediatrician and school counselor are good sources of referrals. Referrals from parents whose children have been in therapy are especially valuable.

If your child has been abused sexually or physically, the best referral sources are your local children's hospital or a hospital that has a special unit for treating abused children, and your local sexual abuse treatment center. You can also call—at no cost—Childhelp USA, a national organization that has therapists on duty 24 hours a day to answer questions and provide referrals across the United States. Childhelp's toll-free telephone number is (800) 4-A-CHILD.

If you suspect that your child has been sexually or physically abused, it is critical that he or she be evaluated in a specialized unit for handling child abuse where the doctors are experienced in the field. Unfortunately, some doctors and hospitals do not have sufficient training in examining abused children and may not only assess your child's condition incorrectly but also exacerbate the trauma. Usually the best evaluation programs are in children's hospitals. In some states, hospitals cannot make assessments for child abuse unless a report has first been made to child protective services.

Another referral resource is child protective service workers who usually are familiar with children's therapists in their area. Less reliable as sources are medical schools and general hospitals in your area; you can call the Departments of Social Work, Psychology, and Psychiatry for names of child counselors. However, you should be cautious about referrals from these sources because some will recommend only the therapists associated with their institution. If possible, obtain an independent confirmation of all institutional recommendations.

When you telephone candidates, be sure to ask each of them whom else *they* would recommend to help your child.

Qualifications

My recommendations about qualifications for child therapists are similar to those for adults: the type of degree held by a child therapist has very little relationship to competence or ability. The woman in my state who is recognized by the experts to whom I spoke as being the best therapist for young children has a master's degree in education. Psychiatrists may in some instances be excellent counselors, but they are expensive and their training may not be as intensive in counseling skills as therapists in other disciplines. Because they are medical doctors, some psychiatrists are more likely to prescribe drugs than engage in therapy with children.

Experience

The therapist's experience in treating children is more important than the type of degree the person has. The experts I interviewed agreed that they would insist on having their children work with someone who had experience in counseling *many* children, more than just one or two. During the initial interview, you should ask specifically how many children your candidate has seen and how many were the same age as your child. You should also ask how many children the therapist has counseled to a *successful* conclusion. If you feel uneasy about questioning a therapist, remind yourself that the therapist works for *you*. You have made a commitment only to see and interview your candidate for an hour; you do not have to hire the person.

The therapist should have a thorough knowledge of child development as well as child psychology. As they mature, children pass through recognizable stages of physical, intellectual, emotional, and social development. They reach critical turning points at each stage which affect personality development and social functioning. The child therapist needs to understand these stages and the developmental tasks which must be completed in each stage in order to determine if your child is progressing normally and if she or he needs special help in certain areas. Ask the therapist how your child's development compares with standard developmental stages.

Finding the right therapist for your child

Once you have established that your candidates have adequate experience in treating children your child's age, many of the basic principles for choosing one of them are the same as those for choosing any other therapist. The most important overall consideration is entirely subjective: how do you and your child *feel* about the therapist? Every child therapist I interviewed emphasized the importance of the therapist being a good "fit" for both parents and the child. There is no scientific test for assuring a good personality match; it depends on whether the therapist's style of communication and beliefs about your child's needs are compatible with yours. The critical question is whether you and your child *like* the therapist or not. You must trust your feelings here.

One of the main qualities the experts asked for in a therapist who works with children is *gentleness*. Other criteria are how much you trust the therapist's opinion, and how much the therapist seems to truly care for your child—and, of course, how comfortable you and your child are with the therapist.

Both parents and the child should interview prospective therapists together before making a selection. The primary consideration is how well your child relates to the therapist; if your child and the therapist do not relate well, healing will not take place. A competent therapist will usually recognize any problems in the development of a therapeutic relationship and suggest referral to another therapist.

When you are interviewing candidates, observe how the therapist and your child interact. Does the therapist treat your child with respect? Does she involve your child in the conversation and use language that your child can understand? Does the therapist invite your child to ask questions about what is being said? Does the therapist treat your child like an object and talk *about* him, rather than talking *to* the child in your presence?

Another important consideration is whether the therapist is patient. For instance, if your child is squirming, does the therapist tell him to calm down and sit in a chair? Or does the therapist give your child a toy or drawing materials or sit on the floor with your child to make him feel more comfortable? The latter responses indicate the therapist's recognition that children are uncomfortable in unfamiliar surroundings. The therapist should be concerned with making your child feel relaxed so that a positive relationship will develop.

The experts I consulted differ on whether the child should be present during the first interview with the therapist. Some say that it is important for the child to participate so that the parents can observe how the child and the therapist interact. With older children, especially adolescents, if the therapist talks to the parents alone first, it may be impossible for the therapist to gain the child's trust because she may believe the therapist has been turned against her by her parents and will not listen to her side of the story. When a teenager is the main client, the experts agree that the teenager should be seen alone first or with the parents.

Some experts believe that parents of younger children may not be able to express themselves freely if the child is present, especially if they are anxious, distressed or angry with the child. They may need an opportunity to talk first to the therapist about their problems with the child.

The experts agreed unanimously that children are helped most when the entire family participates in therapy. The therapist needs to observe the family interacting together in order to understand the child's problems and effectively strengthen the relationship between the child and the family. When children are very young, their family is the whole world. Therapy cannot help a child change if the family dynamics remain the same. In a dysfunctional family, a child usually adapts in a negative or self-defeating way in an effort to survive and make sense out of the chaotic conditions within the home. When the child attempts to change her behavior without family support, she is usually forced right back into old patterns.

If therapy is to be effective, parents must be involved and open to change themselves. Therapy does not work if parents take a child to therapy to be "fixed." It takes courage for families to face family problems and make necessary changes in family dynamics. Where the family is supportive, rapid healing takes place. A good child therapist is one who is able to enlist the support and cooperation of parents and other family members.

A word of caution: sometimes good therapists make parents uncomfortable by recommending that they make changes in their negative behavior patterns. Disrupting established patterns can create so much turmoil and stress it may seem that things are getting worse. It is important not to become discouraged during this stage because things will get better once all family members have a chance to adjust to new behaviors.

The better therapists encourage parents and siblings to attend some sessions together. Just the fact that all members participate and have a commitment to making changes produces remarkable results. Often when fathers are involved, children tend to take therapy more seriously. Some therapists will only see families together, others will only see members individually, and still others will use a combination of individual and family sessions as needed. If the child is very young, the therapist may see the child with a parent until the child feels safe enough to work with the therapist alone. You need to find out what approach your candidate recommends and decide what will best meet your needs and those of your child and your family.

Types of therapy for children

Therapists who work with children use many theories and techniques. Children may be unable to express their thoughts and feelings in adult terms because they have not yet developed sufficient language skills. The consensus among the experts I interviewed was that therapists need to be comfortable and experienced in using a variety of modalities designed to help children express themselves. Therapists who use only one psychotherapeutic approach or a couple of techniques on every child are limited in their capacity to help your child.

Among the long list of modalities for helping children are play therapy, relaxation and guided imagery, hypnotherapy, art therapy, music, dance and movement. The therapist should make a thorough assessment of the child and parents before determining what techniques to use in order to tailor them to suit the child's situation. If a therapist tells you what is going to be done before interviewing you and seeing your child, thank the therapist and leave.

Parents sometimes wonder why they should pay a therapist to play with their child. Simply allowing a child to roll a toy car back and forth alone is not necessarily play therapy, but playing can facilitate therapy. Playing helps the therapist establish a relationship of trust with a child so that the child will be able to express his feelings freely. Good child therapists focus on creating the space and the circumstances under which healing can take place; healing can occur when the therapist simply is present, protective and noncritical while the child establishes a sense of his identity during play.

The main therapeutic value of play is to open channels of communication and give the child an opportunity to express feelings and experiences he may not otherwise be able to communicate. Games and toys are used because they are not threatening to a child and the way a child interacts with them *symbolizes* the child's feelings and problems. For example, if a boy is presented with a number of toys and chooses a toy car which he violently smashes into other cars and objects, he may be expressing anger he cannot verbalize. A young girl who rubs the genital areas of male and female dolls together may be trying to communicate the sexual abuse that she cannot put into words. The way a child plays tells a sensitive and well-trained therapist about her feelings and emotional and intellectual development. Play may also provide nonverbal cues indicating possible conflicts in the family, at school or with the child's peers.

I was skeptical about the effectiveness of using a sand tray with children in therapy before I took a course on its use. A sand tray is like a small portable sandbox which is placed in front of the child along with dozens of miniature figures representing people of various ages, races, and genders; houses, cars, animals, trees, fences, monsters, and sometimes even dinosaurs. If the child is very young, no instructions are given; the child simply begins to pick out toys which he places as he chooses in the sand. An older child may be asked to use the toys to show how he feels, or how he felt when a traumatic event occurred.

It was astonishing to me that children who could not verbalize their trauma or were terrified of talking about it would so readily and clearly express what they felt or what happened to them by the way they selected and placed the miniature toys in the sand tray. One little boy whose father travelled extensively placed dolls representing all of his family members close to his toy house, except his father who was placed at the farthest end of the tray.

The sand tray is more than just a diagnostic tool. After the child arranges toys in the sand, the therapist will talk about what the child is expressing and asks the child what she thinks. Then the therapist helps the child release unexpressed feelings and correct erroneous perceptions the child may have about herself, her parents or her life. Another step is to have the child rearrange the sand tray to show how she would like her life to be. One severely abused child used all the dinosaurs to surround her house and then placed her father outside the ring.

The sand tray and other play therapy tools can be used throughout the course of treatment to ascertain whether the child's feelings have changed, as well as to help them change. Children begin to heal when they enact through play what they want their lives to be like in the future.

You can learn a great deal about a child therapist by the nature of the toys in the office. There should be a variety of toys such as a sand tray, cloth or plastic bats for expressing anger, puppets for acting out painful experiences and emotions, anatomically correct dolls, a doll house with an assortment of dolls, a doctor's kit to help children prepare for a medical examination or release the trauma of one, telephones which can be an effective way of indirect communication for a frightened child, art materials and games. The diversity of games and toys can also give you an idea of how innovative and eclectic therapy will be. Your candidate may not have all of these tools, but the best therapists will have many of them. Asking the therapist to explain how he uses a particular toy can provide helpful insights into his approach to child therapy.

Assessing whether the therapist is sensitive to your child's needs

Another factor in assessing the therapist is whether the office environment is designed to meet the needs of children. Is the office arranged to make children comfortable, with child-sized furniture, books, toys, stuffed animals and games? Is there enough room for a child to play without worrying about knocking over objects? Would you like to be there if you were a child? If the therapist has not given serious thought to designing an office that will make little clients feel safe and comfortable, the therapist may not be sensitive to the feelings and needs of children.

One caveat: therapists who work in government and nonprofit agencies generally cannot choose their office space and do not have the funds to decorate their offices, so their office environments cannot be judged in the same way as those of therapists in private practice.

Preparing your child for the first appointment

Another indication that a therapist is knowledgeable and sensitive to the needs of children is whether you are given information on how to prepare your child for the first appointment. The therapists I consulted routinely advise parents how to explain the therapy process to their children.

In case the first therapist you and your child interview does not provide this information, my experts furnished these suggestions. If the child is two or three, you only have to say, "Let's go see a friend of mommy's." Avoid calling the therapist "doctor"; the word may create anxiety for your child. Sensitive therapists do not use their titles with children. Be sure your child knows that you will be nearby until he is comfortable with the therapist.

With children who are a little older you can explain that you are going to a "talking place" where lots of parents and children go to talk about their worries and troubles. It's a safe place where you can get things off your chest. This person cares about children and is interested in how they think and feel.

If your child is more than nine years old, you can discuss the therapy process in more detail, emphasizing that you care very much about your child and want to do everything you can to make your child happy.

What if your child does not want to go to therapy?

Sometimes children, especially teenagers, may be reluctant to see a therapist and may even adamantly refuse to go. But as I recently told a mother, whose very angry fifteen-year-old daughter had been sexually abused by a neighbor, you do not give children a choice about going, you just take them. Or you might say, "Would you rather see the therapist on Monday or Wednesday?"

If you would not allow your child to refuse to see a doctor for a condition that affects physical health, why would you allow your child to refuse to see a specialist for a condition that affects mental health?

You may have heard the old wives' tale that people must go to therapy voluntarily in order for it to work. Not necessarily so. Part of being a good therapist is demonstrating a caring that gains the child's trust so that therapy can proceed. My experience with adolescents, and I have seen several who were dragged in by their parents or ordered to come by juvenile court, is that the ones who say they do not want to see a therapist usually hurt the most inside and open up fairly easily. Most children's therapists are well seasoned in working with angry, stubborn, oppositional children.

How long will your child's therapy take?

One of the foremost questions in every parent's mind is "How long will therapy take?" No one can give you a definite answer because it depends on so many indefinite factors, such as the age of the child, the nature of the problem, the number of problems, the ability of the therapist, and the involvement and support of family members, to list just a few. In general, the younger the child, the fewer sessions will be needed. And as a rule, the more supportive and involved family members are, the quicker healing will be.

After the child is evaluated, you need to pin the therapist down as to what the treatment goals will be and what treatment plans might best attain these goals. Ask the therapist to explain how the goals and treatment process will be measured. During the course of therapy, you should ask the therapist every few weeks for a verbal progress report. Do not be afraid to challenge and test the therapist; it is your child who is at stake, as well as your time and money.

Always remember, the therapist works for you and your child, and you are entitled to know what is going on in therapy.

The therapist who was the most esteemed by her colleagues gave a candid and enlightening explanation of how she determines whether short- or longer-term therapy is needed. She said she typically sees a child two times before making her evaluation, and in some cases may ask for a third session. She keeps the parents fully informed and involved, frequently asking them if they have other things they want to tell her and what they think of the process so far. Although she acknowledged that she cannot always make an immediate assessment of all the child's problems, she can get a sense of some fairly clear-cut issues that need attention.

Sometimes the work is done in two weeks or two months. In other cases, there is a point after a dozen or so sessions where certain goals have been reached and a choice has to be made as to whether to stop or continue to do deeper work with the child for a longer period in order to resolve more of the child's problems. The child therapists I consulted agreed that it is in the child's best interests to complete all the work while the child is still very young, but they recognized that some parents cannot or will not undertake long-term therapy. If parents are not ready to consider longer-term therapy, the therapist should alert them to trouble signs which may develop over the next few years which would indicate a need for continued therapy.

Medication

WARNING ABOUT MEDICATION FOR CHILDREN: Drugs are often misused with children. One of the most notorious instances is children misdiagnosed as suffering from "attention deficit disorder" ("ADD"), more recently called "attention-deficit hyperactivity disorder" ("ADHD"), and given ritalin. Children who are noisy, demanding and unruly (and who may also be among the brightest and most inquisitive) are all too frequently mislabeled as "ADD or ADHD kids," especially by teachers who are unable to cope with thirty or more children in a classroom.

According to various studies, only 2% to 5% of children actually have ADHD.[1] The primary symptoms of ADHD are the following: The children are inattentive and easily distracted, impulsive, easily and excessively aroused and hyperactive, and they have difficulty delaying rewards. Sometimes children have symptoms which are similar to those of ADHD but they are actually suffering from post-traumatic stress disorder caused by abuse or other trauma, or from depression, family problems, stress, drugs, physical illness or learning disabilities.

To identify accurately whether a child has ADHD, a comprehensive evaluation needs to be performed by a professional who is familiar with characteristics of the disorder. These professionals include the family physician or pediatrician, child therapist, neurologist, family counselors and teachers. In the case of ADHD, it is important for the child to have a thorough evaluation which includes a psychological interview, psychological and educational testing, and a neurological examination to ensure proper diagnosis and treatment. It is wise to obtain several opinions before drugs are used.

It often seems easier to give your child a pill than take him to a therapist for months. But the experts say that a multimodal treatment, one which addresses the medical, emotional, behavioral, and educational needs of the child, is the most effective. Parents need training in understanding ADHD and how to better manage their children, and children need psychotherapy and counseling in methods of self-control, attention focusing, and improving self-esteem. Since no one yet knows the cause of ADHD (the theory that sugar and food coloring are responsible has been discredited), it is important to help your child in a variety of ways. Research indicates that children with ADHD who participate in a long-term supportive treatment program involving multiple types of treatment have better self-esteem, less adolescent delinquency, and a clearly better prognosis into adulthood.

A new approach to dealing with ADHD is proving to be extremely effective. Brainwave biofeedback is being used to help children become more focused and the training apparently works in a very short time. Since biofeedback seems to help children with ADHD, has no negative side effects, and teaches children mental control skills they can use throughout their lives, I would try this option first. (See chapter on brainwave biofeedback, page 254.)

One other caution about medication for children: in cases of depression and anxiety, antidepressants and antianxiety agents are generally not as effective for children as they are for adults. The experts recommended using a combination of psychotherapy and behavior management at home and at school as a first line of treatment rather than hastily prescribing medication in such cases.

I know that you, as a parent, relative or friend, want to do what is best for your child. The undisputed fact is that the earlier you treat your child's psychological problems, the easier it will be for her or him to be healed, thereby sparing the child years of anguish and dysfunction. If children, especially toddlers, who are traumatized or have other psychological problems, are treated immediately, they will not repress their memories, erect the defenses, or form the destructive behavior patterns that can ruin their lives. And therapy for a child usually takes far less time, and money, than therapy for an adolescent or adult.

Evaluating your child's progress and determining when to terminate therapy involve many of the same considerations and issues as in adult psychotherapy. Please refer to the chapters beginning on page 103 and 119 for help in these areas.

With the present knowledge of psychotherapy and medicine, almost all children can be helped. Neurobiologists have even discovered that in cases where part of the brain is damaged, new pathways form to take the place of those that were destroyed. Some children with severe epilepsy have had half of their brains surgically removed and can still function almost completely normally. No matter how hopeless your child's condition appears to be, if you look hard enough you will find someone who has the knowledge to help.

Autism

Autistic children were considered "incurable" until very recently. Autism is a condition which affects young children who withdraw from reality and create their own inner worlds. Some therapists are still unaware that this condition can be treated and may recommend to parents that such children be institutionalized, a euphemism for giving up and warehousing them. However, specially trained therapists have found that contact can be made with autistic children by totally accepting the child where he is, mirroring his actions for long periods each day, and being exquisitely sensitive to the child. The process is long and tedious, but it works for many autistic children.

One therapist worked with a mother who noticed that her baby was displaying unusual symptoms at about five months. Her pediatrician told her not to worry, that nothing was wrong. By seven months the symptoms had increased and the baby was diagnosed as autistic. Fortunately, the mother took the little boy for special therapy. Today he is a happy, "normal" three-year-old.

This story illustrates a couple of important points. First, you know your child better than anyone else does, and you need to trust your instincts, no matter what so-called "experts" say. At the same time, however, you also have to be cautious about being immobilized by a natural desire to deny acknowledging that something is wrong with your child. If you are confused, obtain as many opinions as necessary to develop a clear understanding of what options are available for your child.

Second and most important, do not ever give up on your child. The sciences of psychology and neurobiology are constantly developing. If you cannot find someone who is able to help your child today, there may be someone who can tomorrow.

✓ Interview questions for child therapists

1. Are you licensed in this state?
2. What kind of license do you have?
3. What academic degrees do you have?
4. How many children have you treated?
5. How many children my child's age have you treated?
6. How many children have you seen to successful termination?
7. How long did therapy take?
8. Will you assess how my child's development compares with the standard developmental stages?
9. What type of therapy do you use for children?
10. How do you perceive my child's problem?
11. How do you propose to treat that problem?
12. Will you set goals? (What treatment plan do you propose?)
13. What technique or techniques will you use? (How will you do what you need to do to help my child?)
14. Will you see my child and me together or separately?
15. Will you see the rest of our family?
16. How long will therapy take?
17. How much will therapy cost?
18. Do you qualify for insurance coverage? Medicare or Medicaid?
19. Can I reach you in an emergency or if I have questions between sessions?

✓ Evaluation checklist for your child's therapist

First, verify that each candidate has adequate credentials:

1. Is this therapist licensed by the state?
   (Check with state licensing agency, see page 41.)
2. What type of license does this therapist have?
   (See the chapter beginning on page 44.)
3. What type of degree does this therapist have?
4. Does this therapist have experience in treating children?
5. How many children has the therapist treated?
   How many of your child's age?
6. How many children has the therapist treated to a successful conclusion?

After checking licenses and credentials, rate each candidate separately using the following scale. Then add up the total scores. Compare *both* the totals for each candidate and the individual scores on each question in making your evaluation.

5 = excellent—I feel really good about the response—everything I could hope for in this area

4 = very good—I feel good about the response

3 = average—I feel O.K. about this—acceptable

2 = not very good—a few problems—I feel a little uncomfortable about this

1 = not good at all—several problems or a major problem—I don't feel comfortable about this

0 = terrible—consider eliminating this candidate

If you have given a candidate more than one "0," you probably want to eliminate that one.

1. DO I LIKE THIS THERAPIST?
   (Double your score for this item.)
2. DOES MY CHILD LIKE THIS THERAPIST?
   (Triple the score.)
3. Do I feel comfortable talking to this therapist?

4. Does my child feel comfortable talking to or playing with this therapist?
5. Is the therapist gentle; does he or she treat my child with sensitivity and caring?
6. Does the therapist use words and concepts that my child can understand?
7. Does the therapist pay close attention to my child?
8. Is this therapist patient with my child?
9. *Does the therapist really listen to me and my child?* This is very important—double the score.
10. Does the therapist interrupt frequently instead of waiting until you and your child have had a chance to tell your story?
11. Did the therapist make a diagnosis or say what therapy would be used before thoroughly evaluating your child?
12. Did the therapist invite your child to ask questions about what was being discussed?
13. Did the therapist focus on you and your child rather than talking about himself or herself?
14. Did the therapist ensure that your child was included in the conversation and was talked *with*, not talked about?
15. Do you feel that the therapist treated your child with respect?
16. Are you comfortable with this candidate's views on family participation?
17. Will this therapist keep you informed of your child's progress?
18. Will the therapist be available to talk to you and your child between sessions?
19. Does this therapist make you feel guilty about your child's problems?
20. Is the office environment comfortable for children?
21. Did the therapist have a variety of toys and games available?
22. Were you satisfied with the therapist's description of how he uses a particular toy in therapy?

23. How easy was it to make an appointment with the therapist?
24. Did the therapist take time before your first appointment to tell you how to prepare your child for coming to therapy? (Score 5 for "Yes" and 0 for "No.")
25. Does the therapist insist on being called "Doctor?" (Score 0 for "Yes" and 5 for "No.")
26. Do the theories or techniques this therapist uses with children seem appropriate to you? (Use your common sense here.)
27. Did the therapist answer all of your questions?
28. Is the therapist realistically optimistic about being able to help your child? (You do not want to go to a therapist who is pessimistic or negative about his or her ability to help your child. The therapist's attitude can affect the healing process.)

V

How Do I Choose the Right Type of Therapy

From my own experience as a therapist and as a client in therapy, I do not believe any one theory of therapy can address all the problems of any individual. My preference is to select a therapist who is eclectic—familiar with several theories and many techniques—and willing to use whatever is necessary to help clients improve self-esteem, find inner peace and realize their maximum potential.

However, there may be cases where you may want to hire a therapist for a very specific purpose, such as assertiveness training, communications skills, or breath work, and in that case expertise in only that area is essential.

In order to make an informed decision, you will need to have a rudimentary understanding of the basic principles of psychotherapy and the major schools of thought. The following sections describe and salient features of the most common and most effective theories and schools of psychotherapy.

Although some principles of the founders of psychotherapy are outdated and sometimes incorrect, others continue to be used and expanded upon. Each one of these theories has contributed something important to our understanding of how to heal the human mind. It is helpful to have a general idea of these theories because the candidates you interview may talk about them.

Psychoanalysis/Freudian analysis

Classic psychoanalysis, sometimes called "Freudian analysis," is an intensive, long-term process involving several weekly sessions for four to eight years or more. Classic analysts follow the medical model, where the client is a patient and the analyst assumes an anonymous stance with little self-disclosure or personal reactions. Patients lie on a couch for "free-association activity," which involves saying whatever comes into their minds. They report their feelings, experiences, associations, memories and fantasies.

Psychoanalysis is based on the teachings of Sigmund Freud (1856–1939), the Viennese founder of psychoanalytic theory. Perhaps Freud's greatest contribution to psychotherapy was his realization that past events, especially those in childhood, determine our present behavior. This approach helps clients bring unconscious memories to consciousness so that they can make choices based on new insights. Many of Freud's principles and techniques—such as his concepts of the id, ego and superego; the conscious and unconscious levels of our minds; and ego-defense mechanisms—are still an integral part of modern psychology.[1]

Freud was preoccupied with sex and decided that his patients who claimed to have been sexually molested as children were only fantasizing as a defense against their own sexual desires for their innocent parents. The absurdity of this conclusion is brilliantly demonstrated in the now classic book by Alice Miller, Ph.D., *Thou Shalt Not Be Aware*, which exposes how Freud's misconceptions have kept the western world in the dark about sexual abuse. Dr. Miller uses Freud's own writings to demonstrate how he based his fantasy supposition on his own theory of infantile sexuality, a theory which places the blame on the child rather than on the parent:

"Only Freud had the courage to recognize the importance of sexuality, repressed as it was in the darkest reaches of forgotten childhood. But then, after discovering the prevalence of sexual abuse of children, he distanced himself from his findings and came to see the child as a source of sexual (and aggressive) desires directed at the adult. As a result, parents' sex play with their children could continue under cover of darkness."[2]

Anna Freud recently made her father's letters and other writings available to researchers. These documents contain evidence that toward the end of his life Freud recanted his earlier position about sexual abuse. There is also evidence that Freud himself may have been sexually abused as a child.[3] Freud's repression of his own abuse would explain both his denial of the existence of sexual abuse as well as his obsession with psychology.

Freudian analysis focuses almost exclusively on the reasons for neuroses and dysfunctional behavior. But current research demonstrates that knowing why you act or think a certain way is not enough; you also have to know what to do about it. Understanding also needs to be supplemented with emotional release as well as reprogramming of harmful behaviors and thoughts—Freudian analysis does not address these critical areas.

Psychoanalytic therapy is needlessly lengthy—hourly sessions four or five times a week for four to eight or more years. Even during Freud's time, such immersion in therapy was available only to the very rich.[4] Analysts rarely direct their patients or even have conversations with them; the way analysts obtain information about their patients is by listening to their stream of consciousness, their uncensored speech and how they associate one idea with another. It is a laborious way of searching for tiny pieces of a jigsaw puzzle and trying to fit them together. Newer therapies acknowledge that the client already has the pieces of the puzzle and can describe them if the therapist asks the right questions or can elicit them through a multitude of modern techniques, such as Gestalt and hypnosis.

Modern therapy took the best of Freud and improved on his ideas. Newer approaches incorporate more advanced techniques based on current research. These achieve results in a much shorter period of time because of our greatly increased understanding of human psychology and the effects of trauma.

I do not recommend Freudian analysis because of the length of time and high cost, its unequal treatment of women, and the continuing tendency of some of Freud's adherents to deny the reality of sexual abuse. Freud wrote during the Victorian era of the authoritarian father and unfortunately many of his followers still rigidly adhere to that model. His preoccupation with sex, probably as a result of his own sexual abuse, ignores other important causes of psychological dysfunction and major areas such as social needs and reevaluating harmful decisions.

Although the psychoanalytic approach has been discredited and replaced by more modern methods,[5] Freud's theories remain valuable for an understanding of many facets of human psychology. The best therapists use Freud's work as a foundation, but reject the rigidity of his psychoanalysis.

The Neo-Freudian approach

Freud had little tolerance for colleagues who diverged from his psychoanalytic doctrines and he therefore expelled from his Psychoanalytic Society those who dared to disagree with him.[1] Freud's most famous students rejected the inflexibility of his approach, created their own theories, and incorporated a broader view more consistent with today's holistic approach.

Concepts created by Freud and his revisionists are still very much in use today, but have been improved and expanded. The Neo-Freudians, including Alfred Adler, Karen Horney and Erich Fromm among others, spawned many of the theories of therapy which are in fashion today including Gestalt therapy, the person-centered approach, behavioral therapy, existential therapy, rational-emotive therapy, reality therapy, and family therapy.

Alfred Adler moved away from Freud's biological and deterministic view of human beings (often called the libido theory) toward a social-psychological and nondeterministic view where human beings have the ability to choose and create what happens to them. Adler agreed with Freud that what we become as adults is in large part determined by the first six years of our lives; thus therapy requires an analysis of early memories. However, Adler believed we are motivated more by social urges than sexual ones.

Adlerian therapy emphasizes understanding and confronting our mistakes in thinking. This therapy is active, involving goal-setting and encouraging intervention on the part of the therapist. Adler also had a more eclectic view of psychology than Freud, and applied a wide range of techniques adapted to fit the client's needs. Adlerian therapy is based on a growth model where people are viewed as being in a healthy process of learning and evolution, rather than a medical model, so clients are not seen as sick and in need of being cured, and the client/therapist relationship is one of equals, based on mutual trust and respect.[2]

Carl Jung, a student of Freud's, also broke away from the psychoanalytic fold, although he is not usually grouped with the Neo-Freudians. Jung minimized the importance of the Freudian idea of infantile sexuality and created an expanded concept of the collective unconscious, a transpersonal unconscious. He also got rid of the couch, made psychotherapy more supportive and reduced the number of sessions to one or two a week for a year or so. (For more information on Jung's philosophy, see the chapter on spiritual and transpersonal therapy, page 269.)

The Neo-Freudians recognized that human beings are social animals who do not operate in a vacuum. Their theories took into consideration social interaction, the individual way each of us perceives the world, and also the purpose and reason behind our behavior. They recognized the importance of a positive client/therapist relationship and the value of using a variety of techniques to suit the individual. One of their most significant contributions was the recognition that childhood experiences establish beliefs and patterns in our lives that continue into adulthood and that we must become aware of these patterns and beliefs in order to change them.

I am skeptical of therapists who say, "I'm a Freudian," or "I follow Adler," because the work of both has been superseded by the research and work of many other psychotherapists. It's a little like saying, "I won't drive any car except a Model T." While it is true that the Model T taught us a lot, just as Freud taught us about human psychology, it does not make sense to ignore the modern improvements which make both driving and therapy easier, faster and more efficient. Look for therapists who use Freud, Adler and others as teachers, not gurus, and who are up-to-date on recent advances and techniques.

Gestalt therapy

The therapies we have covered so far all rely on verbal communication to reach their goals. Gestalt therapy made a major breakthrough into the realm of feelings and nonverbal experience. The main premise of Gestalt is that we are responsible for our own lives, and by becoming aware of what we are really experiencing and doing, we learn that we are responsible for what we do, think and feel.

In Gestalt therapy, the focus is on the present, rather than on past events, although clients are encouraged to address "unfinished business"—the unexpressed feelings which have been stored from the past. These feelings of rage, abandonment, guilt, and grief need to be brought to awareness and released in order for healing to take place.

Instead of regular sessions over a long period of time, Gestalt therapy is usually done in workshops lasting a day or weekend. These workshops are designed to be intense, incorporating dramatization and interaction with others to increase self-awareness and evoke hidden emotions. Clients may play roles with other group members or with themselves using an empty chair to represent a family member or another part of themselves.

Gestalt techniques are designed to make people aware of their body language and energy blocks which may appear as tension in the body, stiffness, and nervous gestures. For example, a therapist will ask the client to exaggerate and repeat a gesture or movement which often elicits the feeling and meaning attached to the behavior.

Frederick (Fritz) Perls (1893–1970) was in training as a Freudian analyst when he broke away from psychoanalysis and became the principal founder of Gestalt therapy. Perls wanted to eliminate the split between feeling and thinking. He also rejected the passive, dispassionate role of the Freudian therapist and developed an active, person-to-person relationship where the therapist gives feedback, confronts manipulation and avoidance, and helps his clients explore the fears and blocks that prevent them from taking responsibility for their lives.

Although Gestalt workshops and encounter groups can help you become aware of patterns of behavior and feelings that are blocking your happiness, they have several drawbacks. Sometimes sessions can be so intense that they may provoke a crisis; moreover, since the workshops last for only a day or two, you do not have anyone to follow up after the session to help you work through the crisis. This can be a serious problem for victims of abuse if repressed traumatic memories and feelings start to surface.

Another problem with some Gestalt workshops is that the leaders may have more charisma than training and may lack any real understanding of Perls' conceptual framework and approach. Some can be manipulative. The leaders may also fail to build a relationship of trust with clients or to properly prepare clients for exercises or process them after the exercises.[1] Gestalt therapy demands that the therapist be sensitive and experienced. The therapist must have worked out his own problems so that they do not interfere with the therapy. It is important to obtain recommendations from people who have participated in the workshop you are considering as well as professional recommendations to insure that the leader is qualified and not just hype.

Gestalt methods have made an important contribution to modern therapy and the best therapists make use of these techniques where appropriate. A therapist who uses Gestalt techniques recognizes the importance of dealing with feelings as well as thoughts. On the other hand, practitioners who limit themselves to pure Gestalt therapy may ignore the importance of examining thought processes and mistaken beliefs; fortunately many Gestalt therapists are now adding a cognitive component to their work to change negative thought patterns.

Therapy is most effective when it addresses emotions and thought processes, and when the therapist uses many types of techniques, including Gestalt.

Transactional analysis

Transactional analysis (TA) is an interactional therapy based on the premise that our early decisions affect our present choices. While our past decisions may have been appropriate at the time, they may not be valid now. TA emphasizes our ability to change our lives by making healthier life decisions and eliminating the destructive unconscious games we play. Clients are encouraged to develop a contract with the therapist defining their goals for therapy. This therapy can be done individually but is usually more effective in a group.

TA is perhaps best known for one of its four basic life positions, "I'm O.K.—You're O.K." The other less healthy positions are "I'm O.K.—You're not O.K.," "I'm not O.K.—You're O.K.," and "I'm not O.K.—You're not O.K." These decisions are the result of childhood experiences which determine how we feel about ourselves and others throughout our lives; they rarely change without therapy.[1]

TA recognizes that we all have various "ego states," parts of ourselves which have distinct patterns of behavior, some based on how our parents treated us. The three main TA ego states are the Child, Parent, and Adult, and these provide a framework for analyzing transactions between people and within the individual. Each ego state may contain other parts, such as the Nurturing Parent and Critical Parent in the Parent ego state.[2] Clients are taught how to determine what ego state they are acting from when there is a problem. This awareness allows them to change to a different ego state and handle the situation more effectively.

Clients also learn to recognize the "life scripts" or plans for life they developed as children. These are our life dramas, with all of the characters, scenes and endless repetitions based on the roles we played in our families. TA helps clients rewrite their life scripts and stop playing destructive games like "Kick me" where they set themselves up to be rejected, or "Yes, but" where people who feel helpless ask for help and then reject all suggestions as unworkable.

A drawback of early TA therapy was that it overemphasized cognitive factors and neglected emotions. It is difficult to effect lasting behavior changes at an intellectual level. However, when someone changes a decision while in the emotional state he experienced at the time the decision was originally made, the change will be deeper and more permanent. Some TA therapists add Gestalt techniques to deal with suppressed feelings and this results in a more effective and balanced approach.[3] You will want to find out whether your therapist limits his practice to TA or incorporates other therapies that reach emotional issues.

Behavior therapy

Behavior therapy, sometimes known as behavior modification, encompasses a wide variety of techniques and learning principles which teach people self-management skills. Behavior therapy focuses on *cognition* (thinking) and *changing* present behavior rather than on feelings or the reasons for behavior. A basic assumption of behavior therapy is that all dysfunctional behavior and emotions have been learned and can be changed simply by learning new behaviors, without any insight into the nature or cause of the problem. Thus this therapy is opposite to the Freudian approach which emphasizes understanding of the underlying causes of behavior.

In evaluating behavior therapy, it is important to understand its origins. This therapy is based on experimental research, more with rats than humans. European behaviorists based their work on Pavlov's classic conditioning research with animals. The American founder of behavior therapy, B. F. Skinner, experimented with teaching rats using an apparatus known as the Skinner Box, by rewarding them with food or punishing them with electric shocks according to their performance. Skinner trained pigeons to play ping-pong among other tasks and locked his infant daughter in an enclosed, soundproof, temperature-controlled crib for two years, an experiment which would surely be considered abusive today. Skinner also tested his theories of operant conditioning using positive reinforcement (rewards) and punishment on psychotic patients.[1]

In his autobiographies, Skinner reveals that his family instilled in him a strong sense of right and wrong. His grandmother frightened him with warnings of hellfire and damnation as a punishment for his sins. His father, a lawyer, took him on tours of prisons to demonstrate the consequences of breaking the law. And his mother repeatedly threatened him with censure if he did not act properly. His family environment led him to focus on rewards and punishment as the primary method of changing behavior.[2] He rejected the idea that we have choices and free will, contending that our personalities and behavior are determined by external events, past and present. Skinner is a graphic example of a therapist who needed to heal himself.

Despite his personal problems, Skinner made a significant contribution to modern psychotherapy by developing a theory that deals with learning and observable behavior. Behavior therapy includes many learning strategies ranging from assertiveness and relaxation training to systematic desensitization and positive reinforcement conditioning. Many of these methods have been incorporated into modern models of therapy. Most therapists use some behavioral techniques in clinical practice.

Through his experiments, Skinner came to the conclusion that punishment does not work. When punishment ceases, the behavior returns. This fact has been conclusively confirmed by recent studies which demonstrate that not only is punishment ineffective in changing behavior, but physical punishment, including spanking, creates even greater problems since it teaches children violence.[3]

Most of us who drive are aware that receiving a speeding ticket does not stop us from speeding except while we are still in view of the highway patrol car. And the evidence is overwhelming that sending people to prison does not change criminal behavior.

On the other hand, positive reinforcement is effective in changing some behavior patterns. "Time out," where disruptive children are removed from a reinforcing situation such as from a classroom where they may be getting attention from their peers, is another effective behavioral technique.

A major breakthrough made by behaviorists is their recognition of the importance of having the therapist and client set specific goals. Behaviorists recognized that results cannot be evaluated unless an identifiable goal is established to measure progress. Studies indicate that where client and therapist establish explicit goals at the beginning of therapy, success in most instances is achieved more rapidly than where no goals are set.

Whether you opt for strict behavioral therapy or choose a more eclectic approach, you and your therapist should discuss your goals to make sure they are the same. If your therapy is not working, one of the areas you need to explore is whether your goals need to be modified.

On the whole, however, while behavioral therapy may be useful for helping eliminate a single unwanted behavior, such as smoking or saying "uh" while giving a talk, behavior modification is not appropriate for more complex problems or symptoms caused by abuse or other trauma. Behavior therapy may change your behavior, but will not eliminate suppressed feelings.[4]

In addition, behavior therapy disregards past experiences which may be the cause of present behavior. The treatment of phobias through systematic desensitization is an example. Phobias are debilitating and illogical fears of ordinary objects or situations, such as a fear of heights, open spaces or elevators, which usually manifest as panic attacks. Desensitization is the process of having the client identify the stimuli that evoke fear and then learn relaxation techniques, and later imagine with increasing intensity the fearful objects or situations while still in a state of relaxation. When the client no longer experiences anxiety while imagining the object or situation that was formerly anxiety-producing, the treatment ends.

Although desensitization may cure someone of, for example, agoraphobia (fear of open spaces), the real reason for the feeling of panic persists. Fear of open spaces is frequently a mental symbol or trigger for a more traumatic underlying fear, such as feeling vulnerable, helpless, and alone when being abused as a child. The terror experienced in panic attacks is often caused by repressed fear from a traumatic event which is triggered by a situation which is in some way reminiscent of that trauma.

While desensitization techniques may at first seem to work, enabling people to overcome their fears sufficiently to take a plane flight, pet a cat, or ride in elevators, other debilitating symptoms usually will arise because the reasons for the phobias remain. Unless a person was originally traumatized by an elevator, merely desensitizing him to elevators is not going to solve this problem.

You probably want to eliminate pure behaviorists from your list of candidates unless you want to attain a very specific behavioral goal. The best psychotherapists are familiar with behavioral techniques and include them in their bag of tools, but they also address emotional issues. You may want to question your candidates on their views about behavioral therapy.

Be wary of therapists who focus primarily on scientific research and want to record your sessions for their own studies. Your needs and comfort should always come first. There are therapists who prefer working with rats and therapists who prefer working with people. I would rather have one of the latter as my counselor.

Rational-emotive therapy

Rational-emotive therapy ("RET") adds yet another component to our understanding of psychotherapy. It combines thinking and feeling with deciding and doing. Its founder is Albert Ellis, a psychoanalyst who developed a directive, problem-solving approach to therapy. Aware of the powerful influence our beliefs have on our emotional reactions and behavior, he devised an approach that challenges harmful and mistaken beliefs so people can change those beliefs and alter their feelings and behavior.

Ellis understood that what we believe affects our perception of what we experience. The same event can be regarded as a tragedy or a challenge, a failure or a learning experience; our attitudes determine whether the experience is positive or negative. (Some new philosophies go even further and advocate a totally nonjudgmental attitude toward everything in life based on a belief that no event or emotion is good or bad. All of our experiences are simply to be accepted and lived to the fullest.)

This therapy explains emotional disturbances as the result of irrational thinking that the universe should or ought to be different. We are forced to analyze our "shoulds" and "musts," most of which stem from childhood interpretations of our parents' beliefs.

The A-B-C theory of personality is fundamental to RET practice. A is the Activating event, fact or behavior that precedes an emotional or behavioral Consequence, C. B stands for the Belief system about the event that evokes C, the emotional Consequence. The key is that the *belief*, not the event, causes the emotional response. The therapist intervenes to change inappropriate feelings by Disputing the faulty belief, D, leading to the Effect E, which is intended to be an increase in self-esteem and diminished feelings of anger, anxiety and depression when presented with similar events.[1] A diagram explains the A-B-C theory as follows:

A (Activating event) → B (Belief) → C (Consequence—behavioral and emotional)
                            ↑
                D (Dispute belief) → E (Effect)

An example would be feeling depressed and worthless because you were laid off from your job. Being laid off is A, the Activating event. But the event is not the cause of your depression. Your beliefs (B)—that people in the company did not like you enough to keep you, or that the economy is so bad that you will never find another job in your field, or that people will think less of you because you are unemployed—cause your feelings of depression and worthlessness (C—the consequence).

An RET therapist will help you analyze each feeling and each belief separately and will dispute destructive and mistaken beliefs in order to help you find an alternative way of perceiving the situation which would increase your feelings of self-worth and motivate you to positive action. For instance, the therapist may challenge your belief that people will think less of you because you lost your job by asking whether you would like any of your own friends less if they were in the same boat. Wouldn't you want to help your friend? The therapist might suggest that you use this situation as an opportunity to contact your friends and become closer to them by allowing them to help you. If you can see new possibilities, your feelings about your situation may change. RET places the responsibility for our self-destructive ideas and attitudes directly on us where it belongs.

The A-B-C theory was modified as a self-analysis technique by Maxie Maultsby, a student of Ellis. You can use this process without a therapist as a written exercise. You simply write a short description of the event you want to analyze for A. Then you record all your beliefs or thoughts about the event for B. For C, you describe the feelings you would like to change. Then you dispute your own beliefs by asking yourself if your beliefs are based on fact, whether the belief will help you meet your goals, and whether there are other possible ways of thinking.

Maultsby also created rational-emotive imagery where you can change habits and character traits, such as shyness, by picturing yourself in your mind the way you would like to be. This technique, now more commonly called visualization, has proven to be exceptionally effective in changing behavior and in reaching goals. Swimmer Mark Spitz repeatedly visualized himself winning his five Olympic gold medals long before the games took place. You can reach a goal more easily if you are able to picture yourself doing it in your mind.

The RET approach is extremely valuable even for trauma victims because catharsis alone may not be sufficient for complete healing. Many of us still need to understand our actions and beliefs to come to a complete resolution of our past experiences.

However, RET does not provide a means of releasing repressed emotions based on past traumatic events. RET may change beliefs and even behaviors surrounding present situations, but the emotional energy from past events remains trapped in our bodies and continues to poison us physically and mentally, often overriding our new beliefs.

Also, RET cannot change an unconscious belief because it deals only with *conscious* beliefs. An abuse victim's unconscious belief that she caused her abuse by wetting her pants or that God is punishing her cannot be addressed by the A-B-C theory because the B—belief—is hidden. Even if we change our surface beliefs about an event, that event may continue to precipitate strong emotions and dysfunctional behavior if other unconscious destructive beliefs and strong emotional energy remain unresolved. For these reasons, RET alone will not heal emotional reactions and behaviors due to past trauma, although it is effective in altering those beliefs and reactions which are fully conscious.

Further, RET focuses only on present events, neglecting the client's past history. Effective therapy recognizes that we are a product of our pasts, while at the same time acknowledging that we have freedom of choice which enables us to change our present behavior. The best therapists use a variety of theories and techniques to achieve a healthy balance between dealing with the past and present.

Reality therapy

Although reality therapy used by itself has been largely discredited, I am including it because a few law enforcement agencies and prisons, members of the clergy, and treatment centers for delinquent adolescents still adhere to it. This theory is historically interesting because it attempted to bring a new dimension into psychotherapy—morality and the concept of right and wrong behavior. Reality therapy is usually conducted in groups where accepting responsibility for the consequences of one's actions is emphasized.

Reality therapy was created by William Glasser, yet another psychoanalyst who became disillusioned with strict Freudian theory. He rejected the medical model of psychiatry with its diagnoses and the focus on the past, concentrating totally on present behavior. The central theme of reality therapy is responsibility which, in Glasser's words, is the "ability to fulfill one's needs, and to do so in a way that does not deprive others of the ability to fulfill their needs." His premise is that if we do not fulfill our needs, we may turn to negative addictions and behaviors.

Glasser's theory rests on the assumption that people have choices and the ability to fulfill their needs. He therefore worked to help clients change negative perceptions in order to see themselves as successes rather than victims. He also believed that people could gain control over their lives by adopting what he called "positive addictions," habits such as regular exercise and meditation. He understood that healing does not come by insight and catharsis alone, but must be followed by action—concrete behavioral changes.

Despite many valuable contributions, notably the emphasis on accepting personal responsibility for one's actions, reality therapy has failed to become generally accepted because it is too limited. It ignores past trauma, unconscious feelings and memories, and expression of emotion.[1]

The problem with reality therapy is that it sets the therapist up as an unfettered arbiter of morals and values, a power that can be, and all too frequently is, abused. Although Glasser intended to create a nonjudgmental and supportive atmosphere for therapy, institutions that have adopted his theory sometimes fail to follow this philosophy. Glasser treated his clients as valuable and responsible individuals. Unfortunately some therapists, particularly those in penal institutions, use the basic concepts of reality therapy but really believe their clients cannot change and therefore treat them with a lack of respect. This attitude has been shown to create the expected results—people do not heal. As Glasser discovered, therapists can help people take responsibility for their actions without condemning them and further damaging their self-esteem.

The simple truth is that if people are treated well, as having value, they will act that way. And if they are hurt and treated as if they are bad, they will act badly.

The better therapists may integrate some of the principles of reality therapy into their practices, but have a broader view of human psychology and the methods needed to deal with childhood trauma.

Hypnotherapy

New discoveries in the field of neurobiology and psychology indicate that most psychological problems are the result of traumatic events which were so emotionally painful that we blocked all or a portion of them from our conscious minds. Most children who are traumatized by illness, surgery, a death in the family, neglect or sexual, physical or emotional abuse protect themselves by repressing or forgetting all or part of the traumatic events and the emotions surrounding them. Recent studies show that the most effective way to retrieve repressed memories and feelings is through self-hypnosis.[1] We create our amnesia through self-hypnosis and can use the same process to heal ourselves.

Hypnosis is a natural state, used safely and successfully by people throughout history to attain their goals and desires. The effectiveness of hypnosis as a therapeutic tool has been rediscovered in the last century and is invaluable for treating people suffering from the effects of traumatic events. Under hypnosis, people can remember past trauma and learn to deal with it so that it does not continue to damage their lives.

There are many myths and misconceptions about hypnosis. Grade B movies and television have created a Svengali image of hypnotists who control the minds of unwilling subjects through magic and mysticism. This is totally false.

Hypnosis is a normal everyday phenomenon. You have been in an hypnotic state many times in your life.[2] Have you ever driven your car down a road and all of a sudden realized that you had gone farther than you thought and that you were not aware of how you got there? You did not remember driving past houses or buildings or other streets, but you still drove safely and managed to keep yourself on the road and in the right direction. You were in an hypnotic trance. Did you ever read a book or concentrate on a project so intently that you did not hear someone enter the room and call your name for a couple of minutes? Your intense state of concentration was an hypnotic or altered state.

Researchers have found that we are all in a state of hypnosis for fifteen or twenty minutes out of every two hours.[3] Our minds and bodies operate in two-hour cycles whether we are waking or sleeping. Our waking hypnotic or daydreaming state corresponds to the fifteen or twenty minutes of REM (rapid eye movement or dreaming) sleep we experience at night. Therapists who recognize when clients are in this hypnotic state can use it to help them recover memories. The father of hypnosis, Milton Erickson, M.D., a highly respected psychiatrist, developed this technique to overcome his own paralysis from polio and used it in his practice.[4] Another important discovery about our waking daydreaming state is that, if used properly, it can increase our creativity and productivity.

Contrary to popular myth, hypnosis does not mean sleep. In the movies you see people close their eyes when they are hypnotized, but they are not asleep—they are in a state of intense concentration. In fact, hypnosis is a state of extreme awareness. If you are in an hypnotic state, you are acutely focused. You can be in an hypnotic trance and have your eyes wide open. And no matter how deep your state of hypnosis, you can always come out of it quickly and easily whenever you want. You are aware of what is going on around you at all times. If the telephone rings, you can snap out of hypnosis and answer it. You may feel slightly drowsy for a few minutes or a bit jangled if you come out of hypnosis abruptly, but that is all.

Hypnotists do not possess any special powers. In fact all hypnosis is *self-hypnosis*. You actually hypnotize yourself by allowing yourself to go into a relaxed state. The therapist simply acts as a facilitator to help you relax. No therapist I know uses gold watches, pendants, lights or other devices for hypnotherapy; we simply help people release their tension by focusing on their breathing or relaxing their muscles so they can forget their worries, clear their minds, and become sufficiently comfortable and at ease to access information in their subconscious minds. Many times I merely tell my clients to take four or five deep breaths and they reach this state spontaneously.

You cannot be hypnotized against your will. When people are hypnotized in night clubs, the hypnotist chooses subjects who are willing to be hypnotized and who are susceptible to hypnosis. You have to be willing to relax and recover information, and you must be psychologically ready to do so, or nothing will happen. No one can make you do anything you do not want to do—or believe anything that is not true. Since you are aware of what is happening when you are in a state of hypnosis, no one can implant anything in your mind.

Therapists are finding that the majority of people have repressed traumatic events which adversely affect their lives. Now we can help these people quickly and effectively without years of talk therapy to try to unearth the reason for the client's distress. We do this by a process called regression, which involves helping the client mentally move back through stored memories to the particular memory which is causing the problem.

While this may sound difficult, it is really quite simple because your subconscious mind—what I call your "total intelligence"—knows everything about you. It knows every event that has ever happened to you in your life and where every piece of information you have ever received is stored in your mind. If, for example, I want to know why a client has a fear of cats, I would ask the client under hypnosis if the fear of cats was caused by something which happened in the past. If the response was yes, I would then ask the client to take his mind back in time to the day or memory where he first became afraid of cats. Usually the client is immediately able to retrieve the memory.

If there is more than one memory, I would ask the client to tell me about the next time something happened which made him afraid of cats and I would continue this process until I was sure that I had covered all of the memories which might be the basis for his fear.

People who have suffered childhood trauma can easily regress to the times they were hurt, as long as their subconscious minds determine that they are ready to recover the memories. It is necessary only to request the person to go back to the time of trauma, or to a memory that will explain why they are depressed or angry. Our subconscious or total intelligence contains all of our adult abilities as well as knowledge of all of our memories. The adult portion of the total intelligence understands the instruction and sifts through all of the memories to find the appropriate one.

When a client retrieves a repressed childhood memory, I can actually talk to the client under hypnosis as if the client were the age when the memory took place, because the memory is mentally stored just as it was when it occurred. If the traumatic event took place at five, the client will talk, feel, and act like a five-year-old. This phenomenon allows the therapist to see exactly how the client as a child reacted to the event and to help the child part change harmful perceptions and conclusions about the event.

Most memories are available to your conscious mind and can be recalled by you at any time. If something unpleasant happens—for instance, your boss reprimands you—you can analyze the incident when it occurs or evaluate it later and put it in its proper perspective. Perhaps your boss was in a bad mood and you were not at fault at all. But if the event is so traumatic and emotional that it is immediately blocked from consciousness, it is not available for conscious analysis. The event is stored in your subconscious which continues to experience the raw, unanalyzed emotions you felt when the event took place.

Neurobiologists have discovered that extreme stress creates biochemical reactions in our brains causing our neurotransmitters to shunt traumatic events and emotions to a different part of our brains than the part which processes ordinary events, so that traumatic experiences bypass the part of our minds that analyzes and processes information. Our conscious minds are unable to process the overwhelming emotions we experience during trauma, so traumatic events and emotions are routed to another part of our brain where they are imprinted just as they occur. Our minds store these memories in detail for processing at a later time. Since events have not been analyzed or the emotions released, these memories continue to affect our moods and behavior until they are brought to consciousness so they can be processed and laid to rest.

When something happens to you as an adult that subconsciously reminds you of a repressed traumatic experience, you consciously feel the violent emotions you felt as a child, and you may react the same way. An hypnotherapist can help you bring these suppressed events to consciousness so that you as an adult can look at them objectively, release the violent emotions, and free yourself from the harmful decisions you made as a child.

At this point, it is important to give a warning. YOU SHOULD NOT USE THE REGRESSION TECHNIQUE BY YOURSELF UNLESS YOU ARE WORKING WITH AN HYPNOTHERAPIST WHO TELLS YOU THAT YOU CAN WORK WITH REGRESSION ON YOUR OWN. Although you cannot damage your mind, you can uncover memories with which you are not equipped to deal on your own. This is especially true of victims of severe abuse. I did a lot of my own regression because I was experienced in self-hypnosis, but when I first started, I ended up in the hospital because I uncovered too many memories at once, and became totally overwhelmed.

Regression must be used in a very sensitive way. After all, you are peeling scabs off wounds that your mind found sufficiently painful to cover up with amnesia. Both you and your therapist should work very carefully in this area to make sure you are ready to proceed.

Regression can be used to uncover the reasons for various types of dysfunctional behavior, often with immediate and dramatic results. A writer friend of mine, whom I will call Ray, sought my help because he was stuck in the middle of a children's book he was writing. Although he was pleased with the story and enjoyed writing, he had not been able to write for several months. He contacted me for advice on how to get over his writer's block.

I told Ray that there were a number of possible reasons for the block, but that such blocks were frequently due to fear or resistance to success. He wanted an immediate solution, so I suggested hypnotherapy as a way to reach the heart of the problem quickly. He agreed because he knew and trusted me, but he contended that he could not be hypnotized. I explained that I do not hypnotize anyone, that I would simply help him relax and achieve a state of self-hypnosis if he chose to do so. As with almost all people who claim they cannot be hypnotized, Ray went easily into a relaxed state.

All I did was ask his mind, his total intelligence that knew everything about him, to take him back to a memory which would explain why he had writer's block and could not finish his book. Ray rapidly went from a state of relaxation to one of terror, and came abruptly out of the altered state. He said he was experiencing the same chaotic emotions he felt when he tried to meditate and that he believed he was feeling "the chaos of the universe" and could not continue. Ray had a difficult time accepting the fact that he was feeling chaotic emotions caused by something traumatic he had experienced as a child which had nothing to do with the cosmos, and that his explanation was simply a way of avoiding the memory.

When he finally accepted the possibility that his feelings might be due to something more concrete than universal chaos, Ray agreed to return to a state of self-hypnosis. I asked his mind to show him a memory that he could recover safely and that would explain his chaotic feelings. He quickly regressed to a vivid memory of being beaten with a belt by his father when he was about four years old. He felt overwhelming terror, pain, betrayal, grief, shame, anger, hatred, guilt and confusion—the chaotic emotions the beating engendered in him as a child. He was so young when he was beaten that in his mind his father and mother were his universe, and being beaten created emotional chaos for him.

After he released his painful emotions, I asked Ray what decisions he had made as a child based on the beating. He realized he had concluded that he was to blame for the beating, that it must have occurred because he was bad, and that he was unlovable. After we worked for almost an hour correcting these childish beliefs, I asked him if he had made any other decisions which would explain his writer's block. Ray immediately recovered memories of his father repeatedly saying he wanted to be proud of Ray. Ray hated his father so much because of the beatings that he swore to himself that he would *never* do anything to make his father proud of him. And suddenly Ray realized that although his conscious mind had long forgotten that childhood vow, he had unconsciously adhered to it for more than thirty years of his life! Ray's repressed hatred for his father and his childhood vow were responsible not only for Ray's writer's block, but for his failure to allow himself to achieve any kind of professional success.

During our session Ray decided that he no longer needed to punish his father and he consciously chose to be successful for himself. Two months later, he sent me the completed manuscript of his book.

If I had used traditional talk therapy or other techniques to try to pinpoint Ray's problem, it might have taken years to uncover the suppressed cause, because you can't talk about what you don't consciously remember. While not all sessions are so dramatic or successful, hypnotherapy is certainly one of the most effective therapeutic tools I have found thus far.

Although hypnosis and especially regression are used in therapy almost exclusively to expose traumatic experiences, these processes can also be used to recall pleasurable and positive experiences. Some therapists regress their clients to happy or successful experiences and use those experiences to show their clients that they can recreate positive experiences in the present.

The greatest discovery I made during my own healing from abuse was that I could use hypnotic regression to take myself back in my mind to a time before I was abused. I recovered a vivid memory where I was lying on a blanket in the sunshine playing with my toes. I was two years old. I felt light, totally free of pain, tension and anxiety. My body felt as though it were filled with thousands of tiny champagne bubbles. Somehow I knew that this was the way we are supposed to feel. And I also knew that I was totally good and loving and that this was the way I was born to be. I realized that the wonderful, essentially good part of me which existed from my birth was still alive and untainted by my abuse.

I recovered other happy memories of times before my abuse that helped me wipe out my conviction that because my parents abused me, I must have been a bad person. My memories showed me that as a child all I wanted was to love and be loved. When I realized that

I was born good, I saw that my abuse had changed my *feelings* but it had not changed *me*. That loving, innocent part of me was still alive. My abuse did not kill it. It was the real me. My painful, violent feelings were just an illusory shroud surrounding my essential core, my soul. That core could not be violated. Whatever my parents did to my mind and body, my soul remained untouched.

I have presented this technique in my workshops for therapists across the country and have found that other therapists are also using hypnotic regression to help their clients rediscover this happy, loving part of themselves with the same results. I have regressed many survivors to their early moments of joy, and some have recovered the happy, innocent part of themselves spontaneously, without using hypnosis. I have never found anyone who did not have this essential happy, loving core, although some survivors had to go back to infancy or even into the womb to experience their true natures. It is always there for everyone—we were born that way.

We are only beginning to discover the many benefits of self-hypnosis. Hypnosis can be used to improve self-image, increase confidence, access inner wisdom, control pain, augment our ability to heal, cure physical ailments, improve concentration, solve problems, and expand creativity, to name only a few of its many possible applications. Many people studying hypnosis believe that our present knowledge is just the tip of the iceberg. It is said that we use only ten to fifteen percent of our minds; some people say three percent. Hypnosis may be able to help us access the other eighty-five to ninety-seven percent.

If you suspect that you may have blocked out traumatic memories, you will want to find a therapist who uses hypnotherapy as one technique. Many psychotherapists have taken professional courses in hypnotherapy and are competent to use the technique, although they do not advertise themselves as hypnotherapists. Some therapists use hypnosis but call it relaxation, guided imagery, or inner child work.

Be careful that the person you choose is a trained psychotherapist, rather than an hypnotist who lacks psychological training. In many states, hypnotists and people who are not licensed as hypnotherapists are prohibited by law from doing hypnotic regression. On the other hand, hypnotherapy certifications, as opposed to state licenses, should be scrutinized with care because most are from private organizations rather than established academic institutions and are virtually meaningless.

The suggestions in the chapter "How do I choose a therapist who is right for me?" (page 55) are applicable to hypnotherapists. However, since hypnosis is a highly focused state, you often are more sensitive to and aware of things under hypnosis that you may not be aware of normally. Under hypnosis you may have feelings about your therapist that you did not have before. *Trust those feelings.* If they are negative, find another therapist.

Brainwave biofeedback

Can playing Pac Man with your brain relieve depression, eliminate panic attacks, help you sleep, and even cure drinking problems? The astonishing answer is yes.

This high-tech breakthrough in psychotherapy is EEG biofeedback, sometimes called neurofeedback or brainwave biofeedback. Biofeedback training teaches people to control their brainwaves to achieve desired states of relaxation, concentration, and even ecstasy and expanded consciousness. Biofeedback is being used to treat alcohol and drug addiction, as well as childhood trauma, depression, attention deficit hyperactivity disorder, premenstrual syndrome, insomnia, chronic fatigue, pain, and a variety of other conditions.

EEG biofeedback is a nonintrusive procedure which does not involve drugs. Nothing is injected into the brain. One or more small electrodes connected to an EEG (electroencephalogram) machine are pasted on the scalp. These electrodes pick up and amplify the electrical activity of the brain so it is strong enough to be measured. When the signal exceeds a certain level, the machine emits a tone which means you have at that moment achieved a certain level of activity for a particular type of brainwave.

Electrodes are placed on different areas of the head to amplify and record different brainwaves, producing different tones for each type of brainwave activity. The machine measures brainwaves according to how many times a single wave occurs during one second (wave frequency).

There are three layers in our brains. The first layer, the cortex or gray matter, produces a fast, short rhythm of electrical activity called beta. The beta brainwave is produced during focused attention and everyday activities. People who are depressed tend to have abnormally low beta brainwave activity.

The middle layer of our brains is the emotional area where we experience satisfaction from everyday life events. In this layer we feel relaxation and pleasure which comes from the slower alpha state and the even slower theta state, an hypnogogic or daydreaming state, one reached by experienced meditators. People with addiction problems have too much beta brainwave activity and not enough alpha activity and may use drugs and alcohol to reach an alpha or pleasurable state. Biofeedback training teaches these people to attain pleasurable brainwave states without resorting to addictive substances.

The brain stem is the third level of the brain which produces delta rhythms, the longest and slowest waves, those found in deep sleep. These rhythms are also found in people with head injuries. Brainwave biofeedback is helping some of these individuals recover when they learn to produce the faster beta rhythms.

The training consists of playing computer games such as Pac Man on a monitor and the learning procedure is similar to the children's game of "hotter-colder." "When you are "hot"—producing the desired level of the selected brainwave—a tone sounds and Pac Man lights up and begins to move, chomping dots on the screen. When you are producing a different brainwave, there is no tone and Pac Man remains dark and still. Other games are available and the principles for entraining desired brainwave activity are the same.

The goal of the training is to learn to produce and sustain the desired brainwave. By observing whether Pac Man lights up and moves as you sit in front of the screen, you begin to recognize the mental conditions which create your brainwaves. For example, if you are anxious and trying too hard, Pac Man will not move because the brainwaves created by your anxiety override the alpha or beta brainwaves you want to create.

The amazing part is that you have to do very little during the training. By simply observing yourself playing the game, your scores begin to increase because your mind automatically and unconsciously begins to achieve the desired brainwave activity.

Results are often immediately apparent after the first session. The morning after my first session, I awoke for the first time in my life without feelings of anxiety. I couldn't believe it; I didn't know it was possible to wake up feeling peaceful.

The therapeutic use of EEG biofeedback was discovered by a doctor who wanted to help his son who had epilepsy. The doctor started using an EEG machine for diagnostic purposes to obtain more information about his son's epileptic seizures. He noticed that the seizures decreased when his son's brainwaves were being monitored. The doctor discovered that his son was unconsciously learning to control brainwave patterns associated with seizures merely by watching his own brainwave patterns. When other doctors began using the EEG machine to train epileptics to control their brainwave patterns, they discovered many amazing new applications for the training.

Researchers found that biofeedback training helps children with attention deficit disorders.[1] Hyperactive children are taught to move from alpha and theta brainwave activity toward increased beta—focused attention—activity. The results are spectacular; the training not only seems to increase attention spans but also I.Q. Biofeedback training would appear to be a preferable alternative to drugs since children become permanently calmer and more able to focus on tasks without the dependency or side effects of drugs. There is also evidence that biofeedback may be effective in treating certain learning disabilities.[2]

Eugene Peniston, Ed. D., VA Medical Center, Bonham, Texas, and Paul J. Kulkosky, Ph.D., Psychology Department, University of Southern Colorado, Pueblo, Colorado, expanded the use of EEG biofeedback to treat alcoholics.[3] Up to now relapse rates have been sixty to eighty percent in the year following other types of treatment, including Alcoholics Anonymous programs and stays at expensive hospitals and inpatient clinics. According to an EEG training brochure for therapists from the Menninger Clinic, biofeedback training appears to prevent relapse in up to eighty percent of alcoholics who learn control of alpha and theta brainwaves.

After biofeedback training, many alcoholics can no longer drink alcohol. The brochure states: "Physiologically, brainwave training appears to be related to learned deep central nervous system quieting which alters physiologic functioning in positive ways. For reasons not entirely clear, a number of brainwave trained alcoholics have subsequently been unable to tolerate alcohol intake without becoming acutely ill. With this response to training, the clinical outcome usually is abstinence." The training seems to act in many people like the drug Antabuse. In the early stages of research, some people who took the training for alcoholism became angry when they found they could no longer drink alcohol, so training centers now require people to sign releases consenting to this result before starting the training.

Many applications of EEG biofeedback are being studied and the possible uses appear to be awesome, in the true sense of the word. Psychologists have found that victims of trauma—Vietnam veterans and child and adult victims of abuse—have excessive delta activity in the frontal areas of their brains which is associated with dissociative states. Brainwave biofeedback is being used to help trauma victims integrate their traumatic experiences and relieve their depression and anxiety.

Some therapists are having astonishing results using a combination of biofeedback, hypnotherapy and emotional release with victims of severe childhood abuse who suffer from post-traumatic stress disorder, multiple personality disorder and other forms of dissociation. People with multiple personalities who usually undergo years of other types of psychotherapy find that after thirty to forty treatments all of their personalities are integrated and that they are free from the pattern of dissociation, allowing them to remember and resolve their painful experiences.

Michael Hutchison, the author of *Megabrain Power*, describes the work of Len Ochs, Ph.D., who found that some clients became uncomfortable when their brainwaves reached certain frequency ranges and that ". . . as they willingly relaxed and entered that frequency range, they underwent sudden releases of traumatic material. What was even more exciting was that these sudden releases had powerful, life-transforming effects. It was as if the therapeutic effects of months or even years of traditional "talk" psychotherapy had been compressed into minutes. Ochs concluded that specific traumatic events were coded and stored according to specific frequencies, like library books stored according to call numbers."

Carol Manchester, Ph.D., and her colleagues work with victims of childhood trauma using a combination of biofeedback, hypnotherapy, and other modes of therapy. One of Dr. Manchester's clients is a woman whose sexual abuse by her father began at the age of three. She continued to have sex with her father into her adulthood and had a hysterectomy to prevent herself from becoming pregnant by him. When she started treatment, she had multiple personality disorder and was addicted to drugs and alcohol. After two sessions per day of biofeedback for a total of thirty sessions, her personalities were integrated and she no longer used drugs or alcohol. Dr. Manchester and others have also had success using biofeedback to treat panic attacks, depression, migraine headaches, chronic fatigue, and colitis.

Many victims and perpetrators of violence have been found to have increased delta activity which appears to impede emotional control by cancelling out the executive function of the brain (beta), the part that normally suppresses emotions. Biofeedback helps these people regain control of their emotions thereby decreasing violent behavior. Reductions in violence have been so pronounced that the

State of Kansas is instituting a biofeedback program in its prisons to reduce violence in convicts.

EEG biofeedback is being used successfully to treat depression,[4] epilepsy,[5] fatigue, insomnia, chronic pain, tension headaches, premenstrual syndrome, and an increasing variety of other problems. But biofeedback has benefits other than eliminating problems: therapists are finding that the training increases creativity and imagination.[6] A growing number of people are using the training to improve their minds and expand their creative capacity. Some people report having visions similar to those experienced in deep meditation or shamanic drumming.[7] Others are using biofeedback to achieve whole-brain synchrony, where the right and left hemispheres of the brain are balanced, producing extraordinary experiences of heightened states of consciousness, including feelings of ecstasy and oneness with the universe.

Biofeedback training generally requires thirty or more fifty-minute sessions for alcoholism, and twenty to sixty sessions for other applications. The diagnostic phase usually includes an interview and psychological tests to determine your problem areas and to establish a baseline for treatment, and may in some instances include the creation of a "brain map" using the biofeedback apparatus to chart your brainwave patterns.

Although this method is not a cure-all, it appears to have a great deal of potential and seems to make the recovery process for addiction, childhood trauma, and other conditions easier and faster. One psychologist said he believes this technique is still "experimental," but biofeedback has been around for about twenty years and there is a respectable body of research attesting to its positive results.[8]

If you have an addiction problem, or suffer from depression, chronic fatigue, post-traumatic stress disorder, attention deficit disorder, epilepsy, or any of the other conditions mentioned in this section, it is worth exploring brainwave biofeedback. You should feel some positive results after a couple of sessions; if not, try an-other therapist or therapy.

It is important to find a therapist with whom you feel comfortable and who does a thorough history and evaluation of your symptoms before commencing the treatment. The therapist must be more than a technician or scientist and have a comprehensive understanding of psychology and the effects of various brainwave patterns on behavior and emotions. In a few cases, you can have unpleasant experiences with biofeedback, although biofeedback therapists say adverse effects are reversible. For example, biofeedback can push people into a panic attack or too much alpha training can tip people with bipolar disorder into a manic episode. Brainwave training can also leave some people in a state of rage or fatigue. You need to find a therapist who can handle these situations, who checks your emotional condition before you leave the office, and who is available in an emergency to correct any problems.

I recently tried biofeedback because I wanted to see for myself if the wonderful things I had heard about this treatment could possibly be true. It does seem to be true. After two sessions of left-brain beta training at EEG Spectrum in Los Angeles, I felt noticeably more relaxed and all my daily activities seemed to be easier. However, three weeks later, after returning to my own state, I went to a therapist who recently started using biofeedback and had inadequate training. The technician was not familiar with the equipment and the session did not go well—the benefits disappeared. I returned for sessions in Los Angeles and regained the inner tranquility.

The Menninger Clinic, EEG Spectrum, and several other organizations have sponsored EEG biofeedback trainings for professionals throughout the country, so you should be able to find someone using biofeedback in most large metropolitan areas. You might even convince someone at your local hospital or treatment center to take the course and purchase the equipment. However, you probably want to select a therapist who has some experience as well as training in biofeedback. There are many therapists starting to get into this field so check your therapist's training carefully. Attending one workshop is not enough experience.

For more information and referrals in your area, contact the Life Sciences Institute of Mind-Body Health Inc., 2955 SW Wanamaker Drive, Suite B, Topeka, KS 66614, (913) 271-8686; EEG Spectrum, Los Angeles, California, (818) 788-2083; Carol Manchester, Ph.D., Freshwater Clinic, Inc., Columbus, Ohio, (614) 761-7610; or Austin Biofeedback Center, (512) 447-6998.

Breathing techniques for releasing emotions

One of the most effective ways to release repressed emotions is a simple breathing technique called by various names: "conscious connected breathing," "rebirthing," and "holotropic breath work." Whatever the name, this method generally produces dramatic, immediate and permanent healing effects.

I prefer the term "conscious connected breathing" because it describes the process. When we breathe normally, we tend to breathe automatically, pausing between breaths, and often we do not breathe deeply. In conscious connected breathing, breathing is conscious and one breath immediately follows another without a pause. The person breathes deeply through an open mouth, emphasizing the inhalation and relaxing during exhalation. This way of breathing brings more oxygen into the body which releases the suppressed emotions at a cellular level and brings them to conscious awareness. Continuing to breathe through the emotions that come to awareness allows them to be experienced, expressed and released.

Psychiatrists in World War II found that soldiers who suffered from post-traumatic stress disorder, including hysterical reactions such as paralysis and mutism, were cured through the release of intense emotions.[1] Conscious connected breathing releases the deepest, most intense layers of emotion from past experiences, often those most hidden from our conscious minds, and allows them to be expressed in a safe way. The wonderful news is that once released, those old, painful feelings really *disappear*, leaving you feeling noticeably lighter and happier because the stored emotional energy is gone.

Using conscious connected breathing, I was able to reach the deepest layers of repressed rage, hatred, hopelessness and grief about my abuse, feelings I did not suspect were even there after years of therapy. I knew I felt sad about what my parents had done to me as a child, but conscious connected breathing brought out a depth of grief that made me sob for hours—and left me feeling dramatically lighter and happier. Experiencing the murderous rage and hatred I felt as a child was terrifying, but the lightness and peace I felt afterwards were more than worth it. Now, even when anger is triggered in the present, the old intense rage is gone.

Although many people deny that they have such intense feelings of hatred and rage, I and other therapists have found that such feelings are present in almost everyone, because almost everyone has experienced some form of physical, sexual and/or emotional abuse as a child without having an outlet for the feelings it engendered.

The amount of emotion you expel at each breath work session is up to you because you control how much emotion you feel. If you want to stop evoking emotion, you simply stop the deep connected breathing, relax and breathe naturally. The more breath work sessions you do, the more you will be able to access deeper layers of intense suppressed emotion. Although you may sometimes feel that every last drop of emotion has been wrung out of you, there are usually deeper levels to uncover because we have all suffered a variety of profound psychological wounds.

The number of sessions you need depends on how ready and willing you are to experience intense feelings and to stay with them no matter how strong and unpleasant they are.

Although there is as yet no data on the optimal number of breathing sessions, most people seem to feel as though they are finished after ten to twenty sessions. You will know when you no longer need breath work by the lighter, freer feeling you will experience most of the time in your daily life. Another indication of your progress is whether you stop reacting with exaggerated fear, anxiety, and anger to certain stimuli. When you have cleared yourself of most of your repressed emotions, events that once triggered extreme reactions will no longer bother you. I now catch myself occasionally cursing inconsiderate drivers out of habit, but without the old feelings of rage and helplessness—and I laugh at myself.

Of course you have to continue to release new emotions as they come up in order to remain clear and not build up new stress in your body. The advantage of connected breathing is that once you have learned the technique, you can schedule a session whenever you need one, or work with a partner or by yourself.

The breath process is simple but most people will require the support of a facilitator, at least at first. The depth and intensity of feelings can be frightening and almost overwhelming without the support of someone who is familiar and comfortable with the process. I found I could go deeper and release more with the help of my support person, a massage therapist. After you are comfortable with the process and are able to keep yourself breathing deeply through intense emotions, you may very well be able to continue on your own. A sensitive facilitator will be able to help you reach that point and show you effective ways to move through the emotions that will come up both during and after breathing sessions.

I do not believe your support person needs to be a licensed psychotherapist, although a psychotherapist can help you understand your feelings and reframe hurtful decisions you made as a child. Most people recover enough of the memories or impressions of what happened to them during their emotional release to resolve the trauma and they do not need any further details. It is the emotional release that provides the healing. In fact, a deep emotional release can produce a dramatic alteration in posture, physical appearance, and health.

One of the extraordinary advantages of conscious connected breathing is its ability to reach emotions that were repressed in infancy and even in the womb. Deep breathing techniques were first used by therapists who recognized that trauma caused by the birth process affected people throughout their lives. They called their breathing therapy "rebirthing" and used it to release the repressed intense emotions and pain of being forced from the womb. Now we know the same techniques can be used for later childhood and adult trauma.

Children understand even at a preverbal stage much more than we used to believe. People using this breathing technique have been astonished to find themselves not wanting to be born because during delivery they heard the doctor say they were too big so they were afraid of hurting their mothers. Or they may have heard or felt that their parents did not want them.

The phenomenon of repressing emotions has been explained by the revolutionary research of quantum physicists who discovered that our bodies are not solid as they appear to be, but are composed of atoms and molecules spinning around, some traveling far beyond the visible limits of our anatomy. We are actually ninety percent space.

Quantum physicists also tell us that our emotions are made up of energy particles and that if our emotions are not released through expression, these particles can become trapped as energy in the spaces between the atoms and molecules. When we are under a great deal of stress, we stop breathing and breathe more shallowly, which traps the energy of our emotions in our bodies. Conscious connected breathing helps us release the imprisoned emotions by over-oxygenating our cells and forcing the trapped energy out.

Repressed emotions, these particles of trapped energy, are not simply mental but a physical reality, and healing requires that they be released. That is why it is necessary to deal with the pain of your past and why therapeutic techniques that do not address past traumas are largely ineffective.

Only hypnotherapy and conscious connected breathing seem to be able to reach back to our earliest emotional experiences. Breath work also avoids our western tendency to intellectualize and rationalize our feelings. With breath work, you cannot plan what will come out; whatever emotion is ready to be released will appear. Since the technique works regardless of intellectual capacity or language proficiency, it may be the most effective way to provide psychotherapy for the mentally disabled and disadvantaged. In our society, most people who have a disability have been subjected to enough cruel and humiliating experiences so that breath work could be valuable in releasing the anguish and anger they have repressed. More study is needed on the effectiveness of breath work for this group as well as for children.

In order to heal from any type of abuse or traumatic experience, you must get in touch with all of your repressed painful feelings, accept them and express them in safety. Right now there are not enough traditional psychotherapists in the world to help everyone who needs healing. Conscious connected breathing deserves exploration as a possible means of providing a rapid effective method of healing people at a deep and permanent level on a mass basis without a great deal of expense.

The use of breathing techniques in therapy is a fairly new phenomenon so it may take a bit of searching to find someone qualified to act as a facilitator. Since psychiatrist Stanislav Grof wrote his book, *The Holotropic Mind*, about the amazing effects of connected breathing which he calls Holotropic Breathwork® some psychotherapists are starting to learn the technique, although you do not need a psychotherapist for this work. However, the practitioner you choose should be thoroughly trained in breath work and have experience in using it personally and with clients.

Most important, you should make sure the facilitator has worked on her own problems and is clear of serious emotional problems and blocks that would interfere with your release of emotions. If your practitioner has not dealt with her own anger and hatred, she may not be able to support you through yours and may cut you off prematurely, thereby negating the purpose of the treatment. You should find someone who will encourage you to finish the process no matter how violent your emotions are or how long it takes. Although the usual individual session is $1^{1}/_{2}$ to 2 hours, I have had a couple of sessions that lasted three or four hours.

Being a breath work facilitator takes a special sensitivity, compassion and freedom from personal problems that would interfere with the process. There is no litmus paper test for these qualities; you have to rely on your instincts during your initial interview to determine if you feel you and the facilitator are comfortable working together with intense emotions. I suggest that you try one or two sessions with a couple of candidates before making your final choice so you can experience the process and have a chance to assess firsthand with whom and under what conditions you feel safest and able to release the most emotion. Unlike traditional psychotherapy, a long-term relationship with the same facilitator is not essential. References from friends are extremely helpful in choosing a breath work facilitator.

Psychotherapists have begun to recognize the value of breath work and are starting to refer clients to facilitators. Most large cities now have wellness centers as do some hospitals which can give you the names of facilitators. Breath work therapists frequently advertise in local new age and health magazines and in newspapers or brochures published by health food stores or healing centers. Women's and self-help bookstores can often be helpful in locating breath work practitioners and may also have heard reports from people who engaged them.

Breath work can be done individually or in groups where you work with a partner under the guidance of a facilitator. Whether you choose to work alone and pay a higher fee or learn the process in a group is purely a matter of personal preference. One advantage of groups is that they are often held on weekends for several hours or even a day, so you have time to finish releasing whatever emotions you access that day. A disadvantage is that the facilitator may not be immediately available for another session if you need follow-up help. Sometimes the breath process can release emotions that continue to emerge for a few days following the session and you may want to have someone available for consultation. Before you participate in a group, you may want to ask the facilitator if he will be available for emergencies and further work.

Some facilitators and therapists use evocative music and other sounds during breath work. I went to a facilitator whose husband had recorded segments of classical, African, and other music which not only intensified my feelings, but affected all seven chakras. I found the combination of breath work and music extraordinary and had a powerful spiritual experience. According to Dr. Grof and other therapists, some people experience non-ordinary states of consciousness, including those similar to cosmic consciousness, during breath work. Many people are now using the technique for mind expansion, in addition to clearing repressed memories.

Connected breathing is one of the newest healing techniques and may prove to be the most effective discovered so far. It is certainly worth trying by itself or in conjunction with traditional psychotherapy.

Eye movement desensitization and reprocessing

A new technique, eye movement desensitization and reprocessing ("EMDR"), uses eye movements similar to those accompanying dreams to overcome the effects of trauma and post-traumatic stress disorder. I heard enough positive comments from my colleagues about the process to try it for myself and found it to be surprisingly effective.

A psychologist at the Mental Research Institute in Palo Alto, Dr. Francine Shapiro, first observed the eye movement phenomenon when she was walking in a park thinking of disturbing events. She noticed that while her eyes were moving repetitively, her distressing thoughts seemed to lose their intensity and disappear. She decided to test her eye movement observation on persons suffering from post-traumatic stress disorder as a result of combat in Vietnam, rape, and childhood molestation and discovered that the process was helpful in eliciting repressed memories and that symptoms of post-traumatic stress disorder decreased significantly.[1]

Dr. Shapiro's studies indicate that when EMDR is used with victims of incest, all other similar episodes of molestation by the same perpetrator are reprocessed and lose their power to induce anxiety. After two sessions, an eight-year-old boy's nightmares and fears about the 1989 Northern California earthquake subsided. A woman who was the adult child of an alcoholic was successfully treated for anxiety over a period of four months and was desensitized for memories of abuse by her mother and sexual molestation by a neighbor. And two children who were only able to remember the horrible death of a parent, were able to recall pleasurable memories of the parent after treatment.[2]

No one knows how the EMDR process works in the brain, but the eye movements are similar to those during rapid eye movement (REM) sleep, where the eyes move quickly back and forth during the dream state. According to Dr. Shapiro, this eye movement, during sleep and in the waking state, seems somehow to allow unconscious material to surface so it can be desensitized and integrated.[3] The brain is thereby able to finish processing traumatic experiences and to diminish the fear and anxiety surrounding them.

EMDR involves having the subject visualize a traumatic situation and describe its sensory effects (visual, auditory, kinesthetic, olfactory), while repeating negative statements associated with the scene. The therapist takes pretest measures of the subject's level of emotional distress as well as measurements of the "gut-level" believability of a positive statement the subject would like to substitute for the negative ones. The subject is then asked to follow with his eyes the therapist's finger as it rapidly moves back and forth about a foot away from the subject's face. Some therapists use a plastic pointer to increase the speed of the eye movement. The EMDR procedure often elicits strong emotional responses and may expose repressed memories.

When the movements are completed and the emotions released, the subject is asked to blank the scene out of his mind and to take a deep breath. The subject is then asked to visualize the scene again and measurements of his reactions are repeated. The process is repeated until the subject no longer has a strong emotional reaction to the traumatic event.[4]

Some therapists use a modified version of the technique which includes instructions to the subject to "blink out" the negative statements and feelings as forcefully as possibly while following the therapist's finger or pointer with his eyes. After emotions are released and a sufficient level of desensitization is achieved, the therapist asks the subject to focus on "blinking in" positive statements which are substituted for the negative ones.

I tried the latter procedure and although I was initially skeptical, the experience was powerful. While my mind was saying, "How ridiculous, there is no difference between blinking in and blinking out," my eyes experienced a significant difference in the two types of blinking. I felt as though I were pushing out negative emotions and thoughts, sometimes with tears, during the first stage of the process, and pulling in the positive statements during the second stage. The tests indicated that a clear change had taken place in my attitude. More persuasive for me was the fact that I felt much better in my mind and in my body at the end of the process.

I had chosen to work on a persistent feeling of hopelessness, of not being able to make my life go right no matter how hard I tried. The process brought out emotions as well as some statements my father had made while abusing me that he was going to damage me for the rest of my life, information that I had not recovered through other techniques. My therapist, Dr. Hugh Allred, a university professor and friend, was astute enough to realize that I probably also believed I had no future and reprocessed me to believe I had one. Having a positive future was an entirely new and wonderful thought for me, one I was only too willing to substitute for my long-time view that nothing good would ever happen to me.

Although my experience with EMDR was positive at the time, I am not certain that the results were lasting. My session did not effect a permanent change in my attitude about the future; I have had to do more work around that issue. It may be that I addressed only part of a cluster of issues in my single EMDR session, and that others could have been addressed in additional sessions. While Dr. Shapiro's accounts of her results are certainly glowing, later independent studies although generally favorable did not have the same success rates. Some spectacular successes were documented and most of the test subjects improved, but a few grew worse, some experienced a recurrence of symptoms, and others dropped out of the program because the process did not work for them.[5]

One of the benefits of EMDR is that some people who go through the process can duplicate it by themselves and use it successfully at home. The process can be self-taught and a recent study indicates that it can be effective in a variety of situations, such as eliminating phobic reactions and reducing strong emotional reactions during marital quarrels.[6]

EMDR appears to be a significant breakthrough in dealing with trauma, but by itself is not a miracle cure. My therapist uses EMDR as an adjunct to other types of therapy and I agree this process is best used with other methods. My personal experience is that breath work is more effective in releasing intense stored emotions. On the whole, however, since the procedure is noninvasive and cuts to the heart of traumatic events, I believe EMDR is worth trying. Be sure that your therapist is adequately trained in psychotherapy as well as the eye movement technique because the process can evoke strong emotions and you will need someone who has the experience to deal with them and to help you uncover and change negative thoughts.

Spiritual and Transpersonal Therapies

No discussion of the revolution in psychotherapy would be complete without mentioning the growing number of theories and programs which emphasize the spiritual nature of human beings. These new theories are based on the assumption that have three components—physical, mental or psychological, and spiritual—and that we need to address and heal all three in order to be in balance and whole. Transpersonal therapy may focus exclusively on spiritual issues or combine spiritual and psychological techniques.

Carl Jung was the first Western psychiatrist to introduce a spiritual component into modern psychology. His research and experience with patients led him to believe that we have not only an unconscious part of our mind, but also a part which he called the collective unconscious which connects us all and reflects the history of the human species and the cosmic order. According to Jung, this collective unconscious contains archetypes—inherited ideas or images we all share—derived from the experience of our species, regardless of our nationality or religious beliefs. Thus our minds go beyond the merely personal to something larger and perhaps mystical.

Jung charted the way for an expanded examination of the mystical or spiritual in psychotherapy, an area that therapists up to that time had avoided because it was viewed as unscientific. Given that more than seventy percent of Americans admit to a belief in God or a higher power (or are terrified by the thought of an evil being or devil) and that the same number report having some sort of mystical experience, it only makes sense that psychotherapy should address these issues. The psychotherapeutic profession has finally acknowledged that spirituality is a legitimate area of inquiry for therapists, and transpersonal therapy is now included in university curricula.

Spiritual concerns need to be addressed in therapy because we all have a spiritual aspect, or at least spiritual beliefs. Even a belief that there is no God is still a spiritual belief. Spiritual issues inevitably arise in therapy.

The basis for almost all dysfunction is low self-esteem and most people believe they are bad, evil, and unlovable because they were hurt, neglected, or invalidated in some way. Children usually draw erroneous conclusions about traumatic events which affect their view of themselves and their world for the rest of their lives. If their parents do not love them, children conclude that they are unlovable. The possibility that their parents have problems and may be incapable of showing love does not occur to them. If a parent is angry, the child assumes the anger is caused by something he has done. Young children cannot conceive of the possibility that something outside of them may have caused the anger, or that parents are responsible for their own feelings and responses.

A common example of a damaging childhood conception is the conclusion reached by abused children that they are somehow responsible for their abuse. Young children are at a developmental stage when they are egocentric; they believe that they are the center of the universe and that they cause everything that happens to them. They also quickly learn that they are punished when they are "bad," and since abuse seems like a punishment, they draw the "obvious" conclusion that they must be really bad.

Most children go one step further: they hear that God protects "good little children" and so conclude that if they are being abused, they must be so bad that even God does not love them and is punishing them.

What is worse, children base their view of God on the authority figure in their family who may also be their abuser. They extrapolate from how their parents treat them to their idea of the universe and a higher power. If their authority figure is abusing them, God becomes an abuser. Such beliefs destroy self-esteem and inculcate a frightening view of an unsafe and punitive universe which ruins their lives, until they become aware of their decisions and change them.

Obviously such beliefs must be reexamined. Some therapists may fail to explore their clients' irrational beliefs about God and the universe because they are reluctant to impose their own beliefs on clients or get into the seeming quagmire of religion and spirituality. But victims of abuse cannot be healed unless their erroneous beliefs about God are corrected. Therapists would not hesitate to challenge a client's belief that there was a monster under the bed, so why would they hesitate to confront a belief that there is a monster in the sky?

I believe the most effective therapists are holistic and willing to deal with any issue that affects the client's mental health. Almost all of my clients who have suffered sexual abuse have had at least one mystical experience, usually an out-of-body episode or an encounter with a white light, and want to be able to share their experience with the therapist. These experiences bring victims hope and courage in times of dire need. A positive reaction from the therapist can reinforce the benefits of the experience, while a negative or skeptical one can further destroy the victim's self-esteem as well as trust in the therapist.

The best therapists are open to an exploration of spiritual concerns and have a positive view of the universe and any higher power. Clients have the right to know what religion their therapist practices and if the therapist is open to discussions of spiritual matters. Although you probably cannot have a deep discussion about religion and spirituality in your initial interview with a therapist, if this topic is important to you, you certainly can ask whether or not the therapist addresses spiritual issues and explore his general feelings about the subject.

If you have worked through your major psychological issues and want to explore spiritual ones, you may want to consider transpersonal psychotherapy. Transpersonal psychotherapy has many definitions. *The Journal of Transpersonal Psychology* lists most of the areas covered: "Meta-needs, transpersonal process, values and states, unitive consciousness, peak experiences, ecstasy, mystical experience, being, essence, bliss, awe, wonder, transcendence of self, spirit, sacralization of everyday life, oneness, cosmic awareness, cosmic play, individual and species-wide synergy, the theories and practices of meditation, spiritual paths, compassion, transpersonal cooperation, transpersonal realization and actualization; and related concepts, experiences and activities."

I prefer the definition of psychologists James Fadiman and Kathleen Speeth in *Psychology Handbook*[1] which states the ideal: "Transpersonal psychotherapy includes the full range of behavioral, emotional and intellectual disorders as in traditional psychotherapies, as well as uncovering and supporting strivings for full self-actualization. The end state of psychotherapy is not seen as successful adjustment to the prevailing culture but rather the daily experience of that state called liberation, enlightenment, individuation, certainty or gnosis according to various traditions." Using this definition, transpersonal therapy covers all of the essential elements of successful therapy.

One word of warning: Although a small number of people seem to be able to use religion and spiritual beliefs to leap over all of their psychological problems to a complete healing, most need to clear their psychological issues and behavior patterns in order to heal. No one can tell if you have the ability to heal through spiritual means alone, just as no one knows why some people are miraculously cured at Lourdes in France, while others with the same ailments are not. However, the successes of religious and spiritual methods warrant serious consideration especially when used with more traditional psychotherapy.

The reputable schools of transpersonal and spiritual healing recognize that most people cannot skip over their psychological problems by focusing solely on spiritual issues. Acknowledged spiritual leaders such as Stephen Levine, Joan Borysenko, Dan Millman, and Ram Dass, and the best-selling *The Celestine Prophecy*, teach that you must face your shadow side—your childhood trauma, hidden fears, and anger—in order to reach the spiritual level. Enlightenment means living with awareness in the present physical reality—and awareness means *self-awareness* first of all. You cannot be clear or unconditionally loving without facing your painful, savage, hateful feelings—your inner demons.

While I believe there is undeniable value in transpersonal therapy and use its principles and techniques in my own practice, I strongly believe that you need to be healthy mentally (spiritualists sometimes say "grounded") before you delve too far into the spiritual realm. In cases of severe abuse, spiritual methods alone may be confusing, especially when a victim is just beginning to face abuse issues, and may not provide the support necessary if problems arise. If you have not dealt with repressed trauma and your angry feelings, there is a real danger of overidentification with spiritual concepts and mysticism, or scaring yourself with illusory demons and delusions which can lead to psychosis.

People can develop a delusion based on the story of Jesus Christ where they begin to believe they have the same power as Jesus and have to save the world. They may also have an irrational fear that they will be crucified. Other people may take too literally one of the new age spiritual concepts that we create our reality, which may cause them to think they are somehow mystically responsible for everything that happens in the world. Of course we are responsible for our *perceptions* and our beliefs and reactions to what is around us, but there are many people on this earth and no one person is creating everything that happens.

Another of the tenets common to some transpersonal therapy is based on the Eastern idea that suffering is caused by attachment—the desire for worldly things—and that in order to be free of suffering, we must break free of all attachments and of our ego. This can be very confusing for people because it can be misinterpreted to mean that we must not want or love anything. People can also become psychotic trying to free themselves from their egos. As spiritual leaders acknowledge, you must first have a strong healthy ego before you can transcend it. Thus, transpersonal therapy may be a better choice *after* you have completed psychotherapy and are clear of your most serious childhood traumas.

An enormous number of traditional religions and spiritual options exist and many even have programs specifically designed for survivors of sexual abuse. Many religions now provide counseling for abuse survivors and others make funds available for therapy. Even if you choose to go to a therapist not connected to your church, it is still comforting to know that your church supports you, rather than condemns you as you may fear. And survivors who truly believe that their God loves them and regards them as good heal faster than those who have no such belief.

One program I found to be particularly effective is that of Stephen and Ondrea Levine. The Levines have skillfully combined spiritual philosophy and traditional psychological precepts into various meditations to deal with abuse issues. These meditations include a type of mindfulness meditation for reaching repressed memories which is similar in some ways to self-hypnosis but appears to be more gentle, although it takes longer to reach the buried trauma. Other meditations are for loving-kindness, forgiveness and a powerful "Opening the Heart of the Womb Meditation" included in *Reach for the Rainbow: Advanced Healing for Survivors of Sexual Abuse*. These meditations can be found in Levine's book, *Guided Meditations: Explorations and Healings*.

Many useful spiritual programs exist, from Zen meditation groups to Indian drumming ceremonies, and you will be attracted to those that are helpful to you. However, it is difficult to find therapists who are skilled at handling both the psychological and spiritual aspects of therapy, and delving into the spiritual realm can be dangerous if both you and your therapist are not well grounded.

Too many so-called transpersonal psychotherapists and self-appointed "healers" and "ministers" have little or no counseling skills, have not worked out their own problems, and foster unhealthy ideas of spirituality, using the concepts to control rather than heal; they can do a great deal of damage. You need to be especially careful in checking references and investigating a therapist's qualifications and beliefs when exploring spirituality.

WARNING: You should avoid anything that has any of the trappings of a cult. People who have been victimized often have a tendency to become victims again, allowing others to run their lives and control them. If anyone starts telling you how to think and how to live, or pressures you to spend all your time with them, sign up for additional more expensive courses, or give them lots of money, *run*. You may have been a victim once, but you don't have to become a victim again.

I believe we are physical, mental and spiritual beings. I pooh-poohed the spiritual part for many years—until I learned how potent it could be. Now I know we can heal through any or all of these aspects. Explore spiritual healing when you are comfortable with the idea. It's a part of us that's too wonderful to overlook.

Prayer

Although this is not a religious book, I would be doing you a disservice if I did not include prayer among the techniques for healing both mind and body. Prayer has worked throughout human history and it may be the single most powerful technique for changing your life.

Recently university and medical school studies have demonstrated that prayer *does* in fact work, although we still do not know exactly how.

One of the most fascinating books I have read is *Recovering the Soul* by Larry Dossey, M.D., in which he collects research documenting the effects of prayer and the existence of our souls. Researchers recently studied the effect of prayer on cardiac patients in a San Francisco hospital. The patients, doctors and hospital staff were unaware of the study—only the hospital administrator participated. The researchers obtained lists of patients admitted to the hospital for cardiac problems and divided the lists randomly in half. One half of the patients were prayed for by groups of people out of state and the other half was not prayed for. The results were astounding. There were no deaths in the group that was prayed for, and that group had fewer complications and needed less medication than the other group. This study and others indicate that prayer has a measurable positive effect.

Being a pragmatist, I use prayer because it has worked for me. I have never had a prayer for guidance or help with my psychological problems go unanswered. And because prayer works, I have come to have faith in God, in people, and in the universe. Prayer has been a positive influence on my life and I believe has made me a better person. It has certainly helped me face the painful and difficult issues of my abuse. But most important, praying has made me understand that I am not alone, that I am connected to everything, and that somewhere there is a loving power that cares about me.

It often helps to simply surrender, to turn unbearable pain and uncontrollable emotions over to a higher power. I believe the strongest part of the Alcoholics Anonymous program and its offshoots is the concept of surrendering to a higher power. Sometimes just letting go, giving up our desperate struggle to control, can be the answer.

You may wonder why, if I believe prayer is so effective, I bother with psychotherapy. The answer is that I do not believe God will do it all for us. We were given free will and have to learn to make a good life for ourselves. There is an old Arab saying: "Trust in God, but tie up your camel." God may guide us, but S/He can't live our lives for us. I believe God works through each of us and that we are well-advised to take advantage of the talents and skills we have to offer each other. Perhaps that is what we are here for.

Past-life regression

Past-life regression has become popular as a result of Shirley MacLaine's books and movies such as *On a Clear Day You Can See Forever*. Regression is the process of uncovering repressed memories while under hypnosis and is traditionally used to help people release childhood trauma. However, therapists have occasionally found that clients under hypnosis will appear to relive and describe events that seem to have taken place in another life far in the past. This phenomenon is known as "past-life regression."

Hinduism and Buddhism are based on a belief in reincarnation which assumes that we have a soul which is reborn in human form during many lifetimes. More than half of the world's population accept this belief. An essential part of this belief is a concept called "karma," the cosmic operation of retributive balance by which a person's deeds in one life determine his status and condition in future lives.

According to these religions, people can free themselves from the effects of karma in a number of ways: by becoming aware of past mistakes and changing their behavior, by accepting present tribulations with grace, or by becoming enlightened, thereby transcending the law of karma entirely and enabling them to reincarnate or not at will. Eastern and Western Christian religions agree that anyone can be forgiven for any acts, no matter how serious or numerous, simply by recognizing the error and resolving not to do it again.

The use of past-life regression in therapy is intended to bring to consciousness traumatic events or mistakes in past lives which are believed to be causing problems in this life. There is no concrete evidence that past-life memories are "real," although some people have found historical documentation that the people and events they described under hypnosis actually existed. A fascinating account of a psychiatrist's research into past lives is *Coming Back—A Psychiatrist Explores Past-Life Journeys* by Raymond A. Moody, Jr., M.D.

I am open to the possibility that we may have had other lives or that they are, as one of my therapists suggested, genetic memories from the collective unconscious. If they happen to arise in therapy, such experiences should be used in a positive way to resolve feelings and behaviors that may be impeding the client's ability to be happy.

However, whether or not we have all lived previous lives, I do not believe past-life regression is necessary to therapy. We all have more than enough material in our present lives to work on in therapy. It is easy to avoid dealing with painful present issues by concentrating on past lives.

Even if you accept beliefs about reincarnation and karma, part of that belief system is that you can erase the effects of karma simply by resolving problems in your present life. Delving into past lives is therefore unnecessary and may be traumatic and confuse you about your present reality. I recommend working on present issues in therapy first and waiting until you are mentally strong and grounded before you explore past lives.

You can resolve traumatic past-life experiences simply by understanding why you acted as you did and recognizing that you would not act today as you did before. If you have compassion for yourself and others who commit hurtful acts, then I believe you are free of past karma. You can reach this stage without having specific knowledge of past lives. According to the concept of karma, most of us have been murderers, rapists, thieves, and worse. If you have understanding and compassion for people who commit those acts and realize that you would not commit those acts today, I believe that you will be freed from whatever karmic forces you may have created from such acts. You are not the same person you were in the past. You have a new life with new choices available every second.

One arguably positive aspect of past-life regression is that if memories of childhood trauma in this life are too painful to face, people may be able to address them indirectly by dealing with the same pain or a similar situation through images of a past life. However, I prefer to cut to the heart of the problem and deal with the here and now.

If you are tempted to try past-life regression, I strongly urge you to do so with a competent psychotherapist, rather than a spiritualist, hypnotist, or someone untrained in psychotherapy. If you encounter a painful experience, whether from this life or a past one, you will want a competent guide to help you through the pain safely, someone who has the skills to assist you in resolving the trauma so it no longer affects your life.

Neurolinguistic programming (NLP)

Neurolinguistic programming ("NLP") focuses on excellence and how to replicate it, rather than on curing dysfunction. Using a variety of visualization techniques, NLP methods provide new ways of learning and perceiving problems which help people discover new options and develop new skills.

NLP is described as a system of short-term therapy that produces behavioral changes by creating perceptual shifts, including reframing, through the use of physical movement and linguistics activity. Clients are interviewed to determine what aspect of their lives they want to change, and therapy focuses on changing that specific behavior.

It is difficult not to reject NLP simply on the basis of the exaggerated claims of its proponents, such as the assertion in an NLP brochure that "NLP has decoded the way the brain works and how thinking fits consistent, detectable patterns." The fact is that scientists have been able to discover only a very small fraction of the way our minds work, and new patterns of thinking and processing information are being discovered almost daily.

NLP's tendency toward grandiose advertising is evident in its claims to "cure phobias in less than an hour" and "resolve grief in a single session." The "Fast Phobia Method" involves watching yourself on a mental movie screen going through the experience you want to neutralize. The theory is that by mentally picturing yourself on the screen in various ways—rapid reverse, still pictures, etc.—you neutralize your fears and become more comfortable with the situation. This technique is similar to the desensitization process of behavior therapy and has the same weakness: while it may change a person's reaction to the phobic stimulus, it does not affect the underlying cause of the phobia or eliminate the repressed fear and anxiety which remain stored in mind and body, primed to manifest themselves in other ways.

A slightly expanded version of the "Fast Phobia Method" is supposed to "rapidly reprocess multiple experiences of abuse and trauma." After using the Fast Phobia Process for three unpleasant past experiences, you ask your unconscious mind to sort out your past pleasant and unpleasant experiences. Then you "recode" the unpleasant experiences by mentally seeing them smaller and dimmer in your mind and by visualizing those experiences running backwards like a movie, so you purportedly "disconnect" from them. The next step is to "reconnect" with your pleasant experiences by making them larger, brighter and more colorful in your mind, and then seeing all six of your experiences pass before you while you emphasize the pleasant ones. You then are told to bring this way of thinking about pleasant and unpleasant events into your present and future. This simplistic technique is supposed to resolve your abuse problems.

If I sound angry, I am. Neurobiological and psychological studies show that not only is it impossible to program out suppressed emotions without releasing them, but that a great deal of damage can be caused by artificially trying to change reality in a person's mind. Some therapists have tried to reprogram incest victims with the idea that they had a happy childhood or that the abuse did not occur. But our minds know the truth and attempts to reprogram facts which are obviously inaccurate cause inner conflict and turmoil, especially when we may be already confused by the lies we were told by our abusers.

Although therapists successfully use mental imagery to help clients accept the possibility that *as adults* they now have the power to push their abusers away or run out of the house, attempting to reprogram childhood trauma with lies is a damaging technique. In order to heal, people have to accept and deal with the reality of their abuse; they cannot simply cover up the reality with memories of pleasant experiences.

I have little patience with some of NLP's outrageous claims because I have seen the damage they have inflicted on dozens of abuse survivors. Some are therapists. These people grabbed NLP techniques like a magic talisman, believing they could quickly and easily wipe out intense anguish and years of abuse and dysfunction, only to become disillusioned when they found their inner pain did not disappear and their destructive behavioral patterns continued to ruin their lives. Some NLP trainers prey on people's natural desire to avoid painful issues, leading them to believe that by using the highly intellectual techniques espoused by NLP, they can magically solve their problems without ever having to face unpleasant memories and emotions. Too many people are using NLP as an excuse for avoiding emotional pain.

The founders of NLP are Richard Bandler and John Grinder. Bandler is a computer expert and Grinder a linguist. They became interested in what made people successful and attempted to find out what patterns of thought and learning successful people used so that those patterns could be taught to others.

I have never seen anyone write in a book admonitions similar to those of Bandler and Grinder on the pretext of ensuring quality control: "...we also urge you to attend only those seminars, workshops, and training programs that have been officially designed and certified by Richard Bandler and John Grinder.... Writing both the following addresses is the only way to ensure both Richard Bandler and John Grinder's full endorsement of the quality of services and/or training represented as NLP." What incredible ego not only to assert that you are the only one qualified to teach certain methods but to impugn the competence of people who have paid for your training!

Significantly, most NLP trainers are simply that—trainers. They charge exorbitant prices for workshops and can be mesmerizing performers with a great deal of charisma. But most do not have degrees or training in psychology or counseling and are not licensed to practice psychotherapy. Their real skill is showmanship and the ability to convince you to sign up for more expensive workshops.

The basic flaw in the NLP approach is that humans have an emotional component and are far more complex than computers; we cannot simply be "reprogrammed." Neurobiological research has shown that our brains function differently when recording trauma than when processing other information. Ordinary events are processed in a part of the brain which analyzes them and puts them in perspective so that emotions do not become overwhelming. However, traumatic events may bypass the processing part of the brain and be rerouted to a different area where they are recorded unconsciously exactly as they occur with all of the overwhelming emotions. These memories and emotions must be released and processed consciously so that the stored emotions are not constantly triggered by later events. A basic understanding of the way our brains actually work and how emotions are stored reveals the obvious fallacy in assuming that trauma can be "reprogrammed."

NLP can help you communicate more effectively, remember people's names, and teach you some of the behaviors of successful people, but, as I have seen firsthand with some of my closest friends, including therapists who tried NLP, and with my own experiments, NLP alone cannot eradicate suppressed painful emotions and thus will not bring about inner peace or intimacy.

The NLP approach tends to attract both therapists and clients who do not want to deal with their emotions. If you have suffered childhood trauma or significant emotional distress, NLP alone will merely put an elaborate but temporary band-aid on your wounds. The repressed trauma will remain and your stored emotions will continue to cause you pain.

Another well-publicized criticism of NLP is that some of its techniques tend to be manipulative. For example, a technique called "mirroring" involves getting people to be receptive to you and your ideas by deliberately copying their gestures, body positions, tone of voice, and rate of speech as you interact with them. The assumption is that most people are so wrapped up in themselves that they will not notice the fact that you are mimicking their actions and will unconsciously feel more in tune with you because the actions you reflect are familiar to them and therefore unconsciously reassuring.

I have had long debates with NLP proponents who claim mirroring is not manipulation because both people end up getting what they want. I am not convinced because I think an artificial effort to get what you want by copying people's movements is very different from listening to them and understanding their perceptions and needs. To me, mirroring is simply another highly intellectualized way of avoiding authentic personal interaction which takes into consideration people's feelings. How would you feel if you realized someone had been copying your facial expressions, gestures and movements to get what they wanted?

The most helpful NLP techniques are those that help people improve performance and learning abilities. For example, "anchoring" is a method of reinforcing mental images of peak performances. An illustration of a physical anchor is squeezing your ski pole as you imagine yourself skiing your four best turns. The visualization process is repeated using the three primary methods of learning—visual, auditory and kinesthetic—each coupled with squeezing the ski pole. Later, when you squeeze your pole on the ski slopes, your mind and body are supposed to "remember" the way you made those four beautiful turns and help you maintain that position as you sail down the mountain. Similar techniques are used for remembering names, overcoming shyness, and other behavioral changes.

A few of the leaders in the NLP field, notably Leslie Cameron-Bandler, have recognized NLP's deficiencies in dealing with emotions, especially repressed emotions, and are working to develop methods to release and resolve emotions which can be used with existing NLP techniques and knowledge. It is encouraging to see how many different types of healers are beginning to concentrate on the emotional component, having found that cognitive or even spiritual approaches cannot leap over this crucial element of our psychological makeup. Psychotherapeutic theories seem to be converging as therapists and researchers are finding that all of the approaches have something valuable to offer and that no one theory alone is sufficient for complete healing in most cases.

While I believe some NLP techniques can be helpful if used in conjunction with techniques and theories that address our emotional component, I do not recommend using NLP as the only form of therapy unless you want to focus on a discrete goal like remembering people's names or learning a particular skill. If you are dealing with childhood trauma, NLP has not yet incorporated all of the necessary elements to resolve your problems.

Art and music therapy

Art and music have been used as forms of healing for centuries and their therapeutic value is increasingly recognized today. One of the world's oldest medical documents, the *Ebers Papyrus* (circa 1500 B.C.) prescribed chanting to heal the sick. Modern doctors and therapists find music beneficial for reducing stress, relieving headaches, inducing sleep, acting as an anesthetic during surgery and dental work, improving immunity, and helping Alzheimer's patients to communicate and heart patients to relax.

Some therapists specialize in using art and music as their primary techniques and call themselves art or music therapists. Others use art and music to supplement their work.

Psychotherapists may use art and music as diagnostic tools and to help clients get in touch with their feelings. For those of us who tend to be analytical, art and music provide an opportunity to try new forms of self-expression which may reveal unknown aspects of ourselves. Most of us learned early in life to suppress our emotions, and we may not be conscious of what we are feeling or able to describe our emotions. Drawing a picture about a situation or feeling can give us a concrete way to depict what we feel. People are frequently surprised at what they draw because their pictures vividly convey images, colors, and symbols of sadness, confusion, fear, and anger.

Since music and art are right-brained activities, they stimulate responses which are emotional, intuitive and creative. Scientists have found that most traumatic memories are stored on the right side of the brain, a finding which is consistent with clinical therapeutic experience that music and art can help people access subconscious feelings, thoughts and memories.

People, especially children, draw very clearly what they are thinking and feeling without being consciously aware of what they are doing. For example, if a child is asked to draw his family and he portrays his father as a huge figure towering over the family and colored red, the drawing would probably indicate that the child perceives his father as being threatening and angry. With this knowledge the therapist can begin to explore ways to improve the child's relationship with his father.

When I asked a group of adults who were molested as children to draw how they felt when they were being abused, one woman drew herself in black crayon as a tiny figure, huddled in a box in a corner of the paper. Her picture described better than words ever could the loneliness, fear, depression and helplessness she felt. The act of drawing and then talking about the feelings behind her images enabled this woman to cry and release some of the pain she had repressed.

Renowned psychiatrist Carl Jung analyzed his patients' drawings and discovered universal symbols and archetypes which helped him interpret feelings and past experiences. He found that one of the most commonly used images was a tree symbolizing the artist's view of his life. The shape, size, foliage, root structure, markings on the trunk, and life forms in the tree all have meanings that reveal how the artist subconsciously views his present life and incidents in his past.

When I enrolled in a graduate seminar in Jungian drawing interpretation, I was pretty skeptical; I thought people could probably read whatever they wanted into any drawing and I didn't understand how different people could express the same feelings when they drew a certain object. One of the assigned exercises was to draw a tree—no other instructions were given. The tree I drew was too tall for the paper and the top was cut off. The professor, a psychiatrist, said that meant I felt out of control. He could not possibly have known that I was still in therapy for my childhood abuse and felt very much out of control.

But more astonishing was the fact that even after I *knew* what a tree with a missing top meant, I could not draw a whole tree. The professor told us that sometimes drawing the picture differently could change our feelings and even behavior. I wanted to feel more in control, so when I went home I tried over and over to draw a complete tree—and each time, the top was off the page. I got angry and drove to the store where I bought an enormous sheet of poster paper. But when I drew my tree again, the top was still missing.

It never occurred to me at the time that I always started drawing the tree from the bottom so I could not control its height. My unconscious feelings were so strong that I could not change the way I drew my tree until my feelings changed. Now I can easily draw complete trees on a page, even if I start at the bottom.

I learned that knotholes or markings on the tree trunk universally indicate some kind of trauma, usually childhood abuse or the death of a loved one. What is more remarkable is that the height of the knothole or marking usually indicates the age of the abuse. The age of the trauma is calculated by dividing the total height of the tree into equal sections, one for each year of the artist's present age, and then counting the sections from the bottom of the tree to the knothole.

My old childhood drawings had large knotholes which accurately indicated not only the age my sexual abuse started but covered the four years of its duration. One of my clients placed a knothole on the trunk in proportion to the age six and unconsciously drew the knothole itself as a clear number "6." At the time, she was not consciously aware of the age of her abuse. Subsequently, her mother confirmed that my client's behavior dramatically changed at age six, and my client later recovered more detailed memories which further established abuse at that age.

Yale Medical School surgeon Bernie Siegal, M.D., describes in his book *Love, Medicine and Miracles* how he uses his patients' drawings to determine how they feel about their disease and potential treatments. He has found a direct connection between what his patients draw and the outcome of their treatments. For example, if a patient depicts chemotherapy as yellow light flowing to his body, chemotherapy will probably be successful. On the other hand, if a patient uses black to draw chemotherapy and portrays himself as a skeleton, the outcome will probably not be good.

The fact that we can draw pictures of unconscious feelings and experiences is no longer a mystery. Research has shown that drawing is a right-brained activity which enables us to access our subconscious where all of our experiences are stored. Art therapy is effective because our minds contain knowledge about all of our experiences, conscious and unconscious; the physical act of drawing simply gives us permission to make some of the unconscious knowledge conscious by projecting our feelings and experiences onto what we draw.

It is important for the therapist to let *you* interpret your own drawings first, because your interpretation is the most meaningful since the drawings come from your own mind. I find it useful to ask my clients to pretend their pictures were drawn by a friend. I have them play the role of therapist and tell me what they think their "friend's" picture means. This technique overcomes defenses and enables the client to interpret colors and images more freely with fewer inhibitions.

Frequently clients will say that an obviously angry red and black picture conveys a "happy" feeling. When I ask, "If your friend drew that picture, would you say she was happy?" they usually acknowledge that the picture is not really a happy one. Often I find that clients who initially interpret their pictures as happy are people pleasers who have learned to cover up their true feelings. Becoming aware of this tendency gives clients an opportunity to learn to express their true feelings and acknowledge their own needs.

Drawing can also help change feelings and behavior. When you are aware of how you feel and what you think about yourself, you then have the ability to change. If you can draw a picture differently from what you drew before, you can begin to see yourself and your circumstances differently. If you cannot imagine a goal, you cannot attain it. By drawing something the way you would like it to be, you can visualize it so that your mind can start to create the conditions that can make it a reality. The principle is similar to affirmations, where if you say something to yourself as though it is true such as "I am confident" or "I am lovable," you will begin to believe it. Drawing a belief is an even more powerful way of making your desired belief a reality because drawing combines thought and movement which create new neural patterns in your brain.

Music can also help people become aware of their feelings. Children with behavioral problems are especially difficult to help because they don't understand their feelings or have the ability to describe them with words. Music therapy can open up communication with these children by letting them express their feelings through choosing a piece of music or making the music up. If a child is asked to write a song, she may reveal feelings that she cannot express verbally.

Learning to play an instrument can give a child confidence, and a good therapist will make sure the child can play a tune by the end of the session. Older people can also benefit from learning to play musical instruments, since the ability to play appears to stay the same whether you are forty or ninety. Learning to play increases older people's interest in life because music lessons increase in complexity and people continue to progress.

Music can even help people with degenerative mental conditions. People in the late stages of Alzheimer's disease cannot take care of themselves or communicate effectively and find life confusing and frightening. Playing a simple instrument, such as maracas or drums, stimulates movement and brings some joy into these people's lives.

Researchers are discovering that music can expand our capacity to learn, reason and create. It was recently discovered that listening to Mozart appears to improve spatial reasoning ability—how objects fit together in space and time. The test scores of students at the University of California at Irvine who listened to Mozart improved thirty percent over those of students who sat in silence or listened to modern music for the same amount of time. Although the effects seemed to last only ten minutes, researchers believe that these effects may be more lasting for younger children and are now testing that theory.

If you prefer rap music to Mozart, take heart. After test results showed that the blood pressure rates of people who listened to their favorite relaxing music dropped slightly, researchers designed a study to prove that stimulative music which the listener disliked would cause anxiety and increase blood pressure. However when some test subjects listened to their least favorite music, rap, their blood pressure dropped dramatically, far lower than the group who listened to relaxing music. This phenomenon clearly needs more study.

The fact that a therapist uses art or music is a good indication that he is open to a variety of techniques. If you are in the process of choosing a therapist, you should seriously consider someone who uses art or music as a technique in therapy, if that person also meets your other qualifications.

Body work and massage therapy

Massage and body work are not substitutes for psychotherapy but can be helpful adjuncts. Many physical techniques have a significant positive effect on mental health and psychological problems.

Studies show that we *need* touch as much as or more than we need food and water. During World War II, many babies died in British orphanages simply because they were not held or touched enough. Today the importance of touch for our mental and physical health is widely recognized. Being touched is far more important than the type of body work or massage you choose.

Some people who do massage and other body work call themselves therapists and do in fact counsel their clients because the intimacy may induce clients to confide in them. Some body work practitioners are excellent counselors, but others are not. It is helpful to find out exactly what training your practitioner has as a therapist and counselor, and how much work he has done to resolve his own problems before using him as a substitute for someone trained as a psychotherapist.

Massage and body work are essential elements of healing because we store stress and emotions not just in our minds but in our bodies. Experience with techniques such as rolfing, chiropractic adjustments, acupuncture, and various types of massage have shown that tension and trauma can be released and memories can even be recalled when someone stimulates, adjusts or puts pressure on areas of our bodies.

Stress in our adult lives as well as trauma as children make us lose touch with our bodies. If we do not express our feelings or deal with them at the time they arise, those feelings may be stored in our bodies, resulting in tension, pain, and even disease. Body work can often release the stress of stored feelings so that these symptoms disappear. After a body work session of any kind, your body should feel freer and lighter, and you may notice changes in your posture and facial expression.

As children, if our bodies were beaten, invaded, or used by others for their own ends, we may have blocked out all sensation to protect ourselves. Some of us remain numb. Even if we are no longer numb, we find it difficult to enjoy being touched. Since the touch we experienced as children was painful or shameful, many of us have no idea that touch can be gentle, loving and pleasurable. Learning this wonderful lesson is an important part of healing from physical and sexual abuse.

The most effective way to overcome barriers to enjoyable touch is to experiment with touch in a situation where you are totally in control. This may be with a partner when you take time to explore caressing each other. However, if you don't have a partner, or have one who has not learned to touch you gently and with sensitivity to your needs, a gentle professional massage may be just what you need. Establishing a relationship of trust with your massage therapist can help you improve your future relationships.

Massage is one of the most ancient of the healing arts. Physically, massage improves circulation, relieves tension, soothes sore muscles and reduces stress. In addition to releasing stress and repressed emotions, massage can also enhance vitality.

I recommend trying various types of massage. If one works, continue; if not, try something else. Each type of massage and body work has its own style and purpose. It is important to understand the nature of the treatment and feel comfortable with it and the therapist before commencing. The following are brief descriptions of a few of the available types of massage and body work:

Polarity Massage

This massage balances body energy, promoting relaxation and healing as well as diminishing emotions. Polarity massage involves a minimum of touch and where touch is used, it is so light it is hardly felt at all. I do not pretend to understand how it works. It is based on the energy points discovered in acupuncture. I have been told it balances the positive and negative flows of energy in our bodies. I know only that the effects were dramatic for me. At times when I was in the depths of depression, frozen with fear, or trapped in anger, I felt wonderful and relaxed after just a few minutes of polarity massage.

I also used this technique to relieve pain and assist my healing before and after several operations I have had. The results were quite amazing. Polarity massage is worth trying because it will not hurt you and the results can be remarkable. Since this type of massage involves minimal touch, it can help you develop the trust to experiment with massage requiring more touch.

Swedish Massage

This is a more traditional type of massage which focuses on muscles and joint movement. Depending on the masseur and your preferences, the degree of touch can range from gentle to a much harder and sometimes painful deep tissue massage. Proponents find Swedish massage a soothing, flowing type of massage which they say helps tone muscles and results in a feeling of being cared for. I had an unpleasant experience with an overly vigorous Swedish masseuse, so I know how important it is to specify beforehand how hard you want your massage to be. This massage is usually performed undressed, but you can remain partially clothed.

Acupuncture and Shiatsu (Acupressure)

According to oriental medicine and philosophy, a vital force known as "chi" flows in connected channels or meridians through the body. Acupuncture is an ancient science whereby very thin needles are inserted at specific points in the body on these meridians to increase protective healing energy and release blocked energy. Releasing blocked energy leads to healing, promotes physical and mental health and energy, and diminishes pain. Many western physicians have begun to recognize the effectiveness of Chinese acupuncture and some have learned the procedure and are using it in the United States.

Shiatsu, or acupressure, is a Japanese technique. The word means "finger pressure." Pressure is applied to acupuncture points on the meridians to balance the body's energy and promote health. Applying pressure to acupuncture points also has been used to release blocked energy with many of the same results as with acupuncture.

Both acupuncture and Shiatsu can in some cases release stored memories and emotions. If you are not fond of needles, try acupressure before acupuncture. If you do try the latter, make sure your doctor has the proper training and is *very* experienced.

Chiropractic—Spinal and cranial sacral adjustments

Chiropractic theory is based on the assumption that disease is caused by interference with nerve function, and that manipulation and adjustment of body structures, especially the spinal column, will restore normal functioning. These adjustments are commonly used to improve joint mobility due to injury and stress. Adjustments also appear to release blocked energy and open energy channels in the body, relieving stress and contributing to improved health. Chiropractors also use applied kinesiology, acupressure and other techniques to release stress stored in the body which causes many seemingly "physical" conditions. These techniques often result in the release of repressed memories and emotions, sometimes through vivid flashbacks.

Release of memories seems to occur even more frequently in a relatively new offshoot of chiropractic involving manipulation of the cranial sacral bones of the skull. These delicate cranial sacral adjustments can also change emotional states, eliminating feelings of depression and improving vitality.

My parents brought me up to believe that any doctor without an M.D. from Harvard was a quack, so I did not try a chiropractor until my M.D. could see no possibility of improvement for my neck injury caused when my stopped car was hit from the rear by another car going 55 m.p.h. Even though several friends waxed ecstatic about a certain chiropractor and I had to wait two months to get an appointment with him (always a good sign of customer satisfaction), I went with about the same enthusiasm as going to get my tooth pulled on a doorknob.

It was a miracle. After a session of chiropractic adjustment and a couple of acupressure sessions, I could turn my neck, where before I had to turn my head and shoulders to look behind me, and I had no more pain, even after sitting at my computer for hours. The cranial sacral work also improved my energy, as well as releasing a few more memories I had not resolved. My chiropractor, who is also an osteopath and has studied oriental medicine, kinesiology, homeopathy, and a variety of other methods, is now my primary doctor and I feel physically better than I ever have in my life.

Needless to say, I recommend that you try a chiropractor, with my oft-repeated caveat that you obtain several recommendations and follow the other guidelines for selection in this book. With chiropractors, it is especially important to check credentials to be sure that your condition will be properly evaluated before you get any adjustment because serious injury can result from improper adjustment or from any adjustment with some types of injury. If you have been injured, your chiropractor should take x-rays, or evaluate existing x-rays, before commencing any work on you.

Touch for Health

Touch for Health is a simple holistic system of health care available for people to use by themselves, without any knowledge of medicine or how their bodies work. It measures and corrects muscular and electrical imbalances in the body and it addresses all aspects of health—including structural, nutritional, mental and emotional.

Touch for Health is unique because you can do it by yourself. It was developed by professional chiropractors to teach lay people how to participate in their own healing process. John Thie, D.C., the author of the *Touch for Health* book, believed that any tool for self-enhancement which is safe and easy to use should be available to everyone, regardless of lack of previous training.

Touch for Health is a synthesis of techniques involving skills from modern chiropractic, naturopathy, osteopathy, and ancient Chinese acupuncture. The system uses muscle testing, a biofeedback technique which measures muscle response and effectiveness. Muscle response is pretested, before acupressure points are touched. After acupressure or some other technique is used, the muscle is tested again and changes are noted. These changes are not only physical but may also involve the person's mental and emotional states. A person's negative core beliefs can literally be repatterned out of his body—and it is this repatterning that may cause repressed memories and emotions to surface.

Muscle-testing techniques are also used to determine the need for and effectiveness of treatment. According to Dr. Thie: "We intervene to restore muscle balance which is central to good posture and health. However, we are not just treating muscles. The body is all one thing, a coherent whole, which includes body, mind and spirit."

I have been muscle-tested and been the subject of Touch for Health techniques many times, by my chiropractor and by an Edu-K practitioner (see below), and am constantly amazed and impressed by the results. Kinesiology techniques are being adapted to many disciplines, including psychotherapy, medicine, and nutrition, and I have used them successfully in my own therapy practice. I recommend that you test Touch for Health, Edu-K or some type of applied kinesiology for yourself.

Educational Kinesiology ("Edu-K")

Edu-K merges applied kinesiology (the study of muscles and the testing and balancing of them to restore equilibrium) and learning theory to facilitate learning. Although Edu-K is more commonly known for its success in overcoming learning disabilities such as dyslexia, it has a wide variety of applications and is being used to access repressed traumatic memories and emotions and to eliminate destructive thought and behavior patterns. Developed by Paul E. Dennison, Ph.D., Edu-K uses simple physical movements to alter brain patterning, improve right brain-left brain integration, balance energy, and improve reading ability.

I have found Edu-K exercises extremely effective for releasing emotions and for reducing the intensity of emotional states, as well as for integrating the functioning of the two hemispheres of the brain, and reprogramming harmful decisions. Ann Bogdanich, an exceptionally skilled practitioner employed by school districts and Indian reservations to work with children, used Edu-K to change beliefs deeply ingrained in both my mind and body from abuse, beliefs I could not change intellectually, such as that love was unsafe, and that I did not deserve love, pleasure or success. Repatterning these beliefs also resulted in my recovering additional memories and feelings about my abuse. A few days after the memories subsided, I found that my former defensive thought and behavior patterns based on old childhood beliefs had disappeared.

After other Edu-K sessions, where at the start I had been trapped in strong feelings of depression or anger, I would find myself smiling and feeling wonderful. The changes were so dramatic that I could not deny the power of Edu-K, even though I did not understand the theory and some of the exercises seemed silly.

As a result of my own positive experiences and of my clients I strongly recommend Edu-K, with the caveat that you find someone who is well trained and, if used for therapy, meets the qualifications of a compassionate, kind therapist described in the chapter "How do I find a therapist who is right for me?".

Reflexology

Reflexology is deep massage of the nerve reflex endings in the hands and feet. The benefits of foot massage have been known for centuries; washing of the feet is even mentioned in the Bible. Reflexology is now a modern science based on the discovery that there are points in the hands and feet which connect through channels of energy to organs in the body. Massaging these points in the feet and hands can reduce pain, promote healing of many physical conditions and illnesses, and improve general health. I have used this technique successfully for relieving pain in various parts of my body. There are charts available on the location of points on the hands and feet and corresponding organs, and you can easily learn to do reflexology on yourself and others, either by yourself through books or by someone showing you how.

Mothers of Mercy

When we were children, most of us were not held and hugged as much as we needed to be and this technique is designed to fulfill that basic need. Many of us have also never been held in a gentle, nonthreatening way where nothing is expected of us. Mothers of Mercy are volunteers trained to hold people in a gentle nonsexual way to give people a sense of unconditional love and nurturing. Being held in this way gives them an opportunity to experience the nurturing they missed and may evoke strong emotions. This is the method Mother Theresa uses in India to give babies and others the feeling of love before they die.

I found this technique very powerful when I tried it at a workshop presented by author Stephen Levine and his wife, Ondrea. By appointment, Ondrea simply held people for fifteen minutes each in a private room. I felt awkward because the situation was foreign, but the sense of being held by someone who wanted to do it with no demands or expectations was overwhelming. I realized how much I had missed and longed for this experience, and also the difficulty I had accepting it. Being gently held changed my view of myself and gave me a vivid image of what I wanted in future relationships with a man.

If you try this method, be sure that you have strong feelings of trust and comfort with the person who does it. If you feel uncomfortable, discuss your feelings until you feel comfortable. Most important, if the person who holds you does anything that you feel is sexual, leave immediately. Any kind of sexual overture is totally contrary to the intent of this procedure. Even if you are mistaken, your safety must be your first priority and you can work out your feelings later. The Mothers of Mercy are volunteers, they do not take money for what they do, and they will not be offended if you want to leave.

Trager

This technique involves being rocked and softly shaken in a way that releases stored blocks of energy and patterns in the body so that the body feels freer and more relaxed. Created by Milton Trager,

M.D., this technique is also based on the premise that most of us were not sufficiently held and caressed as children, and that certain types of touch can release grief, pain and other emotions from our bodies. Sessions are usually conducted with the client wearing underwear, but you can keep your clothes on if you wish.

Reiki (pronounced "ray-kee")

This is another technique to channel life-energy by gently placing the hands on the completely clothed body in a specific pattern. Its supporters assert that reiki uses symbols to enhance our natural healing energy and rebalance the energy flow. The flow of energy from the practitioner is said to dissolve blockages of the client's energy allowing toxins to be released, so that the body can reestablish its natural harmony. You can take classes to learn to do this technique for yourself and others.

Many people believe that reiki is effective, and I have personally had some experiences which appear to support that assertion. However, I feel that we all have a natural ability to use our energy to heal others, and reiki makes this process overly complicated and formal. But if you believe you need a structure and group support, reiki may be right for you.

Feldenkrais Method®

Feldenkrais is a kinesthetic technique which uses movement and touch to create learning in the nervous system. It is gentle and may be done in classes or privately. Classes are called "awareness through movement," and use movement to give the central nervous system input and facilitate learning in a way similar to that used by infants. Victims of trauma usually have restricted patterns of movement. The teacher directs students to move in specific ways to create new pathways in the nervous system. Participants learn to move more naturally and with increased flexibility and develop a new sense of themselves and their bodies. This process may also result in the release of repressed memories and feelings.

Individual work is called "functional integration" and is performed on a massage-like table with the client fully clothed. It involves counseling and gentle, nonintrusive touching and moving to enhance learning in the nervous system.

Proponents claim that the Feldenkrais Method works faster and with less pain than physical therapy for overcoming injuries. Ann, a therapist friend of mine whose back was broken in a serious car accident, was told after months of physical therapy that she would have limited movement for the rest of her life. In desperation she tried Feldenkrais and now has almost no limitations. Becky, a courageous and engaging young woman challenged with cerebral palsy, used Feldenkrais treatments to increase her balance and range of motion. She can walk without a wheelchair and was able to live on campus while attending college. I have heard only positive things about this technique and plan to try it myself when I have time.

Rolfing

This treatment consists of ten sessions of massage and pressure, each focusing on a different area of the body. Rolfing is a technique created by Ida Rolf, a Ph.D. in biochemistry, designed to shift the fascia—fibrous tissue around the muscles—in order to release physical and emotional patterns locked in the body. Releasing these patterns can improve flexibility and posture. Some people find that rolfing also releases vivid memories and strong repressed emotions, and enthusiastically endorse it. However, although some practitioners have told me rolfing should not be painful, so many people have reported feeling physical pain with this technique that I am wary of it and would personally prefer a more gentle alternative.

There are so many different types of massage and body work available now which affect mental health, including yoga and the martial arts, that it is impossible to describe them all. We are learning more about the interaction of our minds and bodies every day, and new healing methods are constantly being discovered. I am not familiar with all of the effective techniques and urge you to try those where you have recommendations, no drugs are involved, nothing is injected into your body, and there are no serious risks.

Since many body work practitioners know more than one technique, your relationship with your practitioner is generally more important than the particular technique used. In choosing a practitioner, you can use many of the principles discussed in Part I, pages 39 and 55. The basic rules are the same: Obtain references, interview your candidate *first*, and choose someone you like.

Make sure that you have a safe environment before starting any type of massage or body work by requesting an interview where you can ask questions and state your desires. Be sure you understand what the practitioner will do. If you were abused as a child, tell your practitioner about your abuse and disclose any negative feelings you may have about being touched. Your practitioner should also be aware of your past medical history, especially surgery, accidents, fractures, and sensitive areas. Give specific instructions about whether you want gentle, medium or deep tissue massage, or an absolute minimum of touch. Remember you are paying for your massage or body work and as a consumer you can choose the quality of the experience.

With any type of massage or body work, your body should always be covered except for the area that is being worked on. Many types of massage do not require that you undress, so if you feel uncomfortable with a stranger touching your bare skin, request massage where you can remain clothed. If you do not want to be touched in certain areas, say so. People who suffered abuse as children or battering as adults are often more comfortable beginning with limited massage to the neck, shoulders and back. Remember you can stop the session at any time, with or without a reason.

If you feel uncomfortable even reading about massage or body work, it will be beneficial for you. Touch is one of our most pleasurable senses and abuse has deprived many of us of its benefits. Regaining a sense of our bodies and learning to enjoy touch is essential to complete healing.

In general, I would avoid techniques which make you sign a contract to keep the methods secret because I believe healing should be readily accessible to everyone. Secrecy also prevents techniques from being tested and results evaluated. On the other hand, some effective techniques such as acupuncture and chiropractic adjustments require credentials, licenses, and substantial training to ensure proper treatment, and these requirements are justified given the risks of injury.

I am convinced that healing does not have to be esoteric or complex. You should be able to request an explanation of what is being done and be able to understand it.

Avoid any procedure where you are required to sign up for a series of expensive classes or treatments before you are certain of what you are getting into and sure you will achieve results. You should be able to stop without penalty if you feel uncomfortable.

With any body work technique or massage, you should feel noticeable benefits in the first or, at most, the second session. If not, stop and try something or someone else.

In choosing techniques and practitioners, rely on the recommendations of friends whose opinions you trust, and on your own instincts—your feelings. The whole purpose of massage and body work is *to feel better*. Health, massage and new age magazines and newsletters, women's support groups, and bookstores can be resources for massage and body work practitioners. I have found that the owners of local bookstores often know about local practitioners. It is preferable to have a personal recommendation, but at least ask questions and be sure you are comfortable before commencing a session.

Epilogue

I hope this book has helped you realize that there are many excellent and committed therapists who can help you. You do not have to settle for anyone who is not right for you. Even though you may not believe it now, you know deep down what is best for you and you have the ability to find what you need. Just by reading this book, you have already demonstrated that you have a desire to heal and that you are able to take the steps necessary to help yourself.

Remember that you deserve the best. My favorite quote is from the Buddha who over two thousand years ago said these words during times even more violent and cruel than our own. The concept is just as true today as it was then:

"If you search the wide world over, you will never find anyone more deserving of love than yourself."

Resources

Professional organizations of therapists

The following are not licensing agencies. Check your local telephone directory for the state agency that regulates and licenses therapists. These listings are for the national headquarters of various professional associations for therapists which can refer you to local offices. These associations do not screen therapists and therapists are not required to be members of these associations.

American Association of Marriage and Family Counselors (AAMFC)
225 Yale Avenue
Claremont, CA 91711
(909) 621-4749

American Association of Pastoral Counselors
9504 A Lee Highway
Fairfax, Virginia 22031-2303
(703) 385-6967

American Association of Sex Educators, Counselors & Therapists
5010 Wisconsin Avenue, N.W., Suite 304
Washington, D.C. 20015
(202) 686-2523

American Medical Association (AMA) (psychiatrists)
515 North State Street
Chicago, IL 60610
(312) 464-5000

American Psychological Association (APA)
750 First Street, N.E.
Washington, D.C. 20002-4242
(202) 336-5500

Association for Applied Psychophysiology and Biofeedback (AAPB)
10200 West 44th Avenue, #304
Wheat Ridge, CO 80033-2840
(800) 477-8892
Requests that you send a stamped self-addressed envelope for referrals.

National Association of Social Workers (NASW)
7981 Eastern Avenue
Silver Spring, MD 20910
(301) 565-0333
Professional and institutional inquiries only.
For referrals, call the NASW office in your state capital.

Child abuse and family violence

If you know or suspect that a child is being abused, you are required by law to report what you know to your local police department or state social service or family service agency.

If you are a child who is being abused, you can call these agencies for help, but I also recommend that you call a local child abuse treatment center or legal agency for the protection of children in your area which can help you deal with the police and state agencies.

Crisis Hotlines

Childhelp USA
6463 Independence Avenue
Woodland Hills, CA 91537
Hotline: (800) 4-A-CHILD or
(800) 422-4453
Provides free twenty-four-hour crisis counseling by mental health professionals for adult and child victims of child abuse and neglect, offenders, parents who are fearful of abusing or who want information on how to be effective parents. The Survivors of Childhood Abuse Program (SCAP) disseminates materials, makes treatment referrals, trains professionals, and conducts research.

National Organization for Victim Assistance (NOVA)
1757 Park Road, N.W.
Washington, D.C. 20010
(800) TRY-NOVA (800-879-6682)
Provides free twenty-four-hour crisis counseling, information and referral for crime victims, including rape and sexual abuse.

National Youth Suicide Hotline
National Runaway Switchboard Metro-Help, Inc.
3080 North Lincoln
Chicago, IL 60657
(800) 621-4000 (toll-free)
(312) 880-9860
Provides toll-free crisis counseling, information, and referral to runaway and homeless youth and their families.

Canada

Assaulted Women's Helpline
(416) 863-0511
TDD (416) 516-9738 (for the hearing-impaired)
Provides twenty-four-hour crisis line for women in the Toronto area and will refer to other agencies throughout Canada.

Kidshelp Phone
(800) 668-6868
Provides help for children to age nineteen.

General information

National Victim's Center Infolink
(800) FYI-CALL (800-394-2255)
Provides information and referral to state agencies for victims of violent crime. Operates during regular business hours. (No crisis counseling.)

Childhelp USA (D.C. Office)
5225 Wisconsin Avenue, N.W., Suite 603
Washington, D.C. 20015
(202) 537-5193
Contact for information on Federal programs and legislation.

Military Family Resource Center (MFRC)
Ballston Center Tower Three
Ninth Floor, Suite 903
4015 Wilson Boulevard
Arlington, VA 22203
(703) 696-4555

National Black Child Development Institute
1463 Rhode Island Avenue, N.W.
Washington, D.C. 20005
(202) 387-1281
Provides newsletter, annual conference, and answers public inquiries regarding issues facing black children/youth.

National Center for Child Abuse and Neglect (NCCAN)
Administration for Children, Youth and Families
Office of Human Development Services
Department of Health and Human Services
P.O. Box 1182
Washington, D.C. 20013
(703) 821-2086
Responsible for the Federal government's child abuse and neglect programs. Administers grant programs to states and organizations to fur-

ther research and demonstration projects, service programs, and other activities related to the identification, treatment, and prevention of child abuse and neglect. Clearinghouse provides selected publications and information on child abuse and neglect.

National Center for Missing and Exploited Children
2101 Wilson Boulevard
Suite 550
Arlington, VA 22201
(703) 235-3900
(800) 843-5678
Twenty-four-hour toll-free number for reporting missing children, sightings of missing children, or reporting cases of child pornography. Provides free written materials for the general public on child victimization as well as technical documents for professionals. You will hear a message advising you that all calls are recorded.

National Committee for Prevention of Child Abuse
332 South Michigan Avenue
Suite 1600
Chicago, IL 60604-4357
(312) 663-3520
68 local chapters (in all 50 states). Provides information and statistics on child abuse and maintains an extensive publications list. The National Research Center provides information for professionals on programs, methods for evaluating programs, and research findings.

National Council on Child Abuse and Family Violence and National Crime Prevention Council
1700 K Street, N.W.
2nd Floor
Washington, D.C. 20006
Provides personal safety curricula, including child abuse and neglect prevention for school children and model prevention programs for adolescents. Educational materials for parents, children, and community groups are available.

National Education Association (NEA)
Human and Civil Rights Unit
1201 16th Street, N.W.
Washington, D.C. 20036
(202) 822-7711
Offers training to NEA members. Sells child abuse and neglect training kits and supplemental materials to professionals and the general public.

National Exchange Club Foundation for Prevention of Child Abuse
3050 Central Avenue
Toledo, OH 43606
(419) 535-3232
Provides parent aide services to abusive and neglecting families in 37 cities.

National Network of Runaway and Youth Services
1400 Eye Street, N.W.
Suite 330
Washington, D.C. 20005
(202) 682-4114
Provides written materials, responds to general inquiries regarding runaways and adolescent abuse, and serves as a referral source for runaways and parents.

Parents Anonymous
6733 South Sepulveda Boulevard
Suite 270
Los Angeles, CA 90045
(800) 421-0353 (toll-free)
(213) 410-9723 (business)
1,200 chapters nationwide. National program of professionally facilitated self-help groups. Each state has different program components.

Parents United/Daughters and Sons United/Adults Molested as Children United
232 East Gish Road
San Jose, CA 95112
(408) 453-7616
150 chapters nationwide. Provides guided self-help for sexually abusive parents as well as child and adult victims of sexual abuse.
(Author's note: The Parents United groups for abuse survivors in my area are excellent and free. It is well worth checking out Parents United programs in your area.)

American Humane Association
American Association for Protecting Children
63 Inverness Drive East
Englewood, CO 80112-5117
(303) 792-9900
(800) 227-5242
Professional publications and public inquiries regarding child protective services and child abuse and neglect.
(Author's note: An excellent organization; the first to recognize physical abuse of children.)

Boys and Girls Clubs of America
Government Relations Office
611 Rockville Pike, Suite 230
Rockville, MD 20852
(301) 251-6676
1,100 clubs nationwide serving 1.3 million boys and girls. Offers safety curriculum.

American Academy of Pediatrics
141 Northwest Point Boulevard
P.O. Box 927
Elk Grove Village, IL 60007
(800) 433-9016
For professional and public educational materials, contact the Publications Department. Also has Committee on Child Abuse and Neglect.

Vis-A-Vis/Family Violence Program
The Canadian Council on Social Development
55 Parkdale Avenue
P.O. Box 3505, Station C
Ottawa, Ontario K1Y 4G1
(613) 728-1865

Alcohol and drug problems

These are national organizations. Check your telephone directory for local listings first.

Alcoholics Anonymous (AA)
468 Park Avenue South
P.O. Box 459
Grand Central Station
New York, NY 10163
(212) 686-1100

Al-Anon/Alateen Family Group Headquarters
1372 Broadway
New York, NY 10018
(212) 302-7240

Addiction Alternatives (Rational Recovery)
1851 East First Street
Suite 820
Santa Ana, CA 92705
(310) 372-0244

Adult Children of Alcoholics Central Service Board and Interim World Service Organization
2525 West Sepulveda Boulevard
Suite 200
Torrance, CA 90505
(213) 534-1815

National Clearinghouse for Alcohol and Drug Information and National Council for Alcohol and Drug Information
P.O. Box 2345
Rockville, MD 20852
(301) 468-2600

National Council on Alcoholism and Drug Dependence Hopeline
(800) 622-2255
Toll-free number for referral to your local office.

National Institute of Drug Abuse Workplace Helpline
(800) 843-4971

Brainwave Biofeedback

There are over 100 centers for EEG biofeedback training in the United States. The following organizations may be able to refer you to a center in your area.

Life Sciences Institute of Mind-Body Health Inc.
2955 SW Wanamaker Drive, Suite B
Topeka, KS 66614
(913) 271-8686

EEG Spectrum, Inc.
16100 Ventura Boulevard, Suite 10
Los Angeles, CA 91436-2505
(818) 788-2083

Austin Biofeedback Center
4207 James Casey, Suite 301
Austin, Texas 78745
(512) 447-6998

Carol F. Manchester, Ph.D.
Freshwater Clinic
6065 Glick Road, Suite C
Powell, Ohio 43065
(614) 761-7610
Post-traumatic stress and multiple personality disorders

Miscellaneous

American Self-Help Clearinghouse
St. Clares-Riverside Medical Center
25 Pocono
Denville, NJ 07834
(201) 625-7101
TDD (201) 625-9053 (for the hearing-impaired)
Provides a directory of U.S. and Canadian self-help organizations and literature for starting support groups.

Anxiety Disorders Association of America
6000 Executive Boulevard, Suite 200
Rockville, MD 20852-3801
(301) 231-8368

Educational Kinesiology (Edu-K)
P.O. Box 3396
Ventura, California 93006-3396
(800) 356-2109

Spiritual Emergence Network
The Institute of Transpersonal Psychology
250 Oak Grove Avenue
Menlo Park, CA 94025
(415) 327-2776
Founded by Christina Grof in 1980, this network helps people understand and find appropriate help for crisis states during the transformational process. Refers to local therapists some of whom have experience in psychology and spiritual issues. It is wise to check these recommendations and obtain a second opinion.

Endnotes

How do I know if I need a therapist? (page 6)

1. Baron, R.A. (1992) *Psychology, Second Edition*, Boston: Allyn and Bacon, 583; Eysenck, H. J. (1952) "The effects of psychotherapy: An evaluation," *Journal of Consulting Psychology*, 16, 319–324.

2. Bergin, A.E. et al. (1978) "The evaluation of therapeutic outcomes," in S.L. Garfield & A.E. Bergin (Eds.) *Handbook of Psychotherapy and Behavior Change: An Empirical Analysis* (2nd ed.), New York: Wiley, 139–190; Clum, G.A. et al. (1990) "Behavior therapy better than placebo treatments: Fact or artifact?" *Psychological Bulletin*, 107, 110–113; Shapiro, D.A. et al. (1982) "Meta-analysis of comparative therapy outcomes: A replication and refinement," *Psychological Bulletin*, 92, 581–604.

3. Baron, R.A. (1992) *Psychology, Second Edition*, Boston: Allyn and Bacon, 583; Smith, M. L., et al. (1980) *The Benefits of Psychotherapy*, Baltimore: John Hopkins Press.

4. Baron, R.A. (1992) *Psychology, Second Edition*, Boston: Allyn and Bacon, 583; Howard, K.I. et al. (1986) "The dose-effect relationship in psychotherapy," *American Psychologist*, 41, 159, 164; Orinsky, D.E. et al. (1987) "The relation of process to outcome in psychotherapy," in S.L. Garfield & A.L. Bergin (Eds.), *Handbook of Psychotherapy and Behavior Changes*, 3rd ed., New York: Wiley.

5. Address, Utah Attorney General Jan Graham, Governer's Conference on Victim Rights, April 29, 1993; see Finkelhor, D. 1986/*A Sourcebook on Child Sexual Abuse*. Beverly Hills: Sage Publications, 19.

6. "Inceste: Un Procés D'Assises Sur Cinq." (July 10, 1992) *Libération*, 1–5.

What happens during therapy? (page 13)

1. Van der Kolk, B.A. et al. (1991) "The Intrusive Past: The Flexibility of Memory and the Engraving of Trauma." *American Imago*, 48(4), 425–454.

2. Van der Kolk, B.A. (1988) "The Trauma Spectrum: The Interaction of Biological and Social Events in the Genesis of the Trauma Response," *Journal of Traumatic Stress*, 1: 273–290.

3. Van der Kolk, B.A. (1988) "The Trauma Spectrum: The Interaction of Biological and Social Events in the Genesis of the Trauma Response," *Journal of Traumatic Stress*, 1: 273, 286.

4. Herman, J. (1992) *Trauma and Recovery*. Basic Books: HarperCollins, 124; American Psychiatric Association (1994) *Diagnostic and Statistical Manual of Mental Disorders (Fourth Edition)*, DSM-IV, Washington, D.C.: American Psychiatric Association, 425.

5. American Psychiatric Association (1994) *Diagnostic and Statistical Manual of Mental Disorders (Fourth Edition)*, DSM-IV, Washington, D.C.: American Psychiatric Association, 425.

6. Herman, J. (1992) *Trauma and Recovery*. Basic Books: HarperCollins, 122, and studies cited therein.

Group therapy (page 72)

1. Sgroi, S. M. (1982) *Handbook of Clinical Intervention in Child Sexual Abuse*. Lexington, Massachusetts: Lexington Books, 147–9.

2. Browne, A., et al. (1986) "Impact of Child Sexual Abuse: A Review of the Research." *Psychological Bulletin*, 99(1), 66–77; Burgess, A., et al. (1987) "Abused to Abuser: Antecedents of Socially Deviant Behaviors." *American Journal of Psychiatry*, 144(11), 1431–1346; Runtz, M., et al. (1986) "Adolescent 'Acting-Out' and Childhood History of Sexual Abuse." *Journal of Interpersonal Violence*, 1(3), 326–334; Briere, J., et al. (1986) "Suicidal Thoughts and Behaviors in Former Sexual Abuse Victims." *Canadian Journal of Behavioral Science*, 18(4), 413–423; Briere, J., et al. (1987) "Post Sexual Abuse Trauma: Data and Implications for Clinical Practice." *Journal of Interpersonal Violence*. 2(4), 367–379; McCormack, A., et al. (1986) "Runaway Youths and Sexual Victimization." *Child Abuse and Neglect*, 10(3), 387–395; Janus, M.D., et al. (1987) "Histories of Sexual Abuse in Adolescent Male Runaways." *Adolescence*, 22(86), 405–417; James, J., et al. (1977) "Early Sexual Experiences and Prostitution." *American Journal of Psychiatry*, 134, 1381–1385; Silbert, M.H., et al. (1981) "Sexual Child Abuse as an Antecedent to Prostitution." *Child Abuse and Neglect*. 5, 407–411; Howing, P., et al. (1990) "Child Abuse and Delinquency: The Empirical and Theoretical Links." *Social Work*, 35: 244–49; Swett, C., et al. (1991) "High Rates of Alcohol Use and History of Physical and Sexual Abuse among Women Outpatients." *Am. J. Drug Alcohol Abuse*, 17(1), 49–60; Shearer, S. L., et al. (1990) "Frequency and Correlates of Childhood Sexual and Physical Abuse Histories in Adult Female Borderline Inpatients." *Am. J. Psychiatry*,147: 214–216. For the most recent studies, see Herman, J.L. (1992) *Trauma and Recovery*. Basic Books: HarperCollins, 123–5.

3. Herman, J.L. (1992) *Trauma and Recovery*. Basic Books: HarperCollins Publishing Company, 122-126, and references cited therein.

4. Corey, G. (1985) *Theory and Practice of Group Counseling, Second Edition*. Monterey, California: Brooks/Cole Publishing Company, 6–11.

5. See Madanes, C. (1984) *Behind the One Way Mirror: Advances in the Practice of Strategic Therapy*. San Francisco, California: Jossey-Bass Publishers.

What if I'm sexually attracted to my therapist? (page 96)

1. Corey, G. (1986) *Theory and Practice of Counseling and Psychotherapy, Third Edition*. California: Brooks/Cole Publishing Co., 339.

2. Zamichow, N. "The Dark Corner of Psychology." *Los Angeles Times*, April 15, 1993, A1, A20.

3. Zamichow, N. "The Dark Corner of Psychology." *Los Angeles Times*, April 15, 1993, A1, A20.

What can I do to make being in therapy easier? (page 115)

1. Borysenko, J. (1987) *Minding the Body, Mending the Mind*. Reading, Massachusetts: Addison-Wesley Publishing Company, Inc., 89–109.

2. Benson, H., et al. (1976) *The Relaxation Response*. New York: Avon Books.

3. See Achterberg, J. (1984) "Imagery and Medicine: Psychophysiological Speculations," *Journal of Mental Imagery*, 8(4), 1–14 (spiritual thoughts may have a positive effect on our immune systems).

How do I know when I no longer need therapy? (page 120)

1. Hepworth, D. H. and Larsen, J. (1986) *Direct Social Work Practice: Theory and Skills, Second Edition*. Chicago, Illinois: The Dorsey Press, 577–589.

2. Corey, G. (1985) *Theory and Practice of Group Counseling, Second Edition*. Monterey, California: Brooks/Cole Publishing Company, 116–121, 445–449.

3. *Ibid*, 121–123, 445–449.

Specific problems (page 155)

Depression—Therapy and the use of drugs (page 156)

1. National Institute of Mental Health. *Depression: What You Need to Know*. D/ART/Public Inquiries, Rockville, Maryland. See also *Diagnostic and Statistical Manual of Mental Disorders (Third Edition–Revised)*. (1987) Washington, D. C.: American Psychiatric Association, 228–233.

2. Van der Kolk, B.A. (1988) "The Trauma Spectrum: The Interaction of Biological and Social Events in the Genesis of the Trauma Response," *Journal of Traumatic Stress*, 1: 273–290.

3. "Protracted depression is the most common finding in virtually all clinical studies of chronically traumatized people." Herman, J. L. (1992) *Trauma and Recovery*. New York: Basic Books: HarperCollins, p. 94; see also *ibid*, 108–9, 111, 118; Walker, L. (1979) *The Battered Woman*, New York: Harper & Row; Krystal, *Massive Psychic Trauma*; Tennant, C. C., et al., "The Psychological Effects of Being a Prisoner of War: Forty Years After Release," *American Journal of Psychiatry* 143 (1986), 618–22; Kinzie, J. D., et

al., "PTSD Among Survivors of Cambodian Concentration Camps," *American Journal of Psychiatry* (1984), 645–50.

Alcoholism and drug addiction treatment programs (page 161)

1. Swett, C., et al. (1991) "High Rates of Alcohol Use and History of Physical and Sexual Abuse among Women Outpatients," *American Journal of Drug and Alcohol Abuse,* 17 (1), 49–60; Briere, J. (1988) "Long-Term Clinical Correlates of Childhood Sexual Victimization," *Annals of the New York Academy of Sciences.* 528: 327–34.

2. Seixas, J.S., et al. (1985) *Children of Alcoholism: A Survivor's Manual.* New York: Harper & Row, 189–191.

Sexual and physical abuse (page 167)

1. Cornelia Wilbur, M.D., a former faculty member at the University of Kentucky and the psychiatrist who treated Sybil Dorsett, said about multiple personality disorder: "There are two things we *do* know. The first is that they [people with multiple personality disorder] can get completely well and the other is that by listening to them, you can really learn how the human psyche works." Marsa, L. "The 23 Lives of Lisa Malone." *Woman's Day,* 8/7/90, 36, 39. And see Kluft, R. P. (1987) "An Update on Multiple Personality Disorder." *Hospital and Community Psychiatry,* 38(4), 363, 370.

2. See Finkelhor, D. (1986) *A Sourcebook on Child Sexual Abuse.* Beverly Hills: Sage Publications, 19.

3. "Inceste: Un procès d'assises sur cinq." *Liberation,* July 10, 1992, 1–5.

4. Herman, J.L. (1992) *Trauma and Recovery.* New York: Basic Books, HarperCollins, 111–113, 121; Van der Kolk, B.A. (1988) "The Trauma Spectrum: The Interaction of Biological and Social Events in the Genesis of the Trauma Response," *Journal of Traumatic Stress,* 1: 273, 286.

5. Van der Kolk, B.A. et al. (1991) "The Intrusive Past: The Flexibility of Memory and the Engraving of Trauma." *American Imago,* 48(4), 425–454.

6. Rudy, L. and Goodman, G. (1991) "Effects of participation on children's reports: implications to children's testimony," *Developmental Psychology,* 27: 527–538. See also "Incest: A Chilling Report" (Feb., 1992), *Lear's,* 49–77, 56–7.

7. "Interview: Hollida Wakefield and Ralph Underwager," *Paidika: The Journal of Paedophilia,* Winter 1993, Vol. 3, No. 1, 2–12. When Underwager, a former pastor in Lutheran churches, was asked to "describe a spirituality for paedophiles," he replied in part: "As with all human behavior, I would suggest that paedophiles can say, 'I have chosen; I choose; I will act in this fashion. I believe that the outcome will be good. I will pay the price for that act, whatever the price'."

8. Freyd, Jennifer J. "Theoretical and Personal Perspectives on the Delayed Memory Debate," Ann Arbor, Michigan: A presentation for the Center for Mental Health at Foote Hospital's Continuing Education Conference, August 7, 1993.

9. Herman, J.L. (1992) *Trauma and Recovery*. New York: Basic Books, HarperCollins, 121.

10. Browne, A., et al. (1986) "Impact of Child Sexual Abuse: A Review of the Research," *Psychological Bulletin*, 99(1), 66–77; Burgess, A., et al. (1987) "Abused to Abuser: Antecedents of Socially Deviant Behaviors," *American Journal of Psychiatry*, 144(11), 1431–1436; Runtz, M. et al. (1986) "Adolescent 'Acting-Out' and Childhood History of Sexual Abuse." *Journal of Interpersonal Violence*, 1(3), 326–334; Briere, J., et al. (1986) "Suicidal Thoughts and Behaviors in Former Sexual Abuse Victims," *Canadian Journal of Behavioral Science*, 18(4), 413–423; Briere, J., et al. (1987) "Post Sexual Abuse Trauma: Data and Implications for Clinical Practice," *Journal of Interpersonal Violence*, 2(4), 367–379; McCormack, A., et al. (1986) "Runaway Youths and Sexual Victimization," *Child Abuse and Neglect*, 10(3), 387–395; Janus, M.D., et al. (1987) "Histories of Sexual Abuse in Adolescent Male Runaways," *Adolescence*, 22(86), 405–417; James, J., et al. (1977) "Early Sexual Experiences and Prostitution," *American Journal of Psychiatry*. 134, 1381–1385; Rohsenow, et al. (1988) "Molested as Children: A Hidden Contribution to Substance Abuse," *Journal of Substance Abuse Treatment*, 5, 13–88; Silbert, M. H., et al. (1981) "Sexual Child Abuse as an Antecedent to Prostitution," *Child Abuse and Neglect*, 5, 407–411; Walker, E., M. D., et al. (1988) "Relationship of Chronic Pelvic Pain to Psychiatric Diagnoses and Childhood Sexual Abuse." *Am. J. Psychiatry*, 145: 75–80; Gise, L., M.D. (1990) "Sexual Abuse and Premenstrual Syndrome; Comparison Between Lower and Higher Socioeconomic Groups." *Psychosomatics*, 31: 265–72 (See bibliography.); Howing, P., et al. (1990) "Child Abuse and Delinquency: The Empirical and Theoretical Links." *Social Work*, 35: 244–49; Swett, C., et al. (1991) "High Rates of Alcohol Use and History of Physical and Sexual Abuse among Women Outpatients," *Am. J. Drug Alcohol Abuse*, 17(10), 49–60; Shearer, S. L., et al. (1990) "Frequency and Correlates of Childhood Sexual and Physical Abuse Histories in Adult Female Borderline Inpatients," *Am. J. Psychiatry*, 147: 214–216. For the most recent studies, see Herman, J. (1992), *Recovery and Trauma*. New York: Basic Books, HarperCollins, 123–25.

11. Van der Kolk, B. (1988) "The Trauma Spectrum: The Interaction of Biological and Social Events in the Genesis of the Trauma Response," *Journal of Traumatic Stress*, 1: 273, 286, and citations therein; Wilbur, C. B. (1984) "Treatment of multiple personality." *Psychiatric Annals*, 14(1): 27–31.

12. I am aware of studies which appear to indicate that a small percentage of perpetrators were not sexually abused as children. However, all of these studies merely reflect what the perpetrators interviewed *consciously remembered and were able to report*. We know that many abuse victims completely repress their memories of childhood abuse and not only will fail to

report their childhood abuse, but will argue that they had happy childhoods. Until studies are conducted where perpetrators are questioned under hypnosis, or a reliable substitute is found which is able to measure repressed events, I will remain convinced that abuse is a learned behavior caused by repressed trauma.

13. Herman, J.L. (1992) *Trauma and Recovery*. New York: Basic Books, HarperCollins.

Rape and domestic violence (page 183)

1. Herman, J.L. (1992) *Trauma and Recovery*. New York: Basic Books, HarperCollins, 111–113.

2. Russell, D. (1986) *The Secret Trauma*. New York: Basic Books; Herman, J. (1992) *Trauma and Recovery*. New York: Basic Books, HarperCollins, 111.

3. Lawsuits were filed against the chairman and the college in the Ingham County Circuit Court in Lansing, Michigan, Case Number 91-67922-CZ. The court document and the judgment are available to the public and for use as a precedent by other victims.

4. Hilberman, E. (1980) "The 'Wife-Beater's Wife' Reconsidered," *American Journal of Psychiatry* 137: 1336–47; Herman, J. (1992) *Trauma and Recovery*. New York: Basic Books, HarperCollins, 32, 74–83, 121.

Multiple Personality disorder and ego states (page 187)

1. *Diagnostic and Statistical Manual of Mental Disorders (Third Edition–Revised)* (1987). Washington, D.C.: American Psychiatric Association, 269–270.

2. *Ibid.*, 270–271.

3. Herman, J.L. (1992) *Trauma and Recovery*. New York: Basic Books, HarperCollins.

4. Van der Kolk, B.A., and van der Hart, O. (1991) "The Intrusive Past: the Flexibility of Memory and the Engraving of Trauma," *American Imago* (Johns Hopkins University Press), 48(4), 425–454.

5. National Committee for the Prevention of Child Abuse, "Current Trends in Child Abuse Reporting and Fatalities: The Results of the 1990 Annual Fifty State Survey." (April, 1991).

6. Kluft, R.P. (1987) "An Update on Multiple Personality Disorder." *Hospital and Community Psychiatry*, 38(4), 363, 366.

7. *Diagnostic and Statistical Manual of Mental Disorders (Third Edition–Revised)* (1987) Washington, D.C.: American Psychiatric Association, 269–272.

8. Beahrs, J.D. (1983) "Co-consciousness: A Common Denominator in Hypnosis, Multiple Personality, and Normalcy." *American Journal of Clinical Hypnosis*, 26(2), 100–113; Bliss, E. L. (1980) "Multiple Personalities: A Report of 14 Cases with Implications for Schizophrenia and Hysteria."

Archives of General Psychiatry, 37(12), 1388–1397; Braun, B.G. (1984) "Hypnosis Creates Multiple Personality: Myth or Reality?" *International Journal of Clinical & Experimental Hypnosis*, 32(2), 191–197; Kluft, R.P. (1986) "Preliminary Observations on Age Regression in Multiple Personality Disorder Patients Before and After Integration," *American Journal of Clinical Hypnosis*, 28(3), 147–156; Kluft, R.P. (1987) "An Update on Multiple Personality Disorder." *Hospital and Community Psychiatry*, 38(4), 363–373; Wilber, C.B. (1984) "Treatment of Multiple Personality." *Psychiatric Annals*, 14(1), 27–31.

Eating disorders (page 192)

1. *Diagnostic and Statistical Manual of Mental Disorders (Third Edition–Revised)* (1987). Washington, D.C.: American Psychiatric Association, 65–69.

2. Van der Kolk, B.A., et al. (1991) "Childhood Origins of Self-Destructive Behavior." *American Journal of Psychiatry* 148: 1665–71; Lowenstein, R. (1990) "Somatoform Disorders in Victims of Incest and Child Abuse," in *Incest-Related Syndromes of Adult Psychopathology*, ed. R. Kluft. Washington, D.C. American Psychiatric Press, 75–112; Demitrack, M. A., et al. (1990) "Relation of Clinical Variables to Dissociative Phenomena in Eating Disorders," *American Journal of Psychiatry*, 147: 1184–88.

Anxiety disorders—Panic attacks and phobias (page 198)

1. *Diagnostic and Statistical Manual of Mental Disorders (Third Edition–Revised)* (1987). Washington, D.C.: American Psychiatric Association, 235–253.

2. Statement of Jerilyn Ross, President of the Phobia Society of America, "The Seriousness of Phobia in America." *Congressional Record*, Extension of Remarks, 133:74, May 8, 1987, E 1828–9.

3. Van der Kolk, B.A. (1988) "The Trauma Spectrum: The Interaction of Biological and Social Events in the Genesis of the Trauma Response," *Journal of Traumatic Stress*, 1: 273–290; Herman, J. L. (1992) *Trauma and Recovery*. New York: Basic Books, HarperCollins, 124.

4. Herman, J. L. (1992) *Trauma and Recovery*. New York: Basic Books, HarperCollins, 118–124, and references cited therein.

5. *Ibid*.

6. Weissman, M.M., et al. (1989) "Suicidal Ideation and Suicide Attempts in Panic Disorder and Attacks," *New England Journal of Medicine, 321(18)* 1209-14; 1260-61.

Relationship problems—couples and family therapy (page 203)

1. Broderick, C. (1979) *Couples: How to Confront Problems and Maintain Loving Relationships*. New York: Simon and Schuster, 219.

2. Wilbur, C. B. (1984) "Treatment of Multiple Personality." *Psychiatric Annals*, 41(10), 27–31.

How do I find a good therapist for my child? (page 210)

1. Goldstein, S. *A Teacher's Guide: Attention-Deficit Hyperactivity Disorder In School Age Children*; Children with Attention Deficit Disorders (CH.A.D.D.), American Academy of Child and Adolescent Psychiatry (AACAP), et al. (Fall/Winter 1991) "Medical Management of Children with Attention Deficit Disorders: Commonly Asked Questions." *Chadder*,17–19. For more comprehensive information on ADHD see Goldstein, S., et al. (1990) *Managing Attention Disorders in Children: A Guide for Practitioners*. New York: Wiley Interscience Press.

How do I choose the right type of therapy? (page 227)

Psychoanalysis/Freudian analysis (page 229)

1. Corey, G. (1986) *Theory and Practice of Counseling and Psychotherapy, Third Edition*. Monterey, California: Brooks/Cole Publishing Co., 11–16.

2. Miller, A. (1985) *Thou Shalt Not Be Aware, Society's Betrayal of the Child*. New York: Farrar, Straus, Giroux, 136. See also, Pittman, F. (1987) Turning Points. New York: Norton, 302, and references cited therein.

3. Hunter, M. (1990) *Abused Boys*. Lexington, Mass.: Lexington Books, 295.

4. Corey, G. (1986) *Theory and Practice of Counseling and Psychotherapy, Third Edition*. Monterey, California: Brooks/Cole Publishing Co., 40–41, and references cited therein.

5. Baron, R. A. (1992) *Psychology, Second Edition*, Boston: Allyn and Bacon, 569–70; Corey, G. (1986) *Theory and Practice of Counseling and Psychotherapy, Third Edition*. Monterey, California: Brooks/Cole Publishing Co., 40–41.

The Neo-Freudian approach (page 232)

1. Corey, G. (1986) *Theory and Practice of Counseling and Psychotherapy, Third Edition*. Monterey, California: Brooks/Cole Publishing Co., 11.

2. *Ibid*, 46–71, and references cited therein.

Gestalt therapy (page 234)

1. Corey, G. (1986) *Theory and Practice of Counseling and Psychotherapy, Third Edition*. Monterey, California: Brooks/Cole Publishing Co., 119–147, 144–5.

Transactional analysis (page 236)

1. Corey, G. (1985) *Theory and Practice of Group Counseling, Second Edition*, Monterey, California: Brooks/Cole Publishing Company, 319.

2. Corey, G. (1986) *Theory and Practice of Counseling and Psychotherapy, Third Edition*. Monterey, California: Brooks/Cole Publishing Co., 11–16. For a discussion of ego state therapy, see Watkins, J. G. and Watkins, H. H. (1979) "The Theory and Practice of Ego State Therapy," in *Short Term Approaches to Psychotherapy*, H. Grayson, Editor. New York: National Institute for the Psychotherapies, and Human Sciences Press.

3. Corey, G. (1986) *Theory and Practice of Counseling and Psychotherapy, Third Edition*. Monterey, California: Brooks/Cole Publishing Co., 169.

Behavior therapy (page 238)

1. Corey, G. (1986) *Theory and Practice of Counseling and Psychotherapy, Third Edition*. Monterey, California: Brooks/Cole Publishing Company, 173–177.

2. *Ibid.*

3. *Ibid*, 186; Zastrow, C., et al. (1987) *Social Welfare, Politics and Public Policy*. Chicago, Illinois: Nelson-Hall Publishers, 134–138.

4. Corey, G. (1985) *Theory and Practice of Group Counseling, Second Edition*. Monterey, California: Brooks/Cole Publishing Company, 365.

Rational-emotive therapy (page 241)

1. Corey, G. (1986) *Theory and Practice of Counseling and Psychotherapy, Third Edition*. Monterey, California: Brooks/Cole Publishing Company, 207–241.

Reality therapy (page 244)

1. Corey, G. (1985) *Theory and Practice of Group Counseling, Second Edition*. Monterey, California: Brooks/Cole Publishing Company, 416–417; Corey, G. (1986) *Theory and Practice of Counseling and Psychotherapy, Third Edition*. Monterey, California: Brooks/Cole Publishing Company, 257–258.

Hypnotherapy (page 246)

1. Van de Kolk, B.A. (1988) "The Trauma Spectrum: The Interaction of Biological and Social Events in the Genesis of the Trauma Response," *Journal of Traumatic Stress*, 1: 273, 286.

2. Rossi, E.L. et al. (1991) *The Twenty Minute Break: Using the New Science of Ultradian Rhythms*. Los Angeles, California: Jeremy P. Tarcher, Inc., 7–9.

3. Rossi, E.L., et al. (1991) *The Twenty Minute Break: Using the New Science of Ultradian Rhythms*. Los Angeles, California: Jeremy P. Tarcher, Inc., 7–9, 180–181.

4. Haley, J. (Ed.) (1967) *Advanced Techniques of Hypnosis and Therapy: Selected Papers of Milton H. Erickson, M.D.* Florida: Grune & Stratton.

Brainwave biofeedback (page 254)

1. Lubar, J.F. (1991) "Discourse on the development of EEG diagnostics and biofeedback for attention-deficit/hyperactivity disorders," *Biofeedback and Self-Regulation*, 16(3), 201–225; Lubar, J. F., et al. (1984) "Electroencephalographic biofeedback of SMR and beta for treatment of attention deficit disorders in a clinical setting," *Biofeedback and Self-Regulation*, 9(1), 1–23; Shouse, M. N., et al. (1979) "Operant conditioning of EEG rhythms and Ritalin in the treatment of hyperkinesis," *Biofeedback and Self-Regulation*, 4(4), 301–312.

2. Muehl, S., et al. (1965) "EEG abnormality and psychological test performance in reading disability," *Cortex*, 1, 434–439; Tansey, M. A., et al. (1983) "EMG and EEG biofeedback training in the treatment of a 10-year-old hyperactive boy with a developmental reading disorder," *Biofeedback and Self-Regulation*, 8, 25–37; Tansey, M. A. (1985) "Brainwave signatures. An index reflective of the brain's functional neuroanatomy: Further findings on the effect of EEG sensorimotor rhythm feedback training on the neurologic precursors of learning disabilities," *Int. J. Psychophysiology*, 4, 91–97.

3. Peniston, E.G., et al. (1990) "Alcoholic personality and alpha-theta brainwave training," *Medical Psychotherapy*, 3, 37–55 ("Brainwave treatment resulted in decreased MCMI scales labeled schizoid, avoidant, passive-aggression, borderline, paranoid, anxiety, somatoform, dysthymia, alcohol abuse, psychotic thinking, psychotic depression, and psychotic delusion. . . . EEG brainwave treatment corresponded to significant increases in warmth, abstract thinking, stability, conscientiousness, boldness, imaginativeness, and self-control."); Peniston, E. G., et al. (1989) "Alpha-theta training and beta-endorphin levels in alcoholics," *Alcoholism: Clin. and Exper. Research*, 13, 271.

4. Peniston, E.G., et al. (1990) "Alcoholic personality and alpha-theta brainwave training," *Medical Psychotherapy*, 3, 37–55 ("Brainwave treatment resulted in decreased MCMI scales labeled schizoid, avoidant, passive-aggression, borderline, paranoid, anxiety, somatoform, dysthymia, alcohol abuse, psychotic thinking, psychotic depression, and psychotic delusion.").

5. Cabral, R.J., et al. (1976) "The effects of desensitization techniques, biofeedback and relaxation on intractable epilepsy: Follow-up Study," *J. Neurol. Neurosurg. Psychiatry*, 39, 504–507; Ellertsen, B., et al. (1976) "Clinical application of biofeedback training in epilepsy," *Scandinavian J. of Behavior Therapy*, 5, 133–144; Lantz, D., et al. (1988) "Neuropsychological assessment of subjects with uncontrolled epilepsy: Effects of EEG feedback training," *Epilepsia*, 29(2), 163–171; Lubar, J. F., et al. (1981) "EEG operant conditioning in intractable epileptics," *Arch. Neurol.*, 38, 700–704; Tozzo, C. A., et al. (1988) "EEG biofeedback and relaxation training in the control of epileptic seizures," *Int. J. of Psychophysiology*, 6, 185–194.

6. Peniston, E. G., et al. (1990) "Alcoholic personality and alpha-theta brainwave training," *Medical Psychotherapy*, 3, 37–55 ("EEG brainwave treatment corresponded to significant increases in warmth, abstract thinking, stability, conscientiousness, boldness, imaginativeness, and self-control.").

7. Arrien, A. (1993) *The Four-fold Way*, HarperSan Francisco, 162–171.

8. Siegfried Othmer, Ph.D., has prepared an excellent readable paper entitled "EEG Biofeedback Training: A Journey Toward Personal Autonomy" (June 1994) which is available from EEG Spectrum, Los Angeles, California, (818) 788-2083.

Breathing techniques for releasing emotions (page 254)

1. Wender, P., et al. (1982) *Mind, Mood & Medicine*. New York: New American Library, 312.

Eye movement desensitization and reprocessing (page 266)

1. Shapiro, F. (1989) "Efficacy of the eye movement desensitization procedure in the treatment of traumatic memories." *Journal of Traumatic Stress*, 2, 199–223; Shapiro, F. (1989) "Eye movement desensitization procedure: A new treatment for the post-traumatic stress disorder." *Journal of Behavior Therapy and Experimental Psychiatry*, 20, 211–217; Shapiro, F. (1991) "Eye movement desensitization & reprocessing procedure: From EMD to EMD/R—A new treatment model for anxiety and related traumata." *The Behavior Therapist*, 14(5), 133–135.

2. Shapiro, F. (1991) "Eye movement desensitization & reprocessing procedure: From EMD to EMD/R—A new treatment model for anxiety and related traumata." *The Behavior Therapist*, 14(5), 133–135, 135.

3. Shapiro, F. (1991) "Eye movement desensitization & reprocessing procedure: From EMD to EMD/R—A new treatment model for anxiety and related traumata." *The Behavior Therapist*, 14(5), 133–135, 135.

4. Lipke, H., et al. (1992) "Case studies of eye movement desensitization and reprocessing (EMDR) with chronic post-traumatic stress disorder." *Psychotherapy*, 29(4), 591–595.

5. Marquis, J. (1991) "A report on seventy-eight cases treated by eye movement desensitization." *Journal of Behavior Therapy and Experimental Psychiatry*, 22(3), 187–192, 188–191.

6. Marquis, J. (1991) "A report on seventy-eight cases treated by eye movement desensitization." *Journal of Behavior Therapy and Experimental Psychiatry*, 22(3), 187–192, 191.

Spiritual and transpersonal therapies (page 269)

1. Fadiman, J. & Speeth, K. (1980) "Transpersonal Psychotherapy," *Psychology Handbook* (Herink, R., Ed.). New York: New American Library, 684–686.

Index

A

abuse. *See* alcoholism; cult abuse; domestic violence; drug abuse; sexual abuse; substance abuse
Acevedo, Gary, 10
acupuncture/acupressure, 291, 292, 293
ADD, 219-21
Addiction Alternatives, 306
ADHD, 219-21
Adler, Alfred, 232, 233
adolescents
    eating disorders and, 192-93, 195
    group therapy and, 73, 74-75
    as perpetrators of abuse, 176-77
    risk of suicide among, 153
Adult Children of Alcoholics, 146, 162, 307
Adults Molested as Children United, 305
advice, tips for giving, 149-50
affirmations, 115-16
agoraphobia, 198-99
AIDS, 87, 97
airports, 118
Al-Alon, 162, 306
Alateen Family Group Headquarters, 306
Alcoholics Anonymous, 39, 79, 162, 164, 196, 256, 275, 306
alcoholism, 57-58, 63, 146.
    See also Alcoholics Anonymous
    anxiety disorders and, 201
    childhood abuse and, correlation between, 21, 161
    group therapy and, 73, 79
    the intervention process and,141-42
    treatment programs for, overview of, 161-66
Allred, Hugh, 268
Alzheimer's disease, 284, 287
ambivalence, 109
American Academy of Pediatrics, 306
American Association for Protecting Children, 305
American Association of Marriage and Family Counselors (AAMFC), 301
American Association of Pastoral Counselors, 301
American Association of Sex Educators, Counselors & Therapists, 301

American Humane Association, 305
American Medical Association (AMA), 301
American Psychiatric Association, 53, 156
American Psychological Association, 301
Anatabuse, 256
Angelou, Maya, 18
anorexia nervosa, 192-97.
    See also eating disorders
ANRED (Anorexia Nervosa and Related Eating Disorders, Inc.), 192
antidepressants, 107-8, 156-60.
    See also drug treatment
anxiety
    disorders, 198-202, 308
    "happiness," 7-8
Anxiety Disorders Association of America, 202, 308
Anxiety Disorders Clinic, 199
Arnold, Roseanne Barr, 174
art, 60, 100-102, 284-88
Assaulted Women's Helpline, 303
Association for Applied Psychophysiology and Biofeedback (AAPB), 301
attention deficit disorder (ADD), 219-20
attention-deficit hyperactivity disorder (ADHD), 219-20
Auschwitz, 184
Austin Biofeedback Center, 259, 307
Australia, 8, 38, 167, 169
autism, 221-22

B

Bandler, Richard, 281
battered-child syndrome, 175
battered women, 183-86
behavior therapy, 238-40
Belgium, 8, 176
Benson, Herbert, 118
Berkowitz, Bernard, 59
Bible, 9, 33-34, 150, 294
biofeedback, 102, 160-61, 179, 254-59, 307
body work, 84, 179
    overview of, 289-99
    qualifications for, 50-51
Bogdanich, Ann, 294
Bolles, Richard, 36

Borysenkos, Joan, 118, 272
boundaries, setting, 151
Boys and Girls Clubs of America, 306
brainwave biofeedback, 102, 160-61, 179, 254-59, 307
breath work, 29, 102, 123, 179, 181, 202
   confidentiality issues and, 84
   overview of, 260-65
   qualifications for, 50-51
Brilliant Madness, Living with Manic Depressive Illness (Duke), 101
Britain. *See* England
Buddha, 300
Buddhism, 273, 277, 300
bulimia, 192-97. *See also* eating disorders

C

California, 97
   California Supreme Court, 87, 173
   Medical Board of California, 98
Cameron-Bandler, Leslie, 283
Canada, 8, 167, 169, 303
Celestine Prophesy, The (Redfield), 11, 272
checklists, 9, 42, 53, 64, 66, 80, 111, 113, 133, 223, 224
child abuse, reporting of, 142-43
Childhelp USA, 39, 211, 302-3
children, therapy for, 142-43, 209-26. *See also* adolescents
   autism and, 221-22
   checklists for, 223-26
   drug treatment and, 219-21
   duration of, 218-19
   group therapy and, 73
   preparing your child for, 217-18
   trauma, 210-11, 248-53
   types of, 215-17
China, 291, 293
chiropractic care, 291-92
Christ, 272
clinical social workers, 46-47
Cocaine Anonymous, 162
college students, 73
Coming Back: A Psychiatrist Explores Past-Life Journeys (Moody), 277
confidentiality issues, 84-89
conscious connected breathing. *See* breath work
Conscious Living: The Journey to Cocommitment (Hendricks and Hendricks), 204
cost, of therapy, 33-43, 106, 132, 139. *See also* health insurance

countertransference, 108
couples therapy, 203-7. *See also* marriage therapy
Courage to Heal, The (Bass and Davis), 174
Crawford, Christina, 100
Crawford, Joan, 100
creativity, 100-102, 284-88
crisis hotlines, 302, 303.
   See also emergencies
cult abuse, 104, 167, 175, 201

D

Dateline NBC, 171, 172-73
Daughters and Sons United, 305
death, dealing with, 15, 18, 116
degrees, explanation of, 44-48
Dennison, Paul E., 294
dependence
   on loved ones, 151
   twelve-step programs and, 162-63
   unhealthy, on therapists, 104-5
depression, 153, 156-60
   exercise and, 25, 117, 159
   hospitalization for, 126-27, 130-31
   medication for, 107
   sexual abuse and, 178-79
   symptoms of, 156-57
desensitization, 240, 266-68
diagnosis, 53, 93, 216
Diagnostic and Statistical Manual of Mental Disorders (APA), 53
dissociation, 187-89
diuretics, 193
divorce, 73, 156
domestic violence, 183-86, 302, 303.
   See also sexual abuse
Dossey, Larry, 275
dreams, 16, 105-6
drug abuse, 51-53, 57, 102
   the intervention process and, 141-42
   treatment programs for, overview of, 161-66
Dudam, Tom, 172
Duke, Patty, 101

E

eating disorders, 51-53, 163, 172, 178-79, 192-97
Ebers Papyrus (document), 284
Educational kinesiology (Edu-K), 293-94, 308
EEG biofeedback. *See* biofeedback
EEG Spectrum, 259, 307
Ellis, Albert, 241

EMDR (eye movement desensitization and reprocessing), 266-68
emergencies
  committing clients to hospitals in the event of, 86-87, 89
  hotlines for, 302, 303
  reaching your therapist in the event of, 41
empathetic responding, 58-59
endorphins, 117
England, 8, 38, 167, 169, 289
Erickson, Milton, 49, 247
evaluation, 9-12, 66-67, 103-12
evaluation checklists, 9, 42, 53, 64, 66, 80, 111, 113, 133, 223, 224
exercise, 25, 117, 119, 152, 159, 193
eye movement, 247, 266-68

F
Fadiman, James, 271
False Memory Foundation, 173-75
"false memory" syndrome, 104, 169-76
Family Crucible, The (Napier and Whitaker), 50
family therapy, 47, 79-80, 145-46. See also children, therapy for; marriage therapy
Farm Bureau, 37
Fast Phobia Method, 279-80
Feldenkrais Method, 296-97
finances. See cost, of therapy; health insurance
Fisher, Seymour, 158
Flynn, Errol, 100
Ford, Betty, 141
Ford, Gerald R., 141
foregiveness, 121-22
France, 8, 167, 169, 272
Freshwater Clinic, 259
Freud, Anna, 230
Freud, Sigmund, 104, 229-32
Freudian psychoanalysis, 22, 104, 229-31
Freyd, Jennifer, 174
Freyd, Pamela, 174
Fromm, Erich, 232

G
genetics, 202
Gestalt therapy, 179, 196, 202
  Neo-Freudians and, 232
  overview of, 234-35
  Transactional Analysis and, 236-37

Glasser, William, 244-45
God, 18, 162, 174, 180, 243, 269-70, 273, 275-76
Goodman, Gail, 171
Grinder, John, 281
Grof, Christina, 308
Grof, Stanislav, 263, 265
group therapy, 70-82, 183
  adolescents and, 73, 74-75
  confidentiality issues and, 88
  cost of, 35
  family groups, 79-80
  interview questions for, 80-82
  marathon groups, 76-78
  overview of, 72-82
  sessions, duration of, 31
  the termination stage and, 123-24
  T-groups, 78
  types of, 75-82
guidance systems, 10-11
Guided Meditations, Explorations and Healings (Levine), 273
guilt, 17-18, 29-30, 193

H
"happiness anxiety," 7-8
Harvard Medical School, 14-15, 171, 177-78, 187
health insurance, 35-38, 42
  addiction treatment and, 164
  alternative methods and, 51
  confidentiality issues and, 84-85
  inpatient programs and, 128-39, 164-65
Hendricks, Gay, 204
Hendricks, Kathlyn, 204
Herman, Judith, 187
Hinduism, 277
Hollywood, 100
Holotropic breathwork, 263
Holotropic Mind, The (Grof), 263
homosexuality (sexual orientation), 62, 65
honesty, 62, 144, 151
hormones, 117
Horney, Karen, 232
hospitalization, 86-87, 89, 126-39, 142. See also inpatient programs
  for eating disorders, 195-96
  forms for protection while under, 135-38
  questions to ask before, 133-34
  sexual abuse issues and, 195-96
hotlines, crisis, 302, 303. See also emergencies

How to Be Your Own Best Friend
  (Berkowitz and Newman), 59
Humane Society, 175
Hutchison, Michael, 257
hypnosis, 246-53
hypnotherapy, 2, 16, 19-20, 72, 127, 179, 181
  cost of, 51
  eating disorders and, 194, 195
  overview of, 246-53
  qualifications for, 49
  scheduling, 28

I
incest. *See* sexual abuse
Incest Survivors Anonymous, 79
India, 295
Indian drumming ceremonies, 273
inpatient programs, 125, 164-66, 195-96.
  See also hospitalization
insomnia, 118, 156
insurance. *See* health insurance
Interim World Service Organization, 307
intervention process, 141-42
interviews, 55-65, 69-71
  with child therapists, 210-12, 223-26
  for group therapy, 80-82
  at prospective hospitals, 130-31
  questions to ask, 53-54, 64-68, 80-82, 133-34, 223-26

J
Japan, 291
Jesus Christ, 272
Jourard, Sidney, 63
Journal of Paedophilia, The, 173
Journal of Transpersonal Psychology, 271
Jung, Carl Gustav, 88, 232-33, 269,285

K
Kansas, 258
karma, 277-78
Kidshelp Phone, 303
kinesiology, 293-94, 308
Kluft, Richard, 127
Korean War, 13
Kulkosky, Paul J., 256

L
laxative abuse, 193
legal issues. *See also* licensing
  confidentiality, 84-89
  hospitalization and, 126, 142
  mental distress claims, 85
  rape and, 185
  sexual abuse and, 167-68, 171-77
  therapist/client sexual involvement and, 96-99
"letting go," 121-22
Levine, Ondrea, 273, 295
Levine, Stephen, 272, 273, 295
liability for therapists, 86-89
licensing, 41, 43-54, 96, 98
Life Sciences Institute of Mind-Body Health, 259, 307
Limits of Biological Treatments for Psychological Distress (Fisher), 158
Listening to Prozac (Kramer), 158
Loftis, Elizabeth, 170
Los Angeles County-University of Southern California Medical Center, 199
Lourdes (France), 272
Love, Medicine, and Miracles (Siegal), 132, 286
loved one, therapy for, 140-43

M
MacLaine, Shirley, 277
Manchester, Carol, 257, 259, 307
marriage therapy, 47, 93-94, 203-7.
  See also family therapy
*M*A*S*H* (television program), 14, 17
massage therapy, 289-99, 119
  confidentiality issues and, 84
  qualifications for, 50-51
Maultsby, Maxie, 242
Medicaid, 42, 64
medical insurance. *See* health insurance
Medicare, 34, 42, 64
medication, 28, 93, 106-8
  alternatives to, 117
  for children, 219-21
  for depression, 107-8, 156-60
  hospitalization and, 129-31, 138
meditation, 116-19, 273-74
Megabrain Power (Hutchison), 257
memory syndrome, "false," 104, 169-76
Menninger Clinic, 256, 259
Mental Research Institute, 266
Military Family Resource Center (MFRC), 303
Miller, Alice, 229
Millman, Dan, 272
"mindfulness", 116-17
Minding the Body, Mending the Mind (Borysenkos), 118
money. *See* cost, of therapy; health insurance
Moody, Raymond A., Jr, 277

Mothers of Mercy, 295
Mother Theresa, 295
Mozart, Wolfgang Amadeus, 288
multiple personality disorder, 22, 65, 93, 181, 187-91
    group therapy and, 72
    hospitalization and, 129, 130-31
    sexual abuse and, 174
Munjack, Dennis J., 199
music therapy, 284-88

N
Napier, Augustus, 50
Narcotics Anonymous, 162
National Association of Social Workers (NASW), 302
National Black Child Development Institute, 303
National Center for Child Abuse and Neglect (NCCAN), 303
National Center for Missing and Exploited Children, 304
National Clearinghouse for Alcohol and Drug Information, 307
National Committee for Prevention of Child Abuse, 304
National Council for Alcohol and Drug Information, 307
National Council on Alcoholism and Drug Dependence Hopeline, 307
National Council on Child Abuse and Family Violence, 304
National Crime Prevention Council, 304
National Education Association (NEA), 304
National Exchange Club Foundation for Prevention of Child Abuse, 305
National Institute of Drug Abuse Workplace Helpline, 307
National Institute of Mental Health (NIMH), 156, 200, 201
National Network of Runaway and Youth Services, 305
National Organization for Victim Assistance (NOVA), 302
National Runaway Switchboard Metro Help, 302
National Self-Help Clearinghouse, 308
National Victim's Center Infolink, 303
National Youth Suicide Hotline, 302
Nazi death camps, 184
Neo-Freudian psychoanalysis, 232-33

neuro-linguistic programming (NLP), 279-83
Newman, Mildred, 59
nightmares, 16, 105-6
nurses, psychiatric, 47
nutritional treatment, 196

O
obesity. See eating disorders
obsessive-compulsive disorders, 51-53, 199
Ochs, Len, 257
office design, 60, 217
On a Clear Day You Can See Forever (MacLaine), 277
openness, 62, 63

P
panic attacks, 198-202
Parents Anonymous, 305
Parents United, 79, 305
past-life regression, 277-78
pastoral counselors, 48-49, 84
Pavlov, Ivan, 238
Peniston, Eugene, 256
Perls, Frederick, 234-35
phobias, 198-202
Phobia Society of America, 199
play therapy, 215-17
polarity massage, 290
positive attitudes, developing, 115-16
post-traumatic stress disorder (PTSD), 13-16, 181, 185-86, 199
    "complex," 177-79
    qualifications for treating, 53
prayer, 275-76
premenstrual syndrome, 179
privacy. See confidentiality
Prozac, 158. *See also* antidepressants
psychiatric nurses, 47
psychiatrists
    complex post-traumatic stress disorder and, 177-79
    degrees, explanations, 44-48
    drug treatment and, 107-8
    fees of, 33
psychoanalysis, 229-33
    Freudian, 22, 104, 229-31
    Neo-Freudian, 232-33
psychologists, qualifications of, 45-46
Psychology Handbook (Fadiman and Speeth), 271

Q
qualifications, of practitioners, 44-54, 211-12

R
Ram Dass, 272
Ramona, Gary, 171-73
Ramona, Holly, 171-73
Ramona case, 171-73
rape, 129, 177, 183-86. *See also* sexual abuse
rational-emotive therapy (RT), 163, 241-43
Rational Recovery, 163, 306
Reach for the Rainbow: Advanced Healing for Survivors of Sexual Abuse (Finney), 2, 117, 118, 179, 273
reality therapy, 244-45
rebirthing. *See* breath work
Recovering the Soul (Dossey), 275
referrals, 39-43, 55, 129
reflexology, 294-95
reiki technique, 296
Relaxation Response, The (Benson), 118
religion, 62, 65. *See also* Buddhism; God; meditation; pastoral counselors
   "happiness anxiety" and, 7-8
   poor self-esteem and, 8-9
   twelve-step programs and, 162-63
REM (rapid eye movement), 247, 266-67
repressed memories, 247-53
residential treatment centers, 129, 132-33
ritalin, 219-21
Robert Mondavi Winery, 172
Rolf, Ida, 297
rolfing, 297-98
Rossi, Ernest, 30

S
sand tray, 216
schizophrenia, 129-31, 187
Seattle-Tacoma International Airport, 118
self-defense courses, 185
self-esteem, 8-9, 92, 94, 220
   developing positive, 180
   eating disorders and, 193
   group therapy and, 73, 74
   guilt and, 18
   hospitalization and, 196
   sexual abuse and, 168
   therapists/client sexual involvement and, 98
self-evaluation, 9-12, 111-12
self-mutilation, 130-31
sex therapy, 48, 97
sexual abuse, 1-2, 17, 39, 94, 167-82
   advances by therapists, 96-99
   alcoholism and, 21, 161
   anxiety disorders and, 201
   client/therapist involvement, 95, 96-99, 103
   eating disorders and, 193-97
   "false memory" syndrome and, 104, 169-76
   group therapy for, 24, 71, 74, 79-80
   hospitalization for, 127-28, 130-31, 133, 165
   ideas about creativity and, 100, 101-2
   as passed down in families, 144, 181
   perpetrators, 176
   reporting, 143
   revictimization and, 183-85
   statistics on, 8, 167, 169, 175
   symptoms of, 155-208
   therapists' gender and, 69-71
   therapists' qualifications and, 51-53, 57-58, 63
sexual orientation, 62, 65
Shapiro, Francine, 266, 268
Shiatsu, 291
Siegal, Bernie, 132, 286
Skinner, B.F., 238, 239
sleep states, 30, 118, 246-47
social phobias, 198
social workers, 46-47
sodium amytal, 172
Speeth, Kathleen, 271
Spiritual Emergence Network, 308
spiritual therapies, 269-74. *See also* religion
Spitz, Mark, 242
State University of New York Health Center, 158
strategic therapy, 79-80
substance abuse, 51-53, 57-58, 63, 73. *See also* alcoholism; drug abuse; eating disorders
suicide (suicidal thoughts), 73, 152-53
   anxiety disorders and, 201
   confidentiality issues and, 86
   danger of, hospitalization for, 86-87, 89, 126, 127
   hotlines, 302
support groups, 161. *See also* group therapy
support networks, 118
survival instinct, 150-51
Sweden, 38
Swedish massage, 291

T

termination, 24, 103, 120-25
therapies, types of, 227-99
therapists
    changing, 103-13, 120-125
    checklist for evaluating, 66-67
    counter-transference, 109
    deciding whether you need one, 6-12
    duration of, 22-27, 218-19
    effective, basic characteristics of, 21
    experience, 44-68
    finding potential, 39-43, 210-226
    frequency of sessions, 28-32, 230
    initial interviews with, 55-63
    personality fit, 55-68, 212-13
    progress, 103-14, 120-25
    purpose of, 13-21
    qualifications of, 44-54, 211-12
    referrals to, 39-43, 55, 129
    resistance to, 108
    sessions, length of, 28-32
    sexual advances by, 96-99
    termination of, 24, 103, 120-25
    transference, 108-109
    types of, basic overview of, 44-51
Thie, John, 293
Thou Shalt Not Be Aware (Miller), 229
Touch for Health, 293
Trager, Milton, 295-96
Trager technique, 295-96
Transactional Analysis (TA), 236-37
transference, 108-9
transpersonal therapies, 269-74
trauma, 167-186
Trauma and Recovery (Herman), 187
Twelve-step programs, 162
20 Minute Break, The (Rossi), 30

U

Underwager, Ralph, 173-74
University of California, 87, 171, 288
University of Oregon, 174

V

Vietnam War, 13, 256
Vis-A-Vis/Family Violence Program, 306

W

What Color is Your Parachute? (Bolles), 36
Whitaker, Carl, 50
Wisconsin, 143, 176
World War II, 260, 289

Y

Yale Medical School, 132, 286

Z

Zen meditation, 273

About the author

Lynne Finney is a warm, friendly speaker who has appeared on over a hundred radio and television shows throughout the United States and Canada, including three appearances on Larry King's shows. She presents trainings for therapists, judges, lawyers, and law enforcement personnel on childhood trauma and abuse, and workshops for the public and abuse survivors on how to be happy and healing from childhood trauma.

Lynne has been a law professor, Congressional investigator and Chief Counsel to a U.S. Senator, and under President Jimmy Carter was named as a director of a federal banking agency and served on a White House task force on women's issues. She later became an attorney advisor to the Agency for International Development and was appointed policy advisor on United Nations issues.

After discovering her own childhood abuse in therapy, Lynne went back to graduate school to become a therapist and now specializes in the treatment of childhood trauma and finding ways to help people live happier and more fulfilling lives.

If you would like to contact Lynne about her lectures and workshops, please write to P.O. Box 681539, Park City, Utah 84068-1539.

The Crossing Press

publishes a full selection of titles.

To receive our current catalog,

please call toll-free,

800-777-1048.